PRACTICAL RESEARCH

Practical Research: planning and design

Paul D. Leedy
Professor of Education
The American University
Washington, D.C.

Macmillan Publishing Co., Inc.
New York
Collier Macmillan Publishers
London

Printed in the United States of America

Macmillan Publishing Co., Inc.
866 Third Avenue, New York, New York 10022

Collier-Macmillan Canada, Ltd.

Library of Congress Cataloging in Publication Data

Leedy, Paul D.
Practical research: planning and design.

1. Research I. Title.
Q180.A1L43 001.4'3 73-7347
ISBN 0-02-369240-5

Printing: 3 4 5 6 7 8 Year: 5 6 7 8 9 0

With special appreciation

to

Renie

Table of Contents

About This Book

In a sense this is a do-it-yourself, understand-it-yourself manual. It is not a programmed text, but it will guide you, step by step, in planning and designing a research project, however large or small it may be. This is a *practical* manual, born from years of teaching research methodology to both graduate and undergraduate students and from observing, after the course was over, all their doubts and uncertainties in the face of a practical research undertaking. Many knew the *theoretical* aspects of research methodology thoroughly, yet they had difficulty planning a practical research project, preparing an acceptable proposal, or writing a research report. This may have been because the *practical* base under the theoretical structure was not as supportive as it should have been. Perhaps students had merely done lip-service to research, learning the essentials and proper orientations to theoretical methodology, without coming to grips with the mundane considerations that every researcher must learn if he is to get his project off the ground.

The types of uncertainties are many. Some students are not sure precisely what research is; others do not know how to go about finding the information they need. There are those who are terrified by statistics, and there are those who cannot get a proposal accepted or secure approval for the project they have planned. In these days of grants and financial assistance for research of all kinds, it is particularly important to know, when the need arises, how to present one's ideas for maximum effectiveness.

Many a student has labored over a research project, whether in high school or at the graduate level, only to be told by some instructor after all is done and much energy has been invested that "this was not quite what he expected of the student." Such a reaction is frustrating, comfortless, and unrewarding. To save you from such situations, this book has been written.

The word *practical* is perhaps the most significant word in the title. The practical approach means planning the project properly. It means simple, clear, pragmatic hints on how to get the job done. It is down-to-earth guidance from those who have traveled the road before you, who are aware of the pitfalls and are willing to share with you the wisdom of how to avoid them.

The author of this book does not undervalue the importance of a theoretical approach to an understanding of research. Many times it is basic and required. But a theoretical base is not supportive enough for the practical needs of many students who must get their research off the launch pad of theory into the orbit of creativity. For this, theoretical methodology alone simply does not provide sufficient thrust!

One of the unique features of this book is the "Practicum in Research" section, a part of the end matter. Here, as you pass important milestones in learning the nature of research and how to plan it in the text section of the book, you structure your *own* research project or test your understanding of the basic concepts presented in the text. A high school or college student using this book should be able to write better term papers or research project reports. Similarly, a graduate student should be able to construct an acceptable proposal in a professional manner for his thesis or dissertation committee. Anyone using it should be able to produce a superior research proposal or final document, because he knows precisely what he is doing with respect to research and the demands it makes upon the researcher.

The author is indebted to so many for so much of this book that he refrains from mentioning any one in particular. To his own teachers who, during his doctoral study, gave him the first insight into the need for a book such as this, he pays much respect and acknowledges himself forever in their debt. Next, he wishes to acknowledge with humility the students who, again and again, have begged him to set down for others what they have found to be most helpful in the seminar sessions they have had with him. The same encouragement has come from faculty colleagues in several universities. Those with whom he has discussed the idea and who are engaged in professional research have also encouraged setting down some of the material in this book in permanent form. One esteemed colleague put it in these words, "Tell them the obvious; it may be what no one else has ever thought of telling them!" That is what the author has tried to do. The obvious is frequently so obvious that we feel it is unnecessary to direct the student's attention to it. To those of us who know, the nature of research is so obvious it needs no explanation; the basic reference keys to the library are so well known, we need not tell others about them; the reading of a statistical formula is so simple, we would never think of teaching one who doesn't know what the secret is; a proposal is so commonplace, we would never consider giving explicit instructions on how to write one. All these matters are so very obvious!

Perhaps it is at the very point of the obvious where students lose sight of what we feel there is no need to tell them. This book is an attempt to restore academic sight to those who see either with dim vision or, as in the case of many, with none at all. And our first exercise in seeing will be to try to glimpse what research really is.

P. D. L.

Research and the Tools of Research

1 What Is Research?

Research is a very confusing term.

As commonly used, it has so many meanings that we must understand precisely what we mean when we use it in its scholarly sense. We shall discuss in this book what is commonly referred to as *basic* or *pure research.*

Much that is said about basic research will also be applicable to the many pragmatic varieties of research activity: applied research, action research, developmental research, and so on. The difference between the pragmatic forms and the basic form of research lies in the depth to which basic research probes the underlying causes and meaning of observed phenomena and in the sophistication with which it demands that the collected data of observation be interpreted.

WHAT RESEARCH IS NOT

To understand more readily what research *is,* we should begin by considering what research is *not.* Some of the statements that follow may come as a distinct shock to the conventional way in which you have accepted the meaning of the term *research.* The reason for your surprise may be in part because you have been conditioned to the term in so many connotative frameworks that you may not be sure exactly what the term really does mean. Hence, when many students encounter the term for the first time in a truly professional and academic sense, it bewilders them.

To illustrate, let us take several instances in which the term *research* is used with entirely different meanings. For example, a housewife reads an advertisement and learns that because of "years of research" a new miracle product has been developed which she may now find on the supermarket shelf and which will make her housework easier, do the job faster, and give her more time for other activities.

Her husband, on the other hand, thinks of research in quite a different context. He identifies research with fact-finding surveys of consumer buying power, figures showing customer preferences and needs, charts and graphs detailing company growth and sales improvement, and, in general, the facts and figures representing the corporate economy. This information comes to him through "market research" which the "research analysts" of the company make available to him.

His twelve-year-old son goes to school and the teacher sends him to the library to find the names and the sizes of Columbus's three ships and also their route across the Atlantic. In so doing, she tells him that he is going to the library to do "research" for his history assignment.

His sister in high school has just completed a "piece of research" by writing a "research paper" on the role of the dark lady in the sonnets of Shakespeare. She has, of course, gone through all the motions of the "research" process by gathering her information on note cards, collecting a bibliography, and footnoting her statements in prescribed form. Furthermore, both she and her teacher seem quite serious in thinking of this as a "research project."

Unfortunately, many students have labored under the false impression that looking up a few facts and writing them down in a documented paper is research. Such activity is, of course, nothing more than fact finding and fact transcribing. No amount of transfer of information from one place to another, even though the act of transportation is acknowledged by footnote, can be dignified by the term *research.* Transfer of information, transportation of fact from one place to another, is simply that, nothing more! Yet the strange misconception that fact transferral is research persists; and, even more disconcerting, it grows in magnitude as the student progresses through the formal learning structure from grade school to college and even from college to graduate school. What goes on in the grades and throughout high school, bearing the misnomer of research, is further magnified and encouraged during the undergraduate years in college. The deception is enhanced at the college level by a more glorified terminology. Fact transportation in college is frequently exalted by calling the end product a "research report" or a "research document." Report, perhaps; and document, maybe—but research? Not at all.

The net result of all this is that the student becomes more and more deeply imbued with false concepts and incorrect conditioning. The student has never been taught; rather, he has been permitted to go unwittingly on his way without ever learning the true nature of research. He has never learned the distinguishing characteristics which differentiate true basic research from spurious fact accumulation.

When, therefore, this student comes to graduate study and is faced with his first course in research methodology or a seminar in basic research design, he is frequently unprepared for the discrete and unfamiliar demands that an entirely new academic discipline may make upon him. As a result, he may have a difficult time in fulfilling the exacting demands that writing a thesis or a dissertation requires of him. Consequently, he may give up in despair, or else, after many attempts, write such a mediocre final document that his graduate committee capitulates, despairing of ever getting a piece of real research from such a student.

All this is the result of the student's never having been taught the demands of pure research. Such students are unprepared to conceive of research as a discrete academic discipline. They have never learned the particular way of thinking about facts, not as ends in themselves, but merely as components in a total process whose ultimate aim is to reveal their significance in the quest for the discovery of truth.

WHAT RESEARCH IS

Having discussed at some length what research is not, let us consider what it is. Successful research begins with a proper orientation. It is essentially a way of thinking; it is a manner of regarding accumulated fact so that a collection of data becomes articulate to the mind of the researcher in terms of what those data mean and what those facts say.

Many students need to understand the implications of these statements. They need to see clearly the characteristics of what for many of them is an unfamiliar procedure. Research is simply the manner in which men solve the knotty problems in their attempt to push back the frontiers of human ignorance. We shall discuss these characteristics in the order in which they appear logically in the research process.

Characteristics of Research

Research has seven discrete characteristics which appear sequentially. Every researcher is familiar with these steps, which taken together comprise the particular approach to the discovery of truth which we call research.

• *Research begins with a question in the mind of the researcher.* Man is a curious animal. Everywhere he looks he sees phenomena which arouse his curiosity, which cause him to wonder, to speculate, and to ask questions. He discovers situations, the meaning of which he does not comprehend. By asking relevant questions man creates a favorable attitudinal climate, an inquisitive receptiveness to pertinent fact which is a basic prerequisite for research itself, for research arises from a question intelligently asked in the presence of a phenomenon that the researcher has observed and which puzzles him. By asking the right questions the researcher finds both relevance and direction in his quest for truth.

Look around you. Consider the unresolved and baffling situations that compel you to ask, "Why?" "What's the cause of that?" "What does it all mean?" Here, for example, is a familiar real-life situation: two children begin school from the same neighborhood; both are in the same classroom and have the same teacher. One learns to read and progresses well; the other has great difficulty with reading. Why? What do we really know about human learning and the reading process? What do we not know about human learning and the origin of reading disability in the early grades? These are questions that reveal man's need for knowledge. They are also questions that suggest departure points for research, for through research we can discover the answers in the light of the facts. Research, thus, begins with a questioning and inquisitive mind in the presence of baffling and perplexing fact.

• *Research requires a plan.* Research is not hoping naively that somehow, in some way, you will discover fortuitously the facts that you need or the truth that you seek. It is not aimless, undirected activity: merely "looking something up" in the hope that you may "come across" the solution to your problem. Research, rather, entails a definite plan, direction, and design.

The whole research process should proceed purposively from the awareness of the need to know to the point where the relevant facts speak to the researcher, giving him the answer. And between these two extremes there must be a clear statement of the research problem, a development of hypotheses, a design for gathering and interpreting the data, and finally a test of the hypotheses and an arrival at factually based conclusions. Research is, thus, an orderly procedure, planned and logical in design.

• *Research demands a clear statement of the problem.* Successful research begins with a clear, simple statement of the problem. The perplexing and unanswered questions that the researcher finds indigenous to the research situation must crystallize at the very beginning of the research endeavor in a precise and grammatically complete statement setting forth exactly what he seeks to discover. The reason for this is obvious: before we begin we must understand the problem and look at it objectively. We must see clearly what it is we are attempting to research. We shall say more about the research problem in a later chapter, but the necessity for a concise statement of the central problem that the research aims to solve cannot be overemphasized.

• *Research deals with the main problem through subproblems.* Most researchable problems have within them various other problem areas of lesser breadth and importance.

Because many researchers take neither the time nor the trouble to isolate the lesser problems within the major problem area, they find their research project becoming poorly defined, cumbersome, and unwieldy. From a practical standpoint, therefore, it is more expedient to divide the main problem into appropriate subproblems, all of which when resolved will result in the solution of the main research problem.

To illustrate: University X has been a fast-growing and rapidly changing institution for the past three quarters of a century. Originally conceived as a graduate school with a major emphasis on the social sciences, it has changed direction and emphasis over the years. Now University X is quite a different institution from that which its founding fathers envisioned. Underlying any educational institution is a basic philosophy, a fundamental orientation to the educational milieu in which it exists. A student wishes to determine the basic educational philosophy of University X. Nowhere is this stated explicitly. It is implicit, however, in the history, the structure, the policies, and the way in which the university operates. Moreover, the cumulative result of past events has been responsible for a significant change in direction of the university. Looked at in total perspective, the central issue begins to blur. We can perhaps bring matters back into focus and deal more effectively with the main question of the educational philosophy of University X by considering first some lesser aspects, or subproblems, of the main problem:

1. What was the original educational philosophy of the founders and early administration of the university?
2. What major events have caused a change in that philosophy?
3. What is the present educational philosophy of the university?

These three lesser problems, answered in terms of data derived from documents, addresses, university publications, and similar sources will provide an answer to the principal problem.

- *Research seeks direction through appropriate hypotheses.* Having stated the problem and the attendant subproblems, the subproblems are then each viewed through logical constructs called *hypotheses.* An hypothesis is a logical supposition, a reasonable guess, an educated conjecture which may give direction to thinking with respect to the problem and, thus, aid in solving it.

Hypotheses are a part of our everyday experience; we employ them in the approach to everyday problems. They represent the natural working of the human mind. Something happens. Immediately you attempt to account for the occurrence by a series of guesses, postulates, logical deductions. In so doing, you have been hypothesizing. For example, you flip the switch of your car; the starter grinds; but the car does not start. Here you have a problem for "research." What's wrong? Why doesn't the car start? You now begin a series of reasonable guesses as to the cause of the trouble. In other words, you hypothesize several possibilities:

1. You have no gasoline in the tank.
2. The spark plugs are worn out.
3. Moisture has condensed in the distributor cap, causing a short-circuit.

Each of these assumptions provides direction in seeking out the facts to determine the real reason why the car will not start. At this point you go in search of the facts. You check the fuel tank: it is half full. That rules out hypothesis 1. The motor has just been reconditioned, and new spark plugs were installed. That invalidates hypothesis 2. You glance out of the window of the car. You note that the other automobiles have condensation on them from the humidity and early-morning fog. Hypothesis 3 may lead you to the solution of the problem of your stalled car. To test this hypothesis you remove the distributor cap, wipe out the moisture that is indeed there, and replace it. The car starts. Hypothesis 3 is supported.

Similarly, when you are faced with a problem for research, you make educated guesses to assist you in discovering the solution and in giving you direction in looking for the facts.

• *Research deals with facts and their meaning.* Having now isolated the problem, subdivided it into appropriate subproblems, and posited hypotheses which will suggest the direction in which the facts may lie, the next step is to collect whatever facts seem to be pertinent to the problem and to organize them into meaningful aggregates, capable of being interpreted. We shall suggest methods of such organization in a later chapter. Facts, events, happenings, observations are in themselves merely facts, events, and happenings—nothing more. They are, nevertheless, potentially meaningful. Frequently, however, the significance of the data depends upon the way in which the facts are seen, the manner in which the data are regarded. Often different researchers read entirely different meanings from the same set of data. And, for the researcher, there is no single rule which will guide him unerringly to one "correct" interpretation. Two historians may study the same series of events. Each may be equally competent, both scrupulously honest in their reactions. One may read the meaning of the facts of history one way; the other, viewing precisely the same facts, may arrive at an entirely divergent interpretation. Which one is right? Perhaps both are, or perhaps neither is.

There was a time when we considered that clocks measured time and yardsticks measured space, and in one sense they do; but we further assumed that time and space were two separate and discrete entities. Now we regard both of these factors differently and deal with them within a more sophisticated concept called the time–space continuum. The facts of time and space have always been the same. The difference between the earlier and later concepts is not in the facts themselves, but in the increased keenness of insight that the researcher has had into their meaning.

• *Research is circular.* The research cycle begins simply: a questioning mind is confronted by a perplexing situation. To see his target clearly, the researcher isolates the central problem for research. This central problem is then further divided into subproblems, each of which is an integral part of the larger whole, and all of which collectively comprise the principal research problem. What we have been calling the environment out of which the researchable problem arises is more appropriately called the research universe,[1] and it is potentially fact-laden. The researcher seeks from within the universe for those particular facts which seem to be pertinent to the solution of the problem and its attendant subproblems. His search is facilitated by the construction of tentative hypotheses. They point in the direction of relevant facts. The collected facts are then organized, analyzed, and interpreted for the purpose of discovering what the facts mean. Such discovery aids, in turn, in solving the problem; and this, then, satisfies the question which gave rise to the research originally. Thus, the cycle is completed. Such is the format of all basic research.

Schematically, the "circle of research" might be represented by the diagram on p. 8. This diagram may be thought of more as a helix than as a circle. In the helical process of solving problems, we create still more problems; consequently, research continues progressively onward. To see research in this way is to invest it with a dynamic quality—a far cry from the common view of research as a static, end-in-itself matter.

[1] The term *universe* is perhaps better understood when it is looked at in terms of its elemental meaning. It means simply an "area" surrounding the problem which may contain facts relevant to the problem. Literally, the word signifies the factual area that revolves around the central inquiry, or main problem of the research. The word derives from *unus,* "one," and *vertere,* "to turn": that which turns or revolves around one central inquiry.

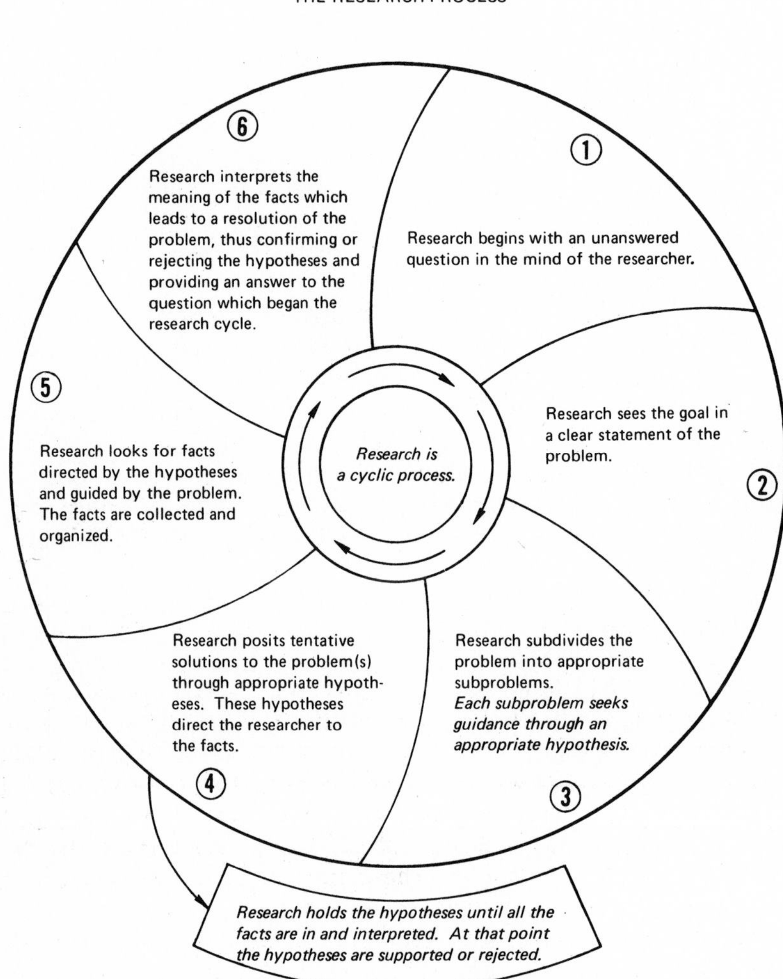

THE RESEARCH PROCESS
Research is a cyclic process.
1
Research begins with an unanswered question in the mind of the researcher.
2
Research sees the goal in a clear statement of the problem.
3
Research subdivides the problem into appropriate subproblems. Each subproblem seeks guidance through an appropriate hypothesis.
4
Research posits tentative solutions to the problem(s) through appropriate hypotheses. These hypotheses direct the researcher to the facts.
5
Research looks for facts directed by the hypotheses and guided by the problem. The facts are collected and organized.
6
Research interprets the meaning of the facts which leads to a resolution of the problem, thus confirming or rejecting the hypotheses and providing an answer to the question which began the research cycle.
Research holds the hypotheses until all the facts are in and interpreted. At that point the hypotheses are supported or rejected.

Practical Application

This book is more than a theoretical discussion of research and its methodology. In addition to the discussion—which is a very practical, grass-roots, "how-to-get-it-done" approach—this manual will provide you with an opportunity to apply those matters that have been discussed. It will provide you with an opportunity to go into the field and to observe research and to evaluate it. These applications of principle to operational research practices will be given in a special section at the back of the book.

We learn to do by doing. You become a researcher by engaging in those activities which provide training in the discipline of basic research. However, at the very outset you should be able to recognize research when you see it. You should also be able to recognize what is not research but masquerades as research. Turn, therefore, to p. 218, where you will find directions for surveying some research studies and evaluating them in terms of the guidelines suggested in the foregoing pages.

2 Tools of Research

Research, as we have pointed out in the preceding chapter, is simply a *systematic quest for undiscovered truth.* It is the search for an answer to an unresolved and perplexing question. In pursuit of his goal, however, the researcher frequently needs to enlist the aid of ancillary areas. These areas are peripheral to the research endeavor itself, but facility with and knowledge of the resources in these areas short-circuit the researcher's route to his objective. The skills and competencies which the researcher has in such ancillary areas of knowledge are called *tools of research.* These are commonly grouped into three categories: (a) bibliothecal tools, (b) statistical tools, and (c) linguistic tools.

Every researcher needs facts, some of which lie in already published documents. Have you, therefore, the independence and the necessary bibliothecal skills to use the library efficiently? Do you know where and how to locate necessary information without wasting time? Do you know the basic references that will aid you in weaving your way expertly through the maze of related literature and important documents which may be corollary but nevertheless essential to the resolution of your problem?

Many research problems deal with quantitative data. Do you have command of statistics so that you may apply appropriate statistical methods to the analysis of your data as a part of the interpretation of their meaning?

Do you read with ease and understanding languages in which data indispensable to the prosecution of your research project are found?

Your ability to handle with competence the tools necessary for the effective execution of your research will speed the research effort and simplify the carrying out of the project. Such an ability will also give the finished study the respectability and stature of genuine research.

Obviously, a manual such as this cannot cover in depth a discussion of the use of bibliothecal tools, linguistic needs, or the theory or application of statistics. There are many appropriate texts which will give you adequate help in these areas. Certain broad guidelines for all researchers can, however, be presented which may clarify for those who need such an elementary introduction some of the essential aspects of tool-of-research areas.

THE LIBRARY

You should be self-sufficient in the library. You should know its principal resources, understand its classification system, and be able to find the shortest route to the information that it contains. One rule is basic: *You learn to use the library by using it.* Nothing will take the place of actual hours of exploration spent in the library getting acquainted firsthand with its particular characteristics and the nature of its holdings. Every library is different. Each has its own emphases, its own personality. There are, however, some practical suggestions which will aid you in achieving facility with this most basic of all tools of research.

Know Your Way Around

The first basic requirement in using any library is to know its layout. When you go into an unfamiliar library, you should explore it quickly from end to end. This is absolutely essential to a later and more detailed knowledge of its resources.

Some libraries have manuals which will give you this information and these are available to students upon request. Inquire at the general circulation desk concerning the availability of such a guide. If there is no such guide, draw your own plan. Learn where the various holdings are located. Indicate on your sketch the location of special collections; the microfilm and microfiche reels, cards, and readers; the audio-visual materials; the reference section; the periodicals section; the vertical file; and the areas in the stacks and in the reference room where the books in the field of your special interest may be found.

Learn to Use the Catalog

The card catalog is the heart of the library and the principal means of locating its holdings. The catalog is a series of drawers containing 3- by 5-inch index cards on which is found the location and a description of each item that the library contains. As a general index to library resources, the card catalog will alert you to the various kinds of materials available: books, films, film strips, tapes, phonograph records, microfilm, microfiche, microprint, maps, pictures, slides, and similar materials. Frequently major topics within collected or edited works are indicated in the catalog by special cards, called author analytical cards or title analytical cards. Thus, if a play by Maxwell Anderson is one of the plays in a collection entitled *Modern American Drama,* it may be indicated by a card cataloged under "Anderson, Maxwell." If a major section of a volume entitled *Great Cathedrals of Western Europe* is given to Chartres cathedral, that fact may be separately indicated by a card in the catalog under "Chartres, Cathedral of," which would refer you to the composite work.

Rules for Catalog Arrangement. In most libraries the cards will be arranged alphabetically by author, subject, and title, but certain rules of precedence within the alphabetical framework are observed by librarians in placing the cards in the catalog. To know the simple rules of precedence is to be able to use the catalog with least loss of time and with greatest efficiency.

Briefly, these rules are (1) books *by* a person precede books *about* a person; (2) collected works usually precede individual works; (3) when the same word is common to (a) a person, (b) a place, or (c) a thing—or the title of a thing—the cards will be arranged in that order; for example:

Lincoln, Abraham (person) precedes cards dealing with
Lincoln, Nebraska (place) which cards precede those relating to
Lincoln Warehouse Corporation (thing)

(4) saints, popes, kings, and others are also arranged in that order of precedence; for example:

John, the Evangelist, Saint, precedes cards relating to
John XXIII, Pope, which cards precede those relating to
John, King of England, which cards precede those dealing with
John of Gaunt, Duke of Lancaster, whose cards precede those of
John, Henry E. (author) whose cards precede those of
John Ericsson Society, The (society, i.e., a thing)

(5) when two persons with the same name are listed, the one with the earlier birth date takes precedence over the one with the later birth date; for example, cards relating to

Girard, Stephen (1750-1831) take precedence over those relating to
Girard, Stephen (1843-1910)

Knowledge of these simple rules will save you a great deal of time, so that you can avoid thumbing through scores of cards, each of which bears a similar heading. Furthermore, knowing what to look for on a card will save you time and effort. Rather than taking the trouble to procure the book itself in order to learn its contents, you can find the book and its contents described in the card catalog.

For example, every catalog card has six separate *zones* of information. Each of these zones presents certain data that are important for an understanding of the book cataloged and for giving a preview of its contents. In reading from the top to the bottom of the catalog card, we shall describe each zone and the particular data it presents. On p. 12 we have analyzed a catalog card, noting in the key the items belonging to each zone. The informational zones are as follows:

- Zone 1, which indicates authorship and/or categorical classification to which the book belongs. In this zone also is placed the classification *call number* of the book.
- Zone 2, which contains the bibliographical data relating to the book: title, subtitle, edition, place of publication, publisher, and date.
- Zone 3, which contains information about the make-up of the book: number of pages (including "front matter" pages, expressed as lower case Roman numerals); presence of illustrations, maps, plates, facsimile pages, and other features, and the height of the book, expressed in centimeters.
- Zone 4, which contains supplementary information concerning the book, usually as to its origin, whether it was originally a series of lectures, a foreign work which has been translated, a reprint, a revision, and other relevant data concerning the origin of the book. The table of contents of the book is also sometimes given in this area of the catalog card.
- Zone 5, which contains the classification data, indicating the categories under which the book may be indexed in the card catalog: the arabic numerals giving the assigned categories under which the book may be cataloged; the Roman numerals, following which appears the name of any other individual connected with the authorship of the book, such as a joint author, an editor, collaborator, or similar person; and the word *Title*, meaning that the book is also to be cataloged under the first significant word of the title.
- Zone 6, which contains the assigned call numbers for the book according to both the Library of Congress Classification System and also the Dewey Decimal

Classification System. At the extreme right is another number, which is the order number for securing a set of catalog cards from the Library of Congress, which issues standard sets of cards for libraries of each book published.

Let us take a card from the catalog and analyze it.

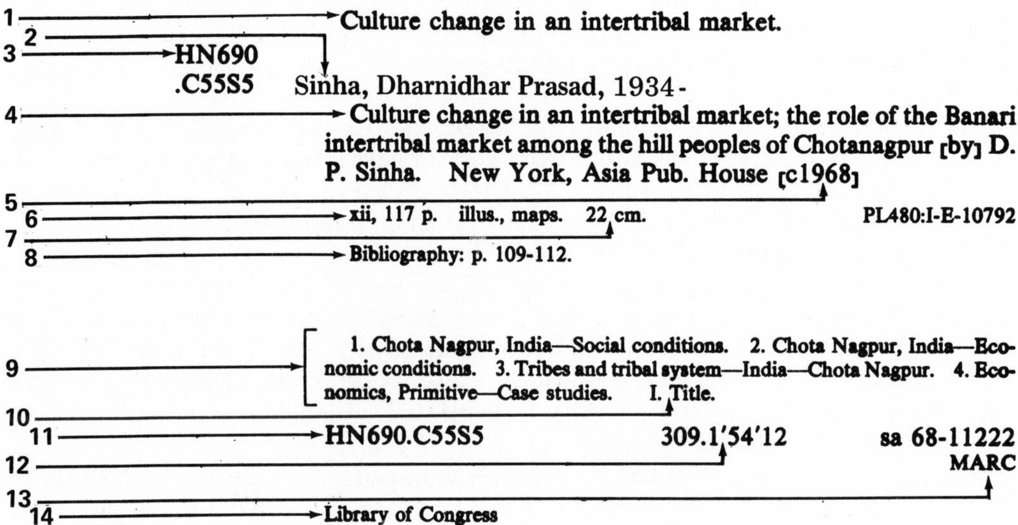

Culture change in an intertribal market.

HN690
.C55S5 Sinha, Dharnidhar Prasad, 1934-
Culture change in an intertribal market; the role of the Banari intertribal market among the hill peoples of Chotanagpur [by] D. P. Sinha. New York, Asia Pub. House [c1968]
xii, 117 p. illus., maps. 22 cm. PL480:I-E-10792
Bibliography: p. 109-112.

1. Chota Nagpur, India—Social conditions. 2. Chota Nagpur, India—Economic conditions. 3. Tribes and tribal system—India—Chota Nagpur. 4. Economics, Primitive—Case studies. I. Title.

HN690.C55S5 309.1'54'12 sa 68-11222
MARC

Library of Congress

The items which are numbered in the left column are as follows:

Zone 1
1. *The classification of the book in terms of its subject matter.*
2. *The author's name, together with birth date.*
3. *The call number (Library of Congress System).*

Zone 2
4. *The title of the book, followed by the subtitle.*
5. *Indicates the copyright date. Information on date of publication does not appear in the book. It has been supplied by quoting a reasonably accurate date as indicated by the brackets.*

Zone 3
6. *The number of pages the book contains. Roman numerals indicate number of prefatory pages. The book also contains illustrations and maps.*
7. *The height of the book as it stands upon the shelf.*
8. *An indication that the book has a four-page bibliography. A description of the contents of the book frequently appears in this area.*

Zone 4 *(None shown on this card.)*

Zone 5
9. *The categories under which the book will be cataloged, in addition to author's name.*
10. *Indicates that the book will also be cataloged by the title.*

Zone 6
11. *The Library of Congress call number.*
12. *The Dewey Decimal call number.*
13. *The order number of this particular set of cards, obtained from the Library of Congress.*
14. *Indicates the "publisher" of the card.*

Perhaps one of the most important features of the catalog card is the classification symbol, found in the upper left-hand corner of the card. This symbol, known as the *call number*, indicates where the book will be found in the library stacks and the type of material it contains. The call number will belong to one of two systems used in classifying the resources of the library: the Dewey Decimal Classification System or the Library of Congress Classification System. Each of these will be discussed briefly.

The Dewey Decimal Classification System. Because the Dewey Decimal Classification System is more widely used than the Library of Congress Classification System, it will be discussed here in greater detail. The Dewey classification is used, for example, in practically all school libraries, in 98 per cent of the public libraries, and in 86 per cent of the college libraries in the United States.[1] Elsewhere in the world, the Dewey Decimal Classification is followed by a majority of libraries in the English-speaking countries and countries now or formerly a part of the British Commonwealth of nations. In addition, it is perhaps the most important single system worldwide and is used in almost every nation on the globe.[2]

The system was conceived in 1873 by young Melvil Dewey, when he was a student at Amherst. He divided all human knowledge into ten major categories as follows:

000	General works	500	Pure science
100	Philosophy	600	Technology, applied science, useful arts
200	Religion	700	The arts
300	Social sciences	800	Literature, belles lettres
400	Language	900	History, biography

Every student should know these ten categories as well as he knows the alphabet. They are a part of his basic knowledge as a researcher, and he will use this information every time he enters a library or consults a card catalog using the Dewey classification.

The system progresses from the preceding ten general classifications to more and more precise subclassifications, based on a decade arrangement. For example, each of the major basic categories is again divided into ten subcategories, thus providing 100 slots into which books may be classified. Each of these 100 slots is again divided into ten further classifications. That makes 1,000 subdivisions. Usually this three-digit thousand category is followed by a decimal point, after which the subdividing continues into tens and hundreds of thousands and even millions of classes. The second subdivision, showing the subclassifications of the ten basic categories, may illustrate this:

000	General Works	100	Philosophy
010	Bibliography	110	Metaphysics
020	Library science	120	Metaphysical theories
030	General encyclopedias	130	Branches of psychology
040	General collected essays	140	Philosophical topics
050	General periodicals	150	General psychology
060	General societies	160	Logic
070	Newspaper journalism	170	Ethics
080	Collected works	180	Ancient and medieval philosophy
090	Manuscripts and rare books		

[1] Thelma Eaton, *Cataloging and Classification: An Introductory Manual,* third edition (Champaign, Ill.: The Illinois Union Bookstore, 1963), p. 65.

[2] Melvil Dewey, *Dewey Decimal Classification and Relative Index,* ninth abridged edition (Lake Placid Club, N.Y.: Lake Placid Club Educational Foundation, 1965), p. 7.

190 Modern philosophy
200 Religion
210 Natural theology
220 Bible
230 Doctrinal theology
240 Devotional & practical
250 Pastoral theology
260 Christian church
270 Christian church history
280 Christian churches & sects
290 Other religions
300 Social Sciences
310 Statistics
320 Political science
330 Economics
340 Law
350 Public administration
360 Social welfare
370 Education
380 Public services and utilities
390 Customs and folklore
400 Language
410 Comparative linguistics
420 English and Anglo-Saxon
430 Germanic languages
440 French, Provençal, Catalan
450 Italian, Rumanian
460 Spanish, Portuguese
470 Latin and other Italic
480 Classical and modern Greek
490 Other languages
500 Pure Science
510 Mathematics
520 Astronomy
530 Physics
540 Chemistry and allied sciences
550 Earth sciences
560 Paleontology
570 Anthropology and biology
580 Botanical sciences
590 Zoological sciences
600 Technology, Applied Science, Useful Arts
610 Medical sciences
620 Engineering
630 Agriculture
640 Home economics
650 Business
660 Chemical technology
670 Manufactures
680 Other manufactures
690 Building construction
700 The Arts
710 Landscape and civic art
720 Architecture
730 Sculpture
740 Drawing and decorative arts
750 Painting
760 Prints and print making
770 Photography
780 Music
790 Recreation
800 Literature, Belles Lettres
810 American literature in English
820 English and Old English
830 Germanic literatures
840 French, Provençal, Catalan
850 Italian, Rumanian
860 Spanish, Portuguese
870 Latin and other Italic literatures
880 Classical and modern Greek
890 Other literatures
900 History, Biography
910 Geography, travels, description
920 Biography
930 Ancient history
940 Europe
950 Asia
960 Africa
970 North America
980 South America
990 Other parts of the world

These expanded classification categories are an extension of the basic ten divisions into which Melvil Dewey originally divided all human knowledge. Although there is little conformity between some of the classes, a cursory glance at the 400 (Philology), 800 (Literature), and 900 (History) categories will show some parallels worth noting. In each of these classes, the same digit means always the same thing: 420 is *English* philology; 820 is *English* literature; 942 designates *English* history. The 2 in each of these designations stands for England.

Another group of symbols, known as *form divisions,* assists the student to understand more clearly the meaning of some Dewey classification call numbers. Form-division numbers are common to all classes and many divisions. Because these numbers recur in various classes the main forms are here defined and their use is explained.[3]

01 Theory

An exposition of the subject treated from the theoretical, philosophical, or psychological point of view, such as R. M. Ogden has used in his book *The Psychology of Art,* 701.

02 Compends, manuals, outlines

A subject treated briefly, or in outline only, as *Epitome of Ancient, Medieval and Modern History,* compiled by Carl Ploetz, which takes the number 902.

03 Dictionaries, encyclopedias

The subject treated in brief, through definitions, or more broadly in a panoramic style. This form number is illustrated by the *Dictionary of Architecture,* edited by Russell Sturgis, which goes in 720.3.

04 Essays, lectures

A book in which the subject is treated in detached chapters rather than as a continuous treatise, such as Brander Matthews' *Essays on English,* which is classified in 420.4.

05 Periodicals

Serial publications of a literary nature or in which the subject is treated in articles, papers, and so on. *The Architectural Record,* 720.5, illustrates this. Periodicals not limited to subject, such as *The Atlantic Monthly,* are classified in 050.

06 Societies

The official publications of societies, such as reports and proceedings. *The Transactions of the Royal Institute of British Architects,* 720.6, is an example. General learned societies are classified in 060.

07 Study and teaching

Books on how to study and how to teach a subject, such as R. M. Pearson's *The New Art Education,* 707. Textbooks are not classified here, but with the general class or as 02 (for example, in 530.2).

08 Polygraphy, collections

Books very miscellaneous in style and treatment, anthologies, chrestomathies, or collected works of an author when it is desirable to keep these together. The Harvard Classics would go in 080 and *The Oxford Book of English Verse* would go in 821.08. This form number has been interpreted to include special collections in some of the classes, e.g., 608 has been used for patents, 708 for art galleries and museums.

09 History

Books in which the history of the subject is told, such as Fletcher's *History of Architecture,* 720.9. This form number can be divided geographically and is used not only for the history of a subject, but also for the local consideration of a subject, even when descriptive rather than historical.

[3]Reprinted by permission from Margaret Mann, *Introduction to the Cataloging and Classification of Books,* second edition (Chicago: The American Library Association, 1943), pp. 50–51.

Before leaving the discussion of the card catalog, a brief amplification should be made of the comment on an earlier page with reference to the call number,[4] which indicated that the call number may provide a clue as to the type of material the book contains.

Let us take a call number and analyze it to see precisely what information it does contain and how you may read it. The call number is

530.12
D597 p
1958

Each level of the preceding call number gives a different type of information. The first set of digits (530.12) is the Dewey Decimal classification number and describes the subject matter of the book numerically. The second level contains information, largely concerning the author and this particular book that he wrote. The third level identifies the edition of the book by giving the publication date of this particular volume. If you refer to the second Dewey subdivision classification given on pp. 14–15, you will begin to see the rationale behind the Dewey Decimal classification symbol:

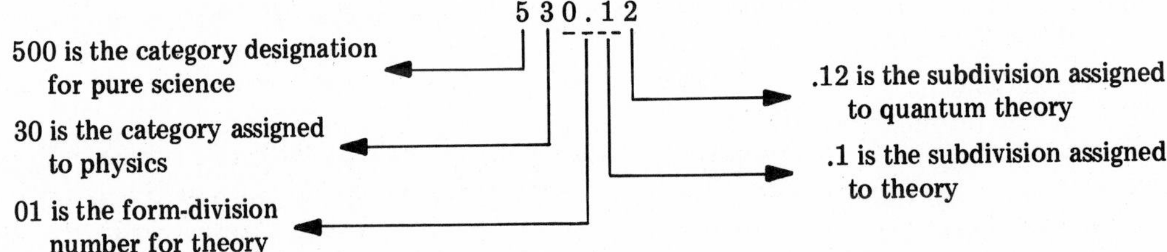
5 3 0 . 1 2
500 is the category designation for pure science
30 is the category assigned to physics
01 is the form-division number for theory
.12 is the subdivision assigned to quantum theory
.1 is the subdivision assigned to theory

From this information, this is the book in the area of physics which deals with the quantum theory. But the next level tells us more:

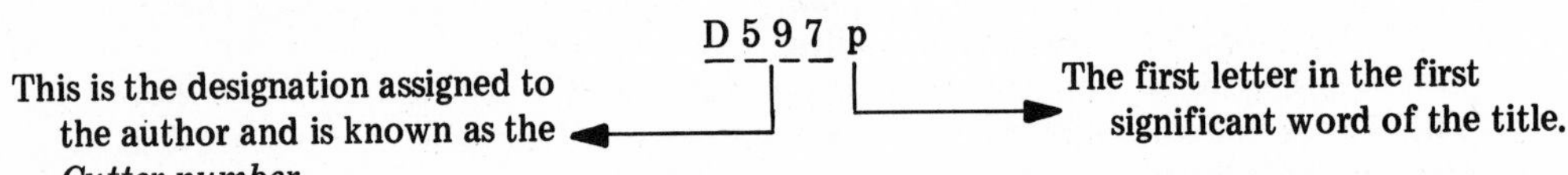
D 5 9 7 p
This is the designation assigned to the author and is known as the *Cutter number.*
The first letter in the first significant word of the title.

The book was, indeed, written by a scientist whose last name begins with the letter *D* and all of his books will bear the designation D597. The book was published in 1958. This, as the title page will show, was the year in which the fourth edition of the famous book by Paul A. C. Dirac, *The Principles of Quantum Mechanics*, was published.

Thus, the call number is a compact numerical code, useful for not only locating the particular book among others on the stack shelf, but providing you, through numerical shorthand, with information about the book, the type of material it contains, and the general area of knowledge to which it belongs.

The Library of Congress Classification System. The second classification system which is in general use, particularly in larger libraries, is the Library of Congress classification system. Instead of a numerical category classification, the Library of Congress system employs a system of letter designations as follows:

A	General works: polygraphy	D	History: general and Old World; topography
B	Philosophy, religion	E–F	History: America
C	History: auxiliary sciences		

[4] See p. 13.

G	Geography, anthropology, folklore	P	Philology and literature
H	Social sciences	Q	Science
J	Political science	R	Medicine
K	Law	S	Agriculture
L	Education	T	Technology
M	Music	U	Military science
N	Fine arts	V	Naval science
		Z	Bibliography and library science

Basic Reference Works

To use the library effectively as a basic tool of research, you should know the shortest possible route to the information you need. The usual approach to instruction in the use of the library is to overwhelm the student with a multitude of titles in the hope that merely by mentioning them he may become aware that such works exist. Unless the student is forced into examining each of them—an exercise which may be time-consuming and only partially satisfactory in meeting the immediate needs of the student—they may remain forever nebulous. This is a fragmentary approach. Without knowing the needs or the specific informational problems for which the student seeks help, it is impossible to mention every usable reference tool and informational aid. Should we attempt to do so, the listing of such resources would fill the remaining pages of this book. There is a better way to attack the problem.

Most students are like the man who died a pauper but who lived in a house built over a buried treasure. They have the riches of the informational world at their fingertips but do not know how to uncover that wealth. There is no informational need a student has that cannot be met by some bibliographical tool. Take, for example, the following questions which might come up in the course of a research investigation. Where would you go to find the information?

> Where may I find the nearest library which has Volume 5 of *The Educator-Journal*, published in Indianapolis, Indiana, from August 1900 to April 1924?
>
> Shortly after Ralph Waldo Emerson published his volume of essays entitled *Conduct of Life*, in 1860, Noah Porter reviewed the book in *The New Englander*. What work should I consult to locate this review?
>
> Shirley Ann Hill received her Ph.D. degree in 1961. What was the title of her dissertation and, briefly, what were her findings?
>
> In 1916 John Dewey published *Essays in Experimental Logic.* The [London] *Times Literary Supplement* reviewed the book. How may I find, in part, what the review said?

Questions similar to these will confront you when you become actively engaged in your research project. Eight keys will unlock for you the treasury of printed knowledge and help answer such questions. These are the master guides to the basic reference literature of research. Every researcher, though he may not have a library, should have a shelf with most of these eight books upon it. It is imperative to know these eight books thoroughly. Every researcher should be intimately acquainted with the format, the content, and the specific purpose of each of them. Here are the eight keys to reference materials:

Alexander, Carter, and Arvid J. Burke. *How to Locate Educational Information and Data.* New York: Bureau of Publications, Teachers College, Columbia University, 1950.[5]

[5] This work is no longer in print. It has been issued under a new title, *Documentation in Education*, edited by Arvid J. Burke and Mary A. Burke.

Burke, Arvid J., and Mary A. Burke. *Documentation in Education.* New York: Teachers College Press, Columbia University, 1967.

Chandler, G. *How to Find Out: A Guide to Sources of Information for All.* Oxford: Pergamon Press, Inc., 1963.

Gates, Jean K. *Guide to the Use of Books and Libraries.* New York: McGraw-Hill Book Company, 1962.

Hoffman, Hester R. *The Reader's Adviser.* Tenth edition. New York: R. R. Bowker Co., 1964.

Murphey, Robert W. *How and Where to Look It Up.* New York: McGraw-Hill Book Company, 1958.

Shores, Louis. *Basic Reference Sources.* Chicago: American Library Association, 1954.

Winchell, Constance M. *Guide to Reference Books.* Eighth edition. Chicago: American Library Association, 1966.

The Master Key to the Library on p. 21 will lead you directly to those pages in each of the preceding eight major reference works where the principal sources of information are described which relate to each of the categories indicated in the left-hand column.

Let's take a typical informational search situation to see how to use the Master Key to the Library. After his retirement from the presidency, George Washington lived for almost three years as a colonial gentleman at Mount Vernon, a few miles south of Alexandria, Virginia. You would like to reconstruct as nearly as possible the times, the events, the ebb and flow of life in that part of Virginia that formed the intimate events of Washington's life. How can you do it? Perhaps the newspapers of the day would give the best picture of Virginia life as Washington knew it. But where does one find such newspapers?

Let us first consult the Master Key. The fourteenth item in the left-hand column is entitled *Newspapers.* We find that every key work, except Hoffman, has a section dealing with newspapers. In Constance Winchell's *Guide to Reference Books*, newspapers are discussed on pp. 150–163. We consult Winchell and find, on p. 151, the following reference to Brigham, *History and Bibliography of American Newspapers, 1690–1820:*

> Brigham, Clarence S. History and bibliography of American newspapers, 1690–1820. Worcester, Mass., Amer. Antiquarian Soc., 1947. 2v. (Repr.: Hamden, Conn., Archon, 1962. 2v. [incl.] Additions and corrections)
>
> AG8
>
> Originally published in the *Proceedings* of the American Antiquarian Society, 1913–27. This cumulated edition, a work of the first importance, includes corrections, additions, and more detailed listings. Arranged alphabetically by state and town, it lists 2120 newspapers published between 1690 and 1820 with indication of location of files in all parts of the country. Historical notes for each paper give title, date of establishment, exact dates of changes of titles, names of editors and publishers, frequency, etc.
>
> The bibliography is followed by lists of libraries and private owners, an index of titles, and an index of printers.
>
> With *American newspapers*, 1821–1936 (AG5), this forms a comprehensive record of American newspaper files from 1690–1936.
>
> Additions and corrections. 1961. 50p. (Repr. from the *Proceedings* of the American Antiquarian Society, April 1961)

Next we go to the card catalog to determine whether the library has Brigham's *History and Bibliography.* It is found with *Ref.* typed over the call number, indicating that this work is in the reference section of the library. Consulting it, we find that at one time or another from 1690 to 1820 eleven newspapers were published in Alexandria, Virginia. George Washington, however, lived at Mount Vernon only from March, 1797, until his death in December, 1799. During that time, however, Brigham reports only two papers, the *Alexandria Times* (1797–1802) and the [Alexandria] *Columbian Mirror* (1792–1800), were published in Alexandria. Each would be appropriate to our inquiry. Brigham lists them, together with the locations where they may be consulted, as follows:

> **Alexandria Times, 1797-1802.**
>
> Daily, Established Apr. 10, 1797, by Thomas & Westcott [John V. Thomas and James D. Westcott], with the title of "The Times. Alexandria Advertiser." In the heading the words "Alexandria Advertiser" were in larger type than "The Times," but the proprietors speak of their paper in the prospectus as "The Times and Alexandria Advertiser," which title is also used as a column heading on the second page. With the issue of Apr. 17, 1799, the title was altered to "The Times; and District of Columbia Daily Advertiser." Thomas retired and the publishers became J[ohn] & J[ames] D. Westcott. With the issue of May 3, 1802, the partnership was dissolved and the paper was published by J. D. Westcott. On July 31, 1802, vol. 8, no. 1641, the paper was discontinued by Westcott, who announced that he would thereafter publish a tri-weekly paper to be called "The Columbian Advertiser," which see.
>
> Lib. Congress has May 20, July 31, 1797-Jan. 1, 1799; Oct. 26, 1799-Apr. 15, 1800; Dec. 2, 1800; Jan. 1-June 15, 1801.
>
> Harvard has Apr. 10-12, 14-21, Nov. 11-14, Dec. 30, 1797; Jan. 1, 6, 8, 1798; Mar. 19, 1801-July 31, 1802, fair.
>
> Georgetown Univ. has Jan. 2-June 29, 1798.
>
> Univ. of Mich. (Clements) has July 2-Oct. 13, 1798.
>
> Wis. Hist. Soc. has Apr. 17-Oct. 15, 1799; Apr. 17, 1800-Oct. 14, 1801; Apr. 16-July 31, 1802.
>
> Am. Antiq. Soc. has May 19, 1797; Apr. 24, 1798; Mar. 4, 1800; July 9, 1801; May 3-July 31, 1802.
>
> C. C. Carlin, Jr., Alexandria, has Apr. 14, 1797.
>
> Univ. of Chicago has Aug. 4, 1797; Oct. 8, 1798.
>
> N.Y. Pub. Lib. has Feb. 4, 1799; Sept. 23, 1801.
>
> Huntington Lib. has Feb. 25, 26, 1800.
>
> **[Alexandria] Columbian Mirror, 1792-1800.**
>
> Semi-weekly and tri-weekly. Established as a semi-weekly Nov. 21, 1792, by John Smith and Ellis Price, with the title of "The Columbian Mirror and Alexandria Gazette." With the issue of Sept. 7, 1793, the partnership was dissolved and Ellis Price became sole publisher. With the issue of Dec. 23, 1793, the paper was changed from semi-weekly to tri-weekly. With the issue of Nov. 29, 1796, Henry Gird, Jun. was admitted to partnership, under the firm name of Ellis Price and Henry Gird, Jun. With the issue of Nov. 21, 1797, Henry Gird withdrew and Ellis Price again became sole publisher. With the issue of Feb. 27, 1798, Price retired and Henry Gird, Jun., became the publisher. In December, 1799, Gird again retired and Ellis Price became publisher. With the issue of Sept. 16, 1800, Price retired, William Fowler became the publisher and so continued to the date of the last issue located, that of Dec. 6, 1800. The last numbered issue is that of Nov. 29, 1800, vol. 8, no. 1184. On Dec. 9, 1800, he sold the paper to S. Snowden & Co., who had just started the "Alexandria Advertiser."
>
> Lib. Congress has Nov. 21, 1792-Nov. 13, 1793; Oct. 3, 1795; Feb. 6, Mar. 1, 1796; Apr. 4, 1797; Aug. 25, 1798; Jan. 2, Nov. 27, 29, 1800.
>
> Harvard has Feb. 28, Mar. 12, 17, May 7, 12, 23-28, June 9, 11, 20, 23, 30, July 4, 7, 16-21, 28, Aug. 6, 13, 15, Oct. 8, Nov. 24, 1795; Jan. 1, Feb. 13, Mar. 5, 8, 17, 19, 24, Apr. 14, 16, 26, May 10, 12, 17, 24, 26, June 16, 28,

30, July 7, 23, 30-Aug. 6, 11-Sept. 3, 10-17, 22, 27, Oct. 4-20, 25-Nov. 8, 15, 17, 22-Dec. 31, 1796; Jan. 2-28, Feb. 2-7, 11, 16-Apr. 11, 15-22, 27, 29, May 18, 25, June 1, 8, 13, 15, 20, 27, July 1, 6, Aug. 12, 19, 31, Sept. 28-Oct. 10, 21, Nov. 2-9, Dec. 5, 1797; Jan. 4, Feb. 8, 10, 22, 27, Apr. 14, 24, May 5, 12, 17-22, 29, 31, June 12, 19, 21, July 21, Aug. 9, Sept. 6, Oct. 9, 27, Nov. 1, 6, 15, Dec. 6, 8, 1798; Feb. 9, 19, 28, Apr. 13, 18, 20, 25, May 11, 14, 23, June 4, 13, 15, 27, July 16, Aug. 6, 10, 15, 22, 27, 31-Sept. 12, 19, 21, 26-Oct. 1, 5-10, 15, 17, 22, 24, 31, Nov. 2-9, 16, 19, 26, Dec. 12, 24, 1799; Jan. 11-16, 21, 25, 30, Feb. 1, 6-13, 18, 20, 27-Mar. 6, 11-22, 27, Apr. 1, 10-24, 29-May 3, 13, 22-31, June 5, 21, 24, July 1, 7, 11, 17, Sept. 16, Oct. 2, 4, 9, 11, 21-28, Nov. 1, 4, 11-15, 27, Dec. 2, 6, 1800.

Am. Antiq. Soc. has Dec. 5, 15, 1792; Jan. 9, 16, Apr. 10, Aug. 24, Oct. 5, 23, 30, Dec. 18, 1793; Apr. 19, May 24, June 19, Aug. 21, 28, 1794; Apr. 30, June 16, Aug. 6, 1795; Mar. 12, Apr. 16, May 5, June 7, 1796; Nov. 7, 1797, Jan. 13, Mar, 13, June 16, 1798; Jan. 10, May 7, 1799; Feb. 27, Mar. 4, Oct. 11, 18, 23, 30, Nov. 1, 4, 18, 25, Dec. 6, 1800.

N. Y. Pub. Lib. has Aug. 4, Dec. 3-31, 1795; Jan. 2-May 7, 12-June 21, 25-July 2, 28-Oct. 11, 15, 18, 22-Nov. 12, 1796; Feb. 15, 1798.

N. Y. Hist. Soc. has Mar. 20, 27, Apr. 6, 10, May 4, 18, 1793; Mar. 7, 1799.

Wis. Hist. Soc. has July 9, Aug. 8, 27, Sept. 15, 17, 1795.

Phil. Lib. Co. has Oct. 22, 29, Nov. 21, 24, 26, Dec. 8, 1795.

Washington & Lee Univ. has Aug. 1, 1795.

Mrs. Lawrence Stabler, Alexandria, has Jan. 21, Feb. 25, 1796.

Boston Pub. Lib. has Jan. 13, 1798.

Univ. of Chicago has Feb. 15, 1799.

Va. State Lib. has Jan. 2, 1800.

Huntington Lib. has Feb. 22, 1800.

On the next page is the Master Key to the Library and Its Resources.

Practical Application

In this section we have been discussing the skills of locating information in the library by means of the Master Key to the Library. Perhaps you will learn to use those Master Keys more effectively and become acquainted with the resources of the library more intimately if we give you a series of project assignments that are similar to those that every researcher faces at one time or another.

Turn, therefore, to Project 2 in the practicum section of this book. There you will be given the opportunity to apply what you have been reading about in these pages.

STATISTICS

Statistics is merely a way of looking at the facts of the real world. This information from our environment reaches us in various ways. Some of it comes in the form of an arithmetic symbol: the size of human aggregations, the intensity of heat, of pressure, of the pull of gravity on physical mass. Other concepts of the not-so-real world we also try to capture by means of numbers: the level of one's intelligence, the strength of one's preferences or beliefs, achievement in academic performance, the worth of an employee to an organization, and so on. Thus, many of the facts of life are statistical.

It is unfortunate, therefore, that so many students regard statistics as a necessary evil lying astride the path of their progress in research. The strange mathematical symbols, the

Master Key to the Library and Its Resources as Based on the Principal Eight Bibliographic Guides for Researchers

To find sources of information about any of the following categories, consult the pages indicated for each basic reference work	Alexander and Burke*	Burke and Burke	Chandler	Gates	Courtney	Murphey	Shores	Winchell
Abstracts	89-99	259-277	44-47	208-209		153	240-241	525-526
Annuals, almanacs	213-214	128-137	48-50	126	II: 79-82†	85-96	88-97	*passim* *See index*
Audio-visual materials	315-316	185-195		134-136		199-203	226-235, 326-339	29-30
Books, guides to	197-241	65-77, 197-256	8-18	107-108, 129-132	I: 18-72, II: 59-82	155-172	190-206	1-64
Dictionaries (*For biographical dictionaries see,* People, books about)	386-395	78-92	81-90	80-88	II: 68-74	97-135	23-55	91 ff.
Directories	361-370	96-105	79	110-117	II: 68-74	173-181	126-135	*passim*
Dissertations and theses	396-404	358-371	29-32	138		43-44, 391		163-167
Encyclopedias	215	138-156	24-29	89-95	*See index Vol. II*	49-84	56-87	81 ff.
Facts (trivia), how to locate	216-217	138-156	48-50	183-184		311-649	136-149	154-165
Government publications	217, 286-304	297-330	55-58	140-146	II: 67-68	183-192	207-225	*passim*
Handbooks and manuals	212-213	128-137		124-128 *passim*	*passim*	*passim*	136-158	*passim*
Indexes	85-125	257-277	38-44	96-109	II: 3, 76, 215, 351, 388, 598	143-153	173-189	144-154
Libraries, how to use	3-84	23-45	1-24	3-79		27-34	1-22 236-247	
Newspapers	100, 371-385	172-184	42-44	105-107	II: 752-755	139-145	159-168	150-163
People, books about	338-370	105-117	172-175	110-117	I: 1008-1018, II: 1-16, 68-74	207-258	98-110	167-197
Periodicals	85-125	257-296	33-44	96-104		137-153	167-172	132-150
Places (geographical locations)		118-127	169-172	176-179		259-310	111-125	441-461
Reference works: general	197-223	65-77	21-24	73-79, 149-153	I: 39-72, II: 59-81	3-25, 170-172	4, 17-22	1-65
Research and report writing	249-257, 396-404	358-371		233-247		35-45		164
Societies and associations	242-262	97-101	50, 52-56, 102-103			541-545		77-81
Statistical information	215, 218, 405-418	157-171	72-73	127, 174, 184	II: 79-80	638-639	144-147	372-387
Textbooks	305-319	152-154			II: 65	163		33
Yearbooks	216, 218-219	129-137		124-128, 151	II: 79-80	*See index*	88-97	*passim*

*This work is no longer in print. It has been issued under a new title, *Documentation in Education,* edited by Arvid J. Burke and Mary A. Burke. Because it has been for so long a standard reference work and is found in so many libraries, it is included here as well as the Burke and Burke title which has superseded it.

†Courtney is a two-volume work. The volume will be indicated by Roman numerals.

multistoried and complex equations, the unfamiliar terminology frighten them unnecessarily. Statistics really is a very simple matter. It is merely a type of language into which the facts of life may be translated; when this is done they are able to speak more clearly and the researcher may see their nature and interrelationships more clearly. The researcher is thus able to see what otherwise he would be incapable of seeing. Put very simply, for those who may feel more comfortable with definitions, a quasidefinition of statistics might be as follows: *Statistics is a language which, through its own special symbols and grammar, takes the numerical facts of life and translates them meaningfully.*

Let us illustrate what we have just been saying. Take an everyday example. Joe is in high school. During the month of February he gets the following daily grades:

92	69	91	70	90	89
72	87	73	86	85	75
84	76	83	83	77	81
		78	79		

These are the raw numerical facts—the data, in researcher's language—directly from a life situation. As they stand in the above array they do not say very much, other than the fact that Joe's performance seems to be broadly inconsistent.

Now suppose we treat these data statistically, employing at first only the very simplest of statistical, or quasistatistical, processes. We shall begin by arranging Joe's grades in a table under the respective day of the week, Monday through Friday, on which the grade was earned.

FEBRUARY				
Mon.	Tue.	Wed.	Thur.	Fri.
92	69	91	70	90
89	72	87	73	86
85	75	84	76	83
83	77	81	78	79

Remember what we have said: Statistics is a means of taking numerical facts and translating them meaningfully. We have put Joe's grades into the most elementary statistical form, a simple statistical array, yet it is sufficient to yield a significant amount of information that was not apparent originally.

We now have the scores within a time sequence. We may now inspect Joe's grades two-dimensionally instead of the straight linear progression as first presented; we may read the grades horizontally as well as vertically. Reading them horizontally, we note that Joe's grades on Monday, Wednesday, and Friday are considerably higher than on Tuesday and Thursday. Throughout the month this pattern is consistent, although in diminishing degree.

As we read the columns vertically, we note an interesting phenomenon. Whereas Joe's grades seemingly deteriorate during each successive week on Monday, Wednesday, and Friday, they steadily improve during successive weeks on Tuesdays and Thursdays. Such behavior of data should alert the researcher; for such an effect, there must be a cause. We shall comment on this later.

Remember the definition: *Statistics takes the numerical facts of life and translates them meaningfully.*

We have already read some meaning into Joe's grades. With a little further treatment of the data, subjecting these grades to one or two additional, although extremely elemental, statistical processes, we shall force the data to tell us much more than they have already done. Let us take the same facts and represent them now in the form of a simple line graph.[6]

Note the difference between the three presentations of the same set of facts. Each has its own unique characteristics: certain particular emphases which no other form of presentation sets forth nearly so well.

[6] For a discussion of reading graphic material, see the author's Chapter IV in *Read with Speed and Precision* (New York: McGraw-Hill Book Company, 1963), entitled "Reading Graphic Presentations—The Ability to See Facts in Action," pp. 76–87.

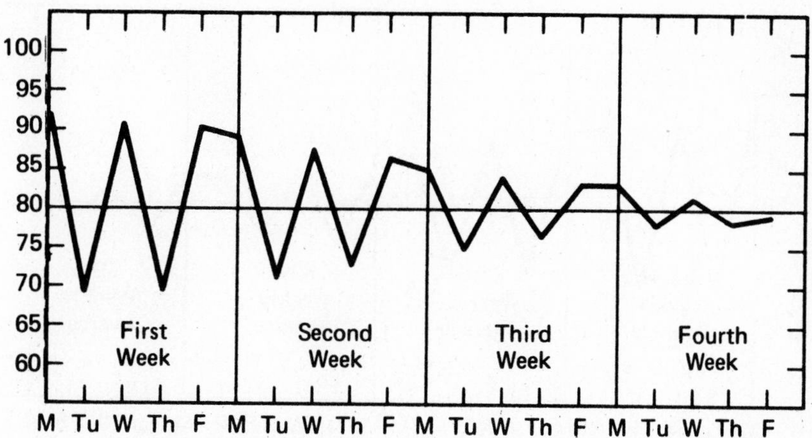

The first set of facts was a mere listing of Joe's grades. It was a straight, linear recounting of the grades in the order in which they were earned. Of all arrays this was the simplest and the least meaningful. The second presentation added the day-month dimension. It placed the data for the first time in a two-dimensional setting. Finally, the line graph presented the most dramatic view of all. It indicated several characteristics not seen so clearly in either of the other displays.

One fact stands out clearly. *Looking at data in only one way yields but a fractional view of those data and, hence, provides only a small segment of the full meaning that those data contain.* For that reason we have many statistical techniques, each of which extracts but one aspect of the meaning from the same set of facts. Each time you rephrase the data into different statistical language, each time you submit the data to a new statistical treatment you derive new insights and see more clearly the full truth those data contain.

Any one set of facts can be viewed from many angles statistically; each view reveals another facet of the total meaning contained within the data. We have already looked at Joe's academic performance in three different ways, but only on a day-to-day basis. Let us now broaden our viewpoint. In contrast to the nervous, daily fluctuations of peak-and-valley achievement, let us level out the jagged irregularities of daily performance into a smooth, total weekly performance. We shall balance statistically the peaks against the valleys week by week. The smoothed-out *average* weekly achievement will be indicated by a dotted line. By so doing, we shall get a whole new insight into Joe's achievement. Instead of its being an erratic zig-zagging between extremes, it will show that very little change occurred in Joe's weekly level of achievement.

The following graph will help to dramatize the situation. The dotted line represents Joe's weekly achievement level. To assist in comparing the daily record with the weekly total, we have superimposed on the weekly average the daily grades in the form of a solid line. The point should be clearly emphasized that *both* records are equally representative of Joe's academic performance; one is not more significant than the other. They merely measure different phenomena. Statistics have already aided us in looking at Joe's achievement in a number of different ways. Now we may see it with still further insight.

We could go on and on, subjecting these data to additional statistical treatment. By so doing we would learn more and more about Joe's academic performance. But that is not the purpose of this discussion. We have merely been illustrating that *as a tool of research* statistics may permit you to see what otherwise you would not see.

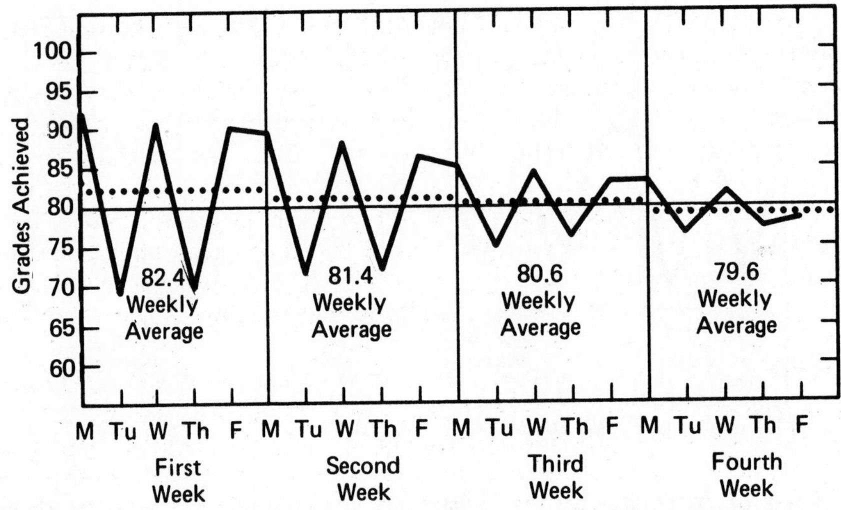

The Role of Statistics

If you know what statistics can and what it cannot do, you may appreciate more fully the role of statistics as a tool of research. If the data are expressed as numerical values, statistics may assist you in four ways:

1. It may indicate the central point around which the universe of data revolves.
2. It may indicate how broadly the universe of data is spread.
3. It may show the relationship of one kind of data to another kind of data.
4. It may provide certain techniques to test the degree to which the data conform to or depart from the fortuitous operations of the law of chance or approximate an anticipated standard.

It may be well to discuss each of these functional roles briefly so that you may see the landscape of statistics at a glance.

• *Statistics may indicate the central point around which the universe of data revolves.* The center of gravitation, or the central axis, for any mass of data is called the *point of central tendency.* One large segment of statistics is devoted to ways of determining the midpoint around which the mass of data is equally distributed. In statistical language, we call the techniques for finding the point of data equilibrium the *measures of central tendency,* the most commonly employed of which are the *median,* the *mode,* or any of the several *means:* the *arithmetic mean,* the *geometric mean,* or the *harmonic mean.* Each of these measures has its own characteristics. As a careful researcher, you will choose the particular indicator of central tendency with full knowledge of its unique capability for really indicating the point of central tendency for any particular set of data and *their* unique characteristics.

Here, as in every other statistical situation, one basic rule applies: *The configurational characteristics of the data dictate the statistical treatment that is most appropriate for any one particular situation.* If the data assume the distribution of the normal curve, they call for one type of central tendency treatment; if they assume an ogee-curve configuration, they demand another method of statistical management. A polymodal distribution may call for a still third type of statistical approach to locate the point of central tendency within the mass of data. Every researcher should bear in mind, therefore, that only after careful and informed consideration of the characteristics of the data and the configurational patterns those data assume, when plotted as a frequency curve, can the researcher select the most appropriate statistical procedure for that particular universe of data.

Too many students of research try it the other way around: they attempt to select the statistical technique before they have adequately considered whether that particular treatment is appropriate to the data characteristics. They say, "I shall find the mean"—having been conditioned by statistics textbooks and courses in basic statistics to think always in terms of the *arithmetic* mean—when the very nature of the data may dictate that the geometric mean or the harmonic mean would be much more appropriate, and that, of all the choices, the arithmetic mean may be certainly the least desirable. Such sensitive discrimination in the choice of the statistical tool is a distinguishing mark of the skilled researcher.

The purpose of this chapter is to discuss statistics merely as one of the tools of research. It makes no pretense at being a résumé of the principles of basic statistics or to supply subject matter. It will be assumed that the student already has this substantive background. For those who wish to learn the fundamentals of statistics or who desire to refresh their minds with reference to statistical principles, a selected bibliography of both programmed and conventional textbook materials is given in Part II of the bibliography section (pp. 183–185).

At this point a further observation should be made with respect to the nature of a statistic. You should always be aware that what statistically seems very plausible, very specific and concrete, may have no counterpart whatsoever within the context of reality. Statistics probably more often than not describe a quasiworld of nonentity rather than depict the real world of everyday life. For example, if you add up a series of grades and divide by the number of students in the class, you may get an average grade of 82 for the class. Having done this you may feel that you have discovered a very substantial fact. If you look down over the class list of individual grades, however, you may be astonished to find that not one student in the entire class actually received a grade of 82! What you accepted statistically as solid fact became empirically an insubstantial nothing in the actual grades earned by the individuals in the class.

Consider the man who read in the newspaper that the Bureau of Census has just announced that the size of the average American family was 3.75 persons. With heartfelt gratitude, he exclaimed, "Thank God, I was the *first*born!" What is acceptable statistically is sometimes meaningless empirically.

All this, however, should not disparage the importance of statistics *as a tool of research* in the hands of the competent researcher. Some statistical concepts, even though they may have no counterparts in the real world, may assist us in understanding the phenomena of the real world with more appreciation and greater understanding than we might otherwise have. Many ideas that we accept as being substantial and use have no real substance. Take the North Pole, for example. The North Pole provides a prime reference point for many essential types of human activity and as a basis of the commerce between nations. It provides a basic reference point for navigation, for terrestrial latitude and longitude, for geodetic measurements, and for many other activities. Yet travel to the Arctic wastes and you will have to imagine that one particular spot on the ice which looks precisely like every other spot on the ice, which stretches from horizon to horizon, is the North Pole. Just so, a statistic is a valuable bench mark, a reference point, even though in the hard world of fact and reality no such point seems to exist. Such is the integral nature of the point of central tendency.

So much, then, for the first of the four functions of statistics as a tool of research.

- *Statistics can show you how broadly the universe of data spreads.* Just as it is important to know where the gravitational center of a mass of data lies, so it is equally important to know how broadly that mass spreads out on either side of the point of central tendency. Both of these determinations—focal point and dispersion range—help us to see the dimensions of a universe of data with greater clarity and to describe it in terms of a two-dimensional relationship. Such determinations are the fundamental baselines from which we may survey the data and describe its other properties. As a surveyor starts from one or two reference points, so the researcher begins by looking at his universe of data from the viewpoint of certain basic statistical bench marks. Because of their descriptive character, these measurements belong to that division of statistics known as *descriptive statistics.*

The usual way of representing a universe of data is by means of the familiar bell-shaped curve, although it is important to remember, as we have previously pointed out, that not all data in the world conforms to such bell-shaped representation.

Much of the natural phenomena, when quantified and expressed in a two-dimensional relationship, *does indeed* assume the Gaussian, or bell-shaped, configuration; and for that reason, such a distribution pattern is often referred to as the *normal curve.*

Consider, however, the two distributions of data represented by the following bell graphs:

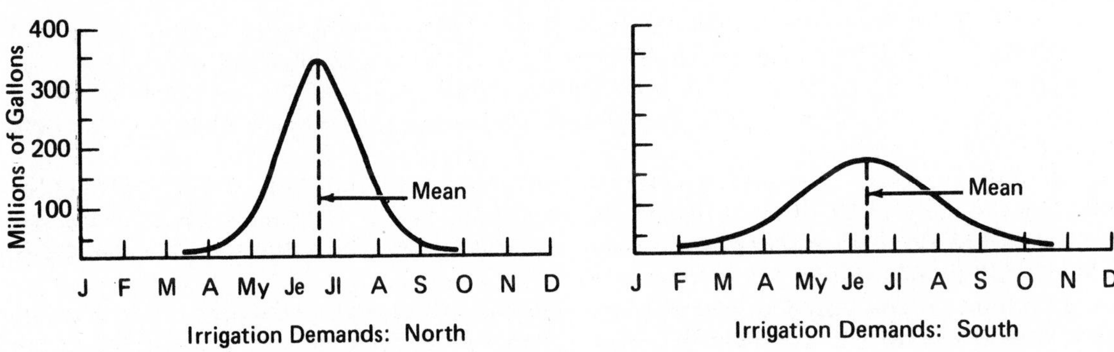

These graphs represent the water consumption for irrigation purposes for an entire year in two separate locations in the United States. One shows the demand in a northern area which has a short growing season, but which also is noted for its hot, dry summers which place an acute seasonal demand on irrigational resources. The other is the water consumption profile for a more southerly region, which has a longer growing season and which is also favored by more rainfall throughout the year. In the northern location the consumption is narrowly spread from mid-March to mid-September, with the greatest demand climaxing severely about mid-June. In the southern location, the demand spreads broadly from mid-January to mid-November. There is no sudden, heavy demand as in the northern location; the consumption instead is a moderate, sustained demand which spreads broadly across most of the months of the year. Both situations use approximately the same volume of water; for both distributions the location of the mean is approximately at the same mid-June point.

We measure the spread in terms of the mean. This spread we call the *dispersion* or the *deviation.* The most commonly employed dispersion measure is, of course, the *standard deviation,* but other measures include the *range* (the *semi-interquartile range* or *quartile deviation* are both variants of the range), the *mean deviation,* and the *coefficient of variance.*

All these measures attempt to tell us something about the spread of the data. That is their only purpose: to give us another dimension from which to view the data more realistically. With a measure of central tendency and with a measure of dispersion, the researcher can see more intimately the configuration, the characteristics, and the nature of the data with which he is working. What comes straight from the observation of natural phenomena as a mere agglutination of characterless digits becomes, by means of statistical treatment, a manageable and meaningful mass of data. By means of a few reference points we can, consequently, survey the whole situation statistically and plot its dimensional characteristics with much more awareness of its essential nature and its mass dynamics.

Let us look again at Joe's grades, this time with reference to both of the statistical dimensions we have been discussing: points of central tendency and measures of dispersion. These might be given in the form of numerical values as follows:

Mean	81	Range	23
Median	82	Average Deviation	6.0
Mode	83	Standard Deviation	6.9

This is the usual way in which these values are reported. Such a presentation does not give us, however, a very concrete picture of exactly what we are talking about. To see more clearly the concepts we have been discussing, let us arrange Joe's grades in a new form—as a linear scale of achievement—with the lowest to the highest grade in increasing order of magnitude.

Think of the median and the mean as fulcrum points. As such, both are points of exact balance, but it is important to understand what each balances. The median is at the precise *numerical* center of the array, with exactly as many grades *in number* above the median as below it. Joe's record has a total of twenty grades. Ten grades will be above the median; ten grades will be below it.

The mean is also a fulcrum point. It is the precise center of all of the amalgamated *values* of the array. The mean balances the *weight* of each of the grades (69 is the lightest of the grades; 92 is the heaviest) and selects the point where the entire statistical mass is in delicate equilibrium around the center of its own gravity.

While we are clarifying the concepts underlying the several terms we have been using, we may say that the *range* is simply the full extent of the data from the lowest value to the highest. Joe's grades range from 69 to 92, a range of twenty-three grade-scale points.

If, however, we wish to explore the degree to which Joe's grades are scattered with respect to the points of central tendency, we must employ one of two commonly used measures of *deviation* or *dispersion:* the less frequently used *average deviation,* which will indicate what the average is of all the deviations from the mean, or the commonly employed *standard deviation.* We shall, in fact, indicate both as a means of comparison.

Let us look at Joe's grades now with these new dimensions indicated on the following array. More and more we are gaining statistical insight into Joe's academic performance. We are seeing more and more what Joe's grades *mean.*

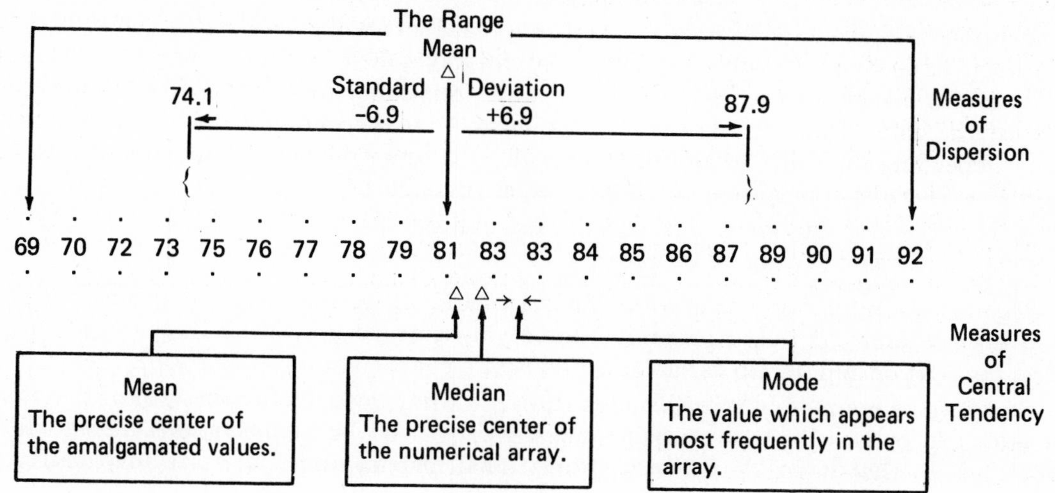

• *Statistics can show you the existence of relationships.* Up to this point, we have been discussing statistics from only one orientational viewpoint. Our statistical concepts have been unidimensional: central tendency and dispersion. Where is the data fulcrum point? How broadly do the data spread? These are phenomena which happen in a geometric plane or in a straight line.

But the facts of life are not always so simple. Life situations cannot be adequately described by a static system where only central balance points and amplitude of dispersion account for the world around us. The *raison d'être* of statistics is that it takes the disparate facts of a life situation and translates these into concepts and formulations that are manageable and meaningful.

In the real world, facts exist not only as gravitational and dispersive integers, but in dynamic relationship with each other. The facts of life have interrelated fields of force. There is a dynamic relevance, for example, between a child's age and his mental maturity, between his age and his growth curve, or between his growth curve and his dexterity index. These are all facts of life exhibiting interdependence. Let one change and it alters the entire structure of relationship. Because many life situations have these interrelated dimensions, one of the functions of statistics is to assist in describing the intensity and the magnitude of such relationships.

Many students regard the mere discovery of a relationship between one kind of data and another as the accomplishment of the objective of research. It is nothing of the kind. We must keep clearly in mind what research is and what it does. Merely to find a relationship between factor x and factor y is to do nothing more than to describe by means of statistics the nature of the data situation. A computer can do as much. But computers cannot do research. They can merely supply the researcher with additional insight into the statistical nature of his data, which indeed he may certainly need, in order to interpret those data into meaningful conclusions.

Such relationships between varying types of data are called *correlations.* The mathematical index, always expressed in terms of a decimal fraction, which describes the degree of relatedness between the factors being correlated is known as the *coefficient of correlation.*

In a very real sense a coefficient of correlation is merely a signpost. It points to a fact: the fact that two things are related. It is a shadowy finger pointing you in the direction of meaningful revelation.

So you have an indication that two sets of data are related. This should spark in the mind of the genuine researcher a barrage of questions: what is the *nature* of the relationship; what is the underlying *cause;* if two things are related, *how* are they related? Answer these questions and you are *interpreting* what the correlation means.

Mention coefficient of correlation and most students will immediately think of only the Pearsonian product moment correlation, commonly called the Pearsonian r. Although the Pearsonian r may be the commonest of all correlational techniques, nevertheless the nature of the data ultimately determines the correlational technique that is most appropriate. Depending upon the nature of the variables to be correlated, the technique must be chosen which is most appropriate to the existing circumstances.

Walter R. Borg has given a succinct presentation of the appropriate correlational techniques for different forms of variables.

Because we have been discussing the various kinds of correlational techniques, we should inspect some of the implications underlying correlation. What happens when we express the relationship of two variables in terms of a coefficient of correlation?

Correlations are merely statistical descriptions. They describe the strength of the bond of relationship between the one variable and the other. At best, correlations are statistical conclusions of what happens within a correlational matrix, and a correlational matrix is

Appropriate Correlational Techniques
for Different Forms of Variables

Technique	*Symbol*	*Variable 1*	*Variable 2*	*Remarks*
Product-moment correlation	r	Continuous	Continuous	The most stable technique.
Rank-difference correlation	ρ	Ranks	Ranks	Often used instead of r when the number of cases is under thirty.
Kendall's Tau	τ	Ranks	Ranks	Preferable to ρ for numbers under ten.
Biserial correlation	r_{bis}	Artificial dichotomy	Continuous	Sometimes exceeds 1; has a larger standard error than r; commonly used in item analysis.
Widespread biserial correlation	r_{wbis}	Widespread artificial	Continuous	Used when you are especially interested in persons at the extremes on the dichotomized variable.
Point-biserial correlation	r_{pbis}	True dichotomy	Continuous	Yields a lower correlation than r; much lower than r_{bis}.
Tetrachoric correlation	r_t	Artificial dichotomy	Artificial dichotomy	Used when both variables can be split at critical points.
Phi coefficient	ϕ	True dichotomy	True dichotomy	Used in calculating inter-item correlations.
Contingency coefficient	C	Two or more categories	Two or more categories	Comparable to r_t under certain conditions; closely related to χ^2 (Chi square).

Reprinted by permission, Walter R. Borg, *Educational Research: An Introduction.* New York: David McKay Co., Inc., 1963, p. 157.

nothing more than a convention for representing graphically two facts of life which presumably have a causal connection with each other.

Let us take a matrix and inspect it. First, there are two types of data, called *variables*, and these are represented as lying in a two-dimensional plane. One type of data is represented by appropriate units on a vertical axis, called the *ordinate.* The other type of data is expressed also by appropriate units, but this time on a horizontal axis, called an *abscissa.*

If we imagine from these units located along the ordinate and the abscissa, vertical and horizontal lines extending from each of these data locations, we will see that the resultant configuration is a grid where the "lines of force" from one type of data intersect with those from another kind of data.

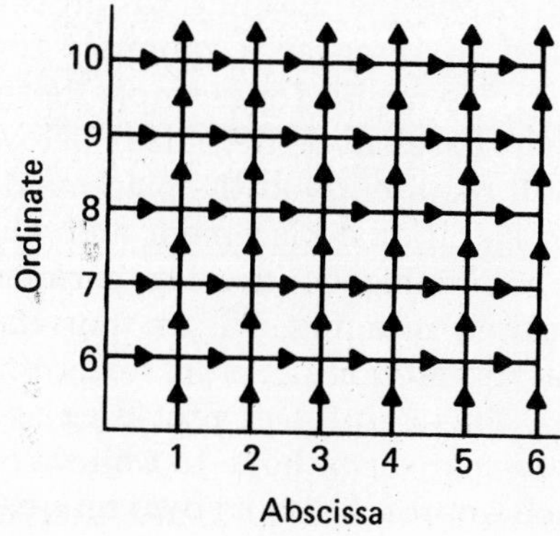

Thus, any one fact expressed in terms of one of these data factors is also expressed in relation to the other data factor and, therefore, is located on the grid at some point where the lines extending from the point of magnitude on each data axis intersect.

Below is a grid representing chronological age (on the ordinate) in relation to grade placement in reading (on the abscissa). We shall identify a particular child with the symbol Δ on the grid. He has made normal progress in reading: at age six he was reading at the first-grade level; at seven, at the second-grade level; at eight, at the third-grade level; and so on. The relationship of age to reading grade expectancy is a perfect one-to-one correspondence; and the straight line that connects these points, in vector fashion, always in a kind of equilibrium between grade expectancy in reading and chronological age, is called in statistics the *line of regression*, which in this case is a line representing perfect, positive correlation, where $r = 1.0$. When we plot in similar fashion the ages and reading achievement levels of other children, we find that some—represented by the symbol ○—are advanced for their age and others—represented by the symbol ●—are lagging with respect to their reading grade expectancy. The following is the resultant correlational matrix.

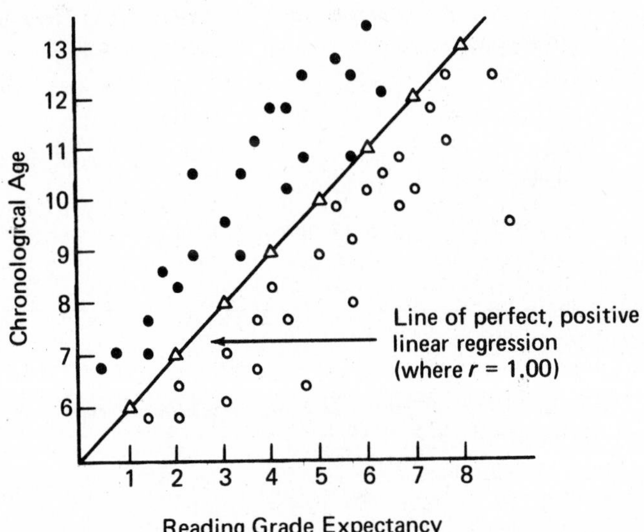

As we inspect the preceding matrix, what can we say about it? We can make statements in two directions. We can (1) *describe* the status quo of the data in terms of its statistical dynamics. This description we express in the form of a coefficient of correlation. We can (2) *interpret* the data within the matrix in terms of certain juxtapositions or remotenesses which seem to hint at significant meanings. Research, by its very nature, goes below mere statistical description to probe the meaning within the individual instances or significant clusters of data in order to discover a rationale for the appearance of such data within the correlational matrix. We might, for example, in the preceding matrix analyze the placement of those data which represent achievement below the level of reading-grade expectancy. Similarly, we might look intently at the placement of the overachievers in reading in order to discover their configurational placement and whatever meanings may be latent within these data. Then, by combining, contrasting, permutating these two subpopulations we are probing these facts for their meaning We are thus attempting to dig under the correlational coefficient to see what its internal structure really is.

Statistical techniques are thus helpful in providing us with overall views and conclusions about data masses that we could not hope to achieve in any other way. And for a full understanding of the data each approach has its own unique contribution to make. What is important, however, is that the researcher be in command, that he know the limitations of *each* approach, on one hand, and how, on the other, each may assist him in entering more fully into the meaning of the data he has at hand.

In all relationship studies, however, you should be alert for faulty logic. A tacit assumption is sometimes made that if one factor can be shown to have a statistical relationship to another, then these two factors must consequently have an influence on each other. In some instances the influence may, indeed, be very intimate and direct, as is the case where chronological age seems to have a very direct bearing upon physical and mental maturity. But to infer that because a correlation exists it, therefore, implies interaction of the correlational variables is very questionable reasoning.

• *One variable correlates meaningfully with another only when there is a common, causal bond that links the phenomena of both variables within the framework of a common relationship.* Take a logically absurd yet statistically demonstrable instance. We could establish a statistically correct correlation between the number of elephants in Siam and the size of the Florida orange crop. The facts may be very clear: as the size of the elephant population increases, the Florida orange crop also increases! To reason, however, that because we can show a positive correlation, there must be a causal bond at the root of that relationship is erroneous. There is no connection whatsoever between the elephant population in Siam and the production of oranges in Florida.

But where in an extreme situation we recognize the absurdity of the reasoning, as in the elephant–orange crop correlation, in research studies we occasionally find this same kind of questionable reasoning. We assume, for instance, that a correlation between low socioeconomic level and poor academic performance implies that one causes the other: *because* the family paycheck is deficient, the achievement of the boys and girls of that family in school is also deficient. And all too many times we assume on the basis of the correlation coefficient alone that one situation determines the other. There may be some causal connection between paycheck and children's grades; again, such an inference may be utter nonsense. Unless we inspect the causal premise very carefully, we may be misled by a statistical statement which in fact may have no validity whatever. If we so reason concerning socioeconomic status and academic performance, it may be very difficult for us to account for all the world's geniuses and intellectual giants who have been born of indigent parents and who have lived in constant companionship with poverty.

Figures may not lie, but the assumptions that underlie some of our figuring may at times be extremely suspect and untrustworthy. The genuine researcher is never content to stop at finding a correlation. He always knows that *below the correlation* in the matrix of the facts themselves lies the all-important area where interpretation of the fact underlying the relationship itself may lead him toward a new area in which he may conceivably experience the discovery of truth.

Perhaps we have said enough about the correlational techniques and their purpose in research. We have yet a fourth subarea to discuss: statistics as a tool for testing nature's fortuitousness.

• *Statistics may test the conformity of research data to that which is found in the anticipated fortuitousness of nature.* This is a new dimension of our statistical discussion. Up to this point, we have shown that all statistics can do for the researcher is to show him an indication of the fulcrum points where the data balances; describe the spread and scatter of the data around a central axis; and indicate the strength of the relationship—the index of homogeneity or heterogeneity—that exists between different kinds of data.

Nature, however, behaves according to rule. Karl Friedrich Gauss discovered that fact and formulated his discovery into a mathematical expression of normal distribution. Natural fortuitousness, Gauss discovered, is expressed in the form of a bell-shaped curve. And this curve has ever since become the *sine qua non* of the statistician. The broad implications of Gauss's curve may perhaps best be shown by this well-known presentation demonstrating its properties and applications.

The following illustration of the characteristics and uses of the normal curve is well worth study. The pivotal axis of static equilibrium is indicated as 0 and represents the point of central tendency. On either side of it, in perfect symmetry—because the curve itself represents the perfect balance of nature—the standard deviation areas are shown. The rest of the scales are relative and informative. Here are the yardsticks by which we measure educational achievement. Against these measuring rods of fortuitous behavior and statistical design each student's ability is judged. Here are the scalar implications of the normal curve.

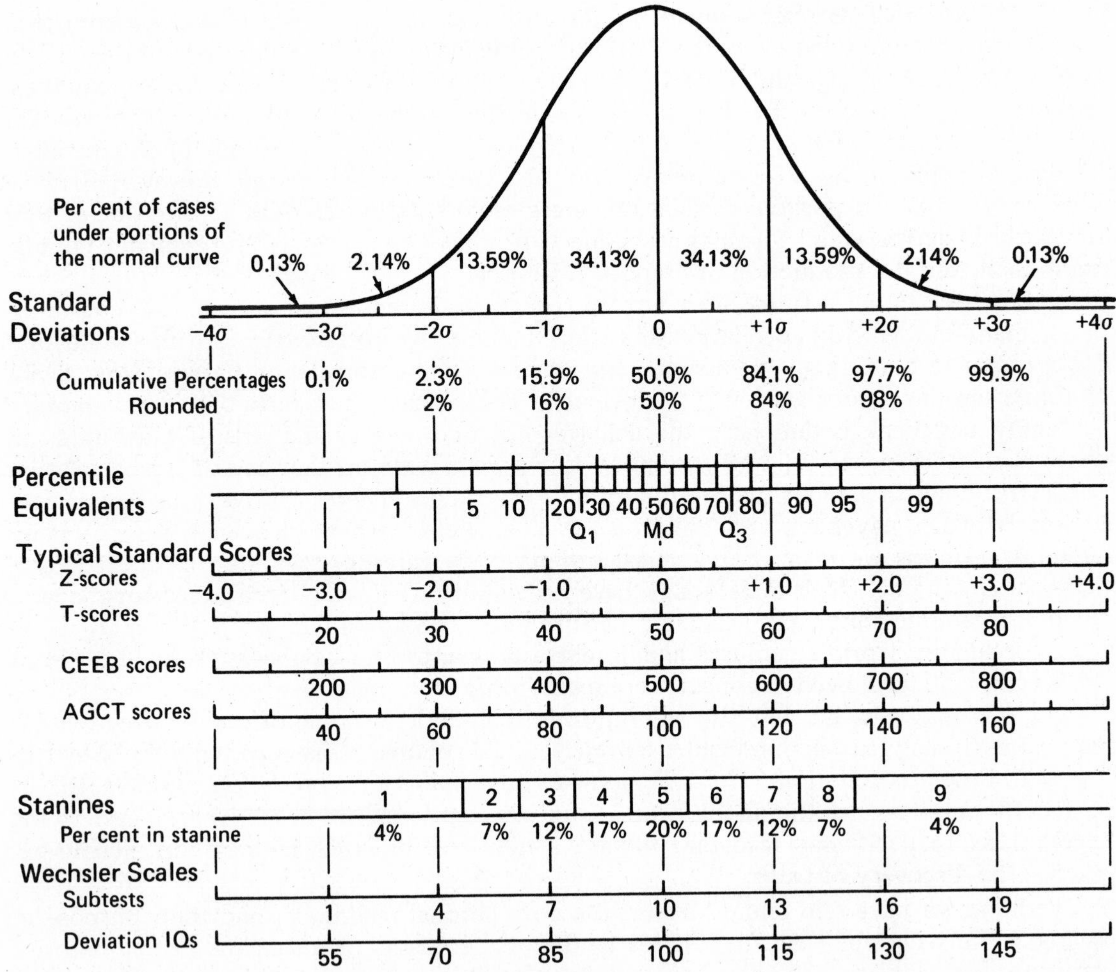

NOTE: This chart cannot be used to equate scores on one test to scores on another test. For example, both 600 on the CEEB and 120 on the AGCT are one standard deviation above their respective means, but they do not represent "equal" standings because the scores were obtained from different groups.

Source: *Test Service Bulletin*, No. 48 (January 1955), The Psychological Corporation.

Because most of the chance phenomena of life conform to a Gaussian curve, statistics can assist the researcher in determining how nearly his data conform or depart from the contour of such a curve. The researcher measures data in much the same way that a carpenter measures a piece of lumber. The carpenter uses a footrule; the researcher employs standards of measurement associated with the normal curve. The principle, however, is the same. In each case, two things are necessary: (1) a standard and (2) an area for measuring.

In the case of the footrule, the standard is the foot, the inch, or its integral fractions. In the case of data, the standard is the normal curve. Compared to the units of the footrule, the mean and the standard deviation are the points of reference for the curve. The Gaussian curve is, in fact, the standard by which phenomena which result from pure happenstance—from the sheer coincidence of nature—are described. The curve is, therefore, a delicate balance of distributed values pivoted statistically about the mean, spreading out on either side in gently fading frequencies into the first, second, third, and fourth standard deviations from that mean. Within a very slight margin, which we usually think of in terms of a 5 per cent variation, nature ideally performs her functions within the range of perfectly predestined curvilinear predictions. These predictions are graphically represented in the form of the well-known Gaussian or bell curve.[7]

Much, however, might happen to upset this delicate balance of natural fortuitousness. Forces, influences, or extraneous dynamics of one kind or another may cause the equilibrium of the normal distribution to be altered or destroyed. When this happens we compare statistically the data that we suspect have been subjected to some outside influence against the data as they should be, according to the normal distribution pattern, and we sometimes find that we may be off course from that indicated by the curve by a significant amount. When that happens we suspect that such aberration is caused by some external force or combination of forces, in addition to those found within the purely natural framework, and that these are exerting their own dynamics within the data system.

We detect the presence of these extraneous forces that cause the difference by means of certain so-called *statistical tests.* A test always implies a standard, or norm, against which any situation to be tested may be appraised. Examples of various statistical tests are the chi square test, Student's *t* test, the *F*-ratio, and other similar procedures. These have only one purpose: to test the conformity of the data which the researcher has to the expectancy of the normal curve.

To establish a statistical base against which a situation may be tested, the researcher relies upon a construct called the *null hypothesis.* The null hypothesis is posited so that the researcher will have a standard against which to test his data statistically. We wish, for example, to test the hunch that a certain method of teaching mathematics will result in the student's understanding more thoroughly the conceptual structure underlying a mathematical process than if he were taught by the purely conventional method. To test our hunch, we posit the null hypothesis that there will be *no* (null) difference in conceptual understanding regardless of the method of teaching. We teach one group by the conventional method; we teach the other by the special method. The procedure is, therefore, similar to the experimental methodology of research. Then we compare results statistically to see whether the special method of teaching did indeed result in a significant difference—by which we usually mean a more than 5 per cent differential over the other group. If we find a "statistically significant difference," we *assume* that the difference resulted from the different method of teaching. It is here, however, that the careful researcher will view very carefully the null hypothesis procedure. The assumption may be entirely warranted and the method of instruction may indeed have caused the increased understanding. On the other hand, some unrecognized external factor may have produced the difference in achievement. In a conclusion resulting from the positing of the null hypothesis, it is possible that what seems like a valid assumption could be incorrect.

It should be clearly pointed out that the testing of the null hypothesis merely results in an indication that points in the direction of further revelation. Merely to find that one method made a difference over another method is really not to find too much. The genuine

[7]Gauss, of course, plotted a curve of error; it was Galton in his studies of heredity who adapted Gauss's curve to describe life phenomena.

researcher will seldom be satisfied with such a foggy resolution of the matter. The real researcher not only will want to know that one method does result in a significantly superior learning process, but he will want to know precisely what made the difference and what the difference is from a qualitative rather than merely a quantitative point of view. Statistics is, therefore, merely the handmaid of the genuine researcher. It is a tool that can reveal that differences do indeed exist. The best research will, however, seldom be satisfied with that fact alone. It will ask more penetrating questions: If the null hypothesis is rejected, then exactly what factors, what influences, what determinants *caused* the statistic to veer out of line from a mere chance occurrence? To discover the fact and degree of divergence from chance expectancy is within the province of statistics; to go beyond this and to read the data in terms of their significance and interpretation—in short, meaning—is research.

A competent researcher will recognize that the rejection of the null hypothesis is a mere symptomatic and surface manifestation of a deeper underlying cause. It is indicative of a concealed dynamic at work which lies at the root of the problem. The best basic research will probe for the deeper and more fundamental causal factors which lie closest to the baseline of the situation. Once these factors are discovered and their meaning is read with accuracy, the researcher is closer to solving the problem for which the whole research process was instituted.

Because the purpose of this chapter is not to teach statistics but merely to give the student the minimal knowledge he needs in order to employ statistics intelligently as a *tool* of research, perhaps one more area should be discussed before concluding this section: namely, how to read statistical language.

How to Read the Language of Statistics

A statistical formula and a cookbook recipe have essentially the same purpose: to give directions in order to produce an ultimate outcome. Look at a recipe. It has a characteristic format. You read it in a particular way. First, with a recipe the reader is usually presented with a list of the ingredients needed; then he follows directions as to the way in which these ingredients are to be combined and processed. In like manner, you read a statistical formula with an equal awareness of its format, the particular demands it makes on the reader, and the arrangement and meaning of its parts. All too many teachers take for granted that students generally know how to read statistical language. One only needs to know students to recognize the fallacy of the assumption. What is it, then, that a student needs to know to read a statistical expression? Perhaps some elementary matters with respect to symbols and conventions in symbol usage may merit review.

Conventions in Symbol Usage. Greek letters generally are used to denote the characteristics of population parameters; Roman letters generally express the characteristics associated with samples. For instance, the population mean is usually indicated by the Greek μ, whereas the sample mean is indicated by M. (Frequently in statistics the italic form of the alphabet is used.) Likewise, σ would denote the standard deviation of the population, whereas s would mean the standard deviation of the sample.

A bar above a symbol, $\overline{X}$ $\overline{Y}$, indicates the arithmetic mean of the several items. Generally, the letters x, y, z denote variables and observations on individual cases. Constants are represented by letters at the beginning of the alphabet. Small letters from the middle of the alphabet, particularly i and j, used as subscripts, indicate reference to specific individuals or groups.

A few other symbols which you should know are the following:

$>$: $a > b$ means "a is greater than b."
$<$: $a < b$ means "a is less than b."
$>>$: $a >> b$ means "a is very much larger than b."

$<<$: $a << b$ means "a is very much less than b."
$\geq$: $a \geq b$ means "a is greater than or equal to b."
$\leq$: $a \leq b$ means "a is less than or equal to b."
$=$ means "equal to."
$\neq$ means "not equal to."
$|a|$ means "the absolute value of a without + or − designation."
∞ means "infinity."
$\sqrt{a}$ means "the square root of a."
H_o means "the null hypothesis."
! means "factorial, or multiply the number by each succeeding number below it to 1." Thus, 4! means $4 \times 3 \times 2 \times 1 = 24$.

Subscripts and Exponents. Common to statistical expressions are small letters or figures written slightly below a quantity. These are called *subscripts.* They function as adjectives, or qualitative descriptors, which tell what kind of quantity is indicated. For example, in the expression M_g the subscript g tells the kind of M, where M stands for the mean. If read as a literal translation of the symbol, one would read it as the "mean geometric" or the geometric mean.

Where a small symbol is written slightly above the quantity, it is called an *exponent.* An exponent is a quantitative descriptor: it tells not what kind, but how much. M^2, for example, is read "M squared," meaning of course that M is multiplied by itself, thus increasing the value of M.

Summation. Another symbol which is frequently seen in equations is the summation sign. It is an overgrown Greek upper-case sigma, Σ, and it simply means "add." Sometimes it, too, has smaller symbols below and above it to indicate the limits of the additive process. For instance,

$$\sum_{i=1}^{N}$$

which simply means, "add all the items from 1 ($i = 1$) to N (the last item)." Thus, if you had the series 1, 2, 3, 4, 5 and it was expressed as

$$\sum_{i=1}^{5}$$

it would mean, with respect to the preceding series, $1 + 2 + 3 + 4 + 5 = 15$.

Multiplication and Division. Multiplication is indicated in one of two ways: either by two quantities standing in juxtaposition to each other, as XY, or by a quantity in parenthesis juxtaposed to another quantity or symbol, for example, $(a + b)(a + b)$ or $N(N + 1)$.

A horizontal line always means *divide.* Furthermore, the quantity below the line is always divided into the quantity above the line. Thus,

$$\frac{1}{3}$$

means divide 1 by 3, or divide 3 into 1. Likewise,

$$\frac{\Sigma X}{N}$$

means divide N into the sum (Σ) of all the X's.

How to Read a Statistical Formula

A statistical formula is merely an expression in the shorthand of statistical symbols which gives directions for obtaining a specific answer to a problem. The problem is always stated to the left of the equal sign. Everything to the right of the equal sign is directive in nature—it tells you what to do. Here are, however, some basic guidelines which may help you to read statistical statements:

1. Know what each symbol in the equation means. Following each equation is usually a listing of the symbols employed in the equation with the specific meaning of each, except where these are the common symbols with which every student of statistics should be familiar, e.g., Σ , $\sqrt{\ }$, $|a|$, and similar symbols, most of which have been discussed already in this chapter.
2. Begin at the extreme *right* and read toward the *left*. This is the reverse of the normal reading direction.
3. Where there are quantities in parentheses, begin inside the parenthesis and perform the operations indicated there *first*. Work from left to right. For example, take this expression: 5(6 + 2)(3 + 4). Add the 3 + 4 first; then add the 6 + 2. Now you have 7 and 8. Go back to the extreme right. Multiply 7 × 8 = 56; then multiply this by 5 (working always toward the left).
4. Where there is an exponent, do as it directs.
5. Perform all the operations *above* the line first.
6. Then perform the operations *below* the line.
7. Effect the division, indicated by the horizontal line.
8. Finally, perform the operation that is indicated by the all-encompassing symbol.

With respect to the points just discussed, take, for example, the following formula:

$$s = \sqrt{\frac{\sum_{i=1}^{N}\left(X_i - \overline{X}\right)^2}{N}}$$

Where $\overline{X}$ = the arithmetic mean
X_i = each individual observation
N = the number of cases
s = the standard deviation of the sample

Now let's read that expression according to the preceding directions.

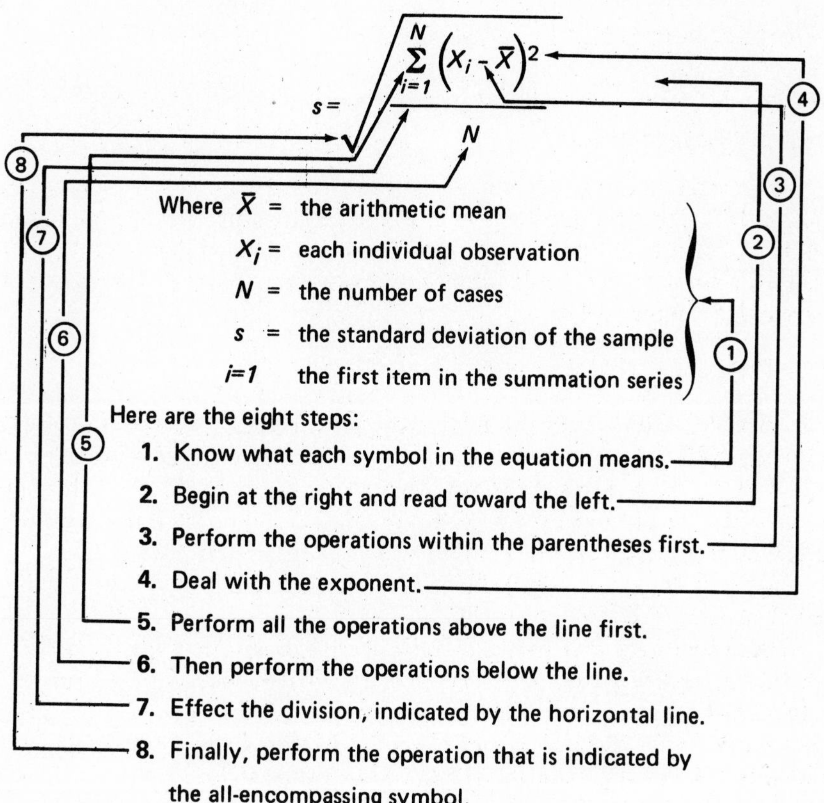
$s = \sqrt{\frac{\sum_{i=1}^{N} (X_i - \bar{X})^2}{N}}$
Where $\bar{X}$ = the arithmetic mean
X_i = each individual observation
N = the number of cases
s = the standard deviation of the sample
$i=1$ the first item in the summation series
Here are the eight steps:
1. Know what each symbol in the equation means.
2. Begin at the right and read toward the left.
3. Perform the operations within the parentheses first.
4. Deal with the exponent.
5. Perform all the operations above the line first.
6. Then perform the operations below the line.
7. Effect the division, indicated by the horizontal line.
8. Finally, perform the operation that is indicated by the all-encompassing symbol.
1
2
3
4
5
6
7
8

Conclusion

We have said enough about the role of statistics as a tool in the hands of the researcher. That, of course, was the primary purpose of this section. The section has, however, a secondary purpose: to help the student to see that statistics is a system devised so that data which at first glance seem disparate might be induced to divulge something of the specific dimensions characteristic of statistical articulation—central tendency, dispersion, relatedness and conformity to or divergence from mere chance. It is hoped that by now you will recognize that statistics is logical, systematic, and reasonable; that it is not a terrifying, impassable chasm which lies astride your path.

The primary purpose of this section has been to give you an overall view and provide a rationale for thinking about statistics so that you might know what it can and cannot do, and by understanding its capabilities, be better able to appreciate the way in which the tool of statistics might help you solve your research problem.

Research Planning and Design

3 The Research Proposal

THE FUNCTION OF THE PROPOSAL

A proposal is as essential to successful research as an architect's drawing is to the building of a house. No one would start the construction of a house by rushing out to dig a hole in the ground for the foundation. Before turning a shovelful of earth, many questions must be answered, many decisions made. What kind of a house do you plan to build? Will it be a two-story, a split-level, or a ranch type? How will the house be placed on the building site? Where will the openings be located? What kind of heat will it have? Where will the electrical outlets and switches be placed? What floor plan and traffic pattern do you wish to have? We could go on and on. Every one of these questions is extremely important, and each must be answered specifically before the construction can begin. Even then, after you have made all these decisions, do you immediately begin digging? Not at all! Yet another preliminary phase remains. The architect now draws a plan of the entire structure, showing to the fraction of an inch precisely where every detail will be located. Insofar as possible, nothing is left to chance. The writer of a proposal does similarly. In the section of his proposal entitled "The Data and Their Treatment," he spells out precisely every detail of acquiring, arranging, processing, and interpreting the data. Continuing with the analogy of the architect, he next draws an elevation of the building, showing the exterior on all sides and picturing precisely how the building will appear when it is finished. The researcher does precisely this in sketching the Outline of the Proposed Study in the appropriate section of the proposal. To build a house in any other way than we have described would be too costly, too prone to mistake, too open to hazard. In building a house, there is too much money involved to play around with trial and error. In doing research there is also too much investment of time, effort, and frequently money to rush into it without a clearly conceived design. It is this design that the proposal aims to provide before the actual research activity begins.

Doing research cannot be left to whimsy or happenstance. Foresight, purposeful decision, and careful consideration of important details of procedure and design must take place before an elaborate data-gathering operation is set in motion. Every critical item of the entire research process must be thoroughly thought through, must be clearly set down for study, must be given evaluative and common-sense study before the inauguration of activity itself. The function of the research proposal is to provide this objectivity and critical insight.

PLANNING IS IMPORTANT

Clear, systematic planning is essential to the success of research at any level. It is as necessary for your own research efforts as it is in seeking the cause or cure of multiple sclerosis or putting a man on the moon. That these latter projects are more complex and sophisticated than what you may be planning does not alter the fact that your own research project needs systematic, thorough planning as much as they do before the actual activity begins.

The heart of all research planning is the *research proposal.* The proposal is as essential to the research effort as the architect's plan is to the construction of a building. Each is a basic plan of procedure. Each deals with the problems: defining them, identifying the data or the materials to be used in resolving them, delineating methods by which either the materials will be utilized or the data will be processed and interpreted.

The research proposal is highly important. It affords the researcher and others an opportunity to evaluate the total design before an inordinate expenditure of effort, time, and perhaps money is invested in the project. A careful inspection of the proposal will reveal the degree to which the researcher has thought through the details of his investigation. It will show whether he has envisioned the dimensions of the task and whether he has considered the problems involved in the acquisition of the data and their subsequent treatment and interpretation. A sound proposal prevents mistakes. It prevents the frustration of misdirected effort on ill-conceived research. As you can look at an architect's plans and tell whether the proposed building will be adequate for its intended use, so by considering the research proposal carefully, the researcher can tell whether the methodology he has indicated and the data he will have available will result in the probable solution of his problem. Proposals are important also in many other ways. For the award of a grant subsidy or for the underwriting or endorsement of any sizable undertaking, a well-written proposal is a prime requirement. Major research projects frequently are approved or rejected on the basis of the proposal alone. It is essential, therefore, to set forth clearly the problem and to indicate precisely the manner in which you propose to resolve it within the framework of the scientific method. Whether you seek the funding of a project from a grant foundation or whether you seek to show your professor or your graduate committee that you have the ability to plan and carry out an investigation independently, a clear, well-written proposal is indispensable. Nothing is a substitute for an explication of problem and procedure.

Because of the central importance of the proposal in all research, this chapter will discuss the nature of the proposal, its purpose, parts, and rationale. In the everyday world, and quite divorced from the narrower field of academic research, the ability to construct an effective proposal is a skill that is in increasingly high demand. The ability to present ideas forcefully is important, no matter what field one is in. Proposal writing helps to focus your thinking on important and critical details; it assists in isolating central issues and in considering the best action to take in solving problems. Other names for what is essentially a proposal are *prospectus, plan, outline, statement,* and *draft.*

Purpose and Style of a Proposal

The purpose of the proposal is to present clearly and unambiguously the problem to be researched, to discuss the research efforts of others who have worked on collateral or related problems, to set forth precisely the data necessary for solving the problem, and to indicate specifically how these data will be treated and interpreted. A proposal should further indicate the reason for the study, present the qualifications of the researcher, and indicate the principal bibliography in the problem area.

• *A proposal is a straightforward document.* It should not be cluttered with extraneous matter. It begins with a straightforward statement of the problem to be researched. It stands upon its own feet; it needs no explanatory props. There is no necessity for introduction, prologue, or statement of reasons why the researcher became interested in the problem or feels a burning need to research it. That may be interesting, but none of it is necessary or appropriate. Nor does it aid you to think straight to the point, a prime requirement of an acceptable proposal. Whatever does not contribute directly to the delineation of the problem and its solution must be eliminated. Anything else only obscures and is a diversionary tactic on the part of the student, who many times is not sure either of his problem or of his ability to come to grips with it. A proposal is like an architect's drawing: clean, clear, and economical. It contains all that is necessary; not one detail more.

• *A proposal is not a literary production.* An architect's drawing is not a work of art, and a proposal is not "literary" (in the sense of being consciously a piece of fine writing). The mission of neither is to be artistic; the purpose of both is to communicate clearly. As an architect's drawings present an idea of construction with economy of line and precision of measurement, so a proposal, with an economy of words and precision of expression, indicates how a research project is to be executed to completion. It provides no opportunity for fine writing, for literary composition, for verbal extravagance. Quite the contrary, it is generally stylistically stark and prosaic in expression.

Proposals offer no opportunity for the flowers of rhetoric, but they do present a challenge to the writer. They provide an opportunity to express ideas, thoughts, and procedures in language which is clear, sharp, and precise. It furnishes the writer of the proposal a chance to show with what ultimate clarity and precision he can state a research problem, how accurately he can delineate the scientific approach to the treatment of the data, and with what consummate coherence he can establish the logical validity of his conclusions. To those who have been nurtured in the idea that writing should be stylistically interesting and artistically creative, the preceding statements may come as a shock. But to write a superb proposal calls for skills of expression upon the part of the writer which are equally as demanding as forging an unforgettable sentence.

• *A proposal is clearly organized.* Organization of ideas is conventionally represented by a technique known as *outlining.* In an outline, the main ideas are placed closest to the left-hand margin and designated by Roman numerals. Subsidiary ideas, in degrees of lesser and lesser importance, are indented farther and farther to the right, forming a kind of inverted "stairway." Each succeeding step is labeled by A, 1, a, (1), (a) to indicate the relative "level" of importance of the idea. This device, however, has its limitations. It permits only the expression of a group of words or a short sentence to suggest the idea. The thought cannot be explained, expanded, or enlarged upon as is possible in the conventional paragraph style of writing. On the other hand, paragraph development does not lend itself well to the convention of the outline. However, traditional paragraph writing provides a way to show the relative importance of the several parts of the composition. This is done by the use of a system of conventionalized headings which efficient readers recognize immediately. Each chapter of this book, for example, has followed the outline form of writing, although you may not have been aware of that fact. The relative importance of each section, as it has related to all of the other sections, has been shown by the use of appropriate headings. The headings have signalled to the reader the relative importance of each section. Look at Chapter 1. It followed this outline:

I. What is research?
   A. What research is not.

B. What research is.
  1. Characteristics of research.
     a. Research begins with a question in the mind of the researcher.
     b. Research requires a plan.
     c. Research demands a clear statement of the problem.
     d. Research deals with the main problem through subproblems.
     e. Research seeks direction through appropriate hypotheses.
     f. Research deals with facts and their meaning.
     g. Research is circular.
  2. Practical application.

When you read the chapter, did you see it arranged in the form of this outline?

Headings Show Organization

The organization of the thought was shown by the headings.

THE CENTERED HEADING

appears in the manuscript as we have represented it here, typed in all capitals; in manuscript writing it is always reserved for the major divisions of thought. The printer, because of his wide variety and weights of type face, can be much more versatile than the manuscript writer, who must rely upon the limitations of the typewriter alone to express the thought and its relative degrees of importance. In printed material, centered headings are always set in the largest type size, and although the printer may not always center them, they are usually reserved for chapter headings of a book and other divisions of prime importance in the document. In outline style, such headings would ordinarily correspond to those parts of the outline which would be assigned the Roman numerals I, II, III, and so forth.

The Free-Standing Sidehead

which we have printed here to show how it would appear in typescript is written in capitals and lower case with each word of the heading underscored. No punctuation follows the free-standing sidehead. The initial letters of the principal words are capitalized, the rest of the word and also the prepositions and articles of the title are in lower case. In print, such free-standing sideheads are usually italicized; they are *always* so in typescript. Italicization in manuscript is indicated by *underlining the words to be italicized.* Note that the spaces are not underlined. The reason is obvious: you cannot italicize a space.

In importance, the free-standing sidehead is next below the centered heading. In an outline this level would ordinarily be represented by the A, B, C level under the Roman numeral.

The paragraph sidehead. The paragraph sidehead, as the name indicates, is a heading set into the paragraph, as we have done here. It always has a period as terminal punctuation. Only the first word of the paragraph sidehead begins with a capital letter, all the rest of the words of the heading are typed in lower case. The heading indicates the next degree of thought subordination under the free-standing sidehead level, and would normally correspond to the 1, 2, 3 level in the conventional outline. The paragraph sidehead is always italicized (underlined). Normally in typing, two or three spaces follow the period of the paragraph sidehead before the paragraph proper is begun for sake of ease of reading.

Should the student desire a fourth-level heading, such further diminution of thought importance is indicated by a centered heading, but this time quite different from the heading-of-first-importance discussed above. We have shown this type of heading in the sample proposal in Appendix A. It is

The Fourth-Level Heading

which is centered, in capitals and lower case, *not* italicized. Such a heading would indicate an importance of thought corresponding to the a, b, c level in the conventional outline.

Now, as far as we have gone in this chapter, by translating the several types of heading into conventional outline form, the organization of the chapter assumes the following form:

III. The research proposal.
   A. The function of the proposal.
   B. Planning is important.
      1. Purpose and style of a proposal.
         a. A proposal is a straightforward document.
         b. A proposal is not a literary production.
         c. A proposal is clearly organized.
      2. Headings show organization.

So much for the stylistic and mechanical matters. Now, let us look at the content and organization of the proposal.

Content and Organization of a Proposal

Proposals follow a simple, logical form of presentation. Although there are many ways to arrange the items within the proposal, the following outline of the proposal is the one we shall follow in this text:

I. The problem and its setting.
   A. The statement of the problem.
   B. The subproblems.
   C. The hypotheses.
   D. The delimitations.
   E. The definitions of terms.
   F. The assumptions.

II. The review of the related literature.

III. The data, their treatment, and their interpretation.
   A. The data.
      1. The primary data.
      2. The secondary data.
   B. The criteria governing the admissibility of the data.
   C. The research methodology.
   D. The specific projected treatment of each subproblem.
      1. Subproblem 1. (*The subproblem is here restated.*)
         a. The data needed.
         b. Where the data are located.
         c. How the data will be obtained.
         d. How the data will be treated and interpreted.
      2. Subproblem 2. (*Here, again, the subproblem will be restated and will be subjected to the four steps,* a, b, c, d. *Then each subproblem will be given similar treatment.*)

IV. The importance of the study.

V. The qualifications of the researcher.

VI. The outline of the proposed study.

VII. The selected bibliography

Practical Application

At this point you are now ready for a practical application of the subject matter which has been discussed in this chapter. Turn to Appendix B, Practicum in Research, p. 222, Project 3. Here you will find an opportunity to apply the principles discussed in this chapter.

4 The Problem and Its Setting

WHERE ARE RESEARCH PROBLEMS FOUND?

Problems for research are everywhere. Take a good look at the world around you. It teems with researchable problems. Whatever arouses your interest, tweaks your curiosity, and raises questions for which there are as yet no answers; or, where there are answers but in which the answers are in some dispute as to their validity, here is fertile ground for the discovery of a researchable problem. The human race does not have the final word on most of the questions which are important to it. Inspect any segment of life, any circumstance in the world around you, any of the phenomena happening at this moment, any of the events that swim before your eyes. In all these situations lie innumerable problems to claim the attention of the researcher.

Where does the area of your interest lie: in agriculture, chemistry, economics, education, electronics, engineering, health sciences, languages and literature, medicine, music, political science, physics, sociology, zoology or, perhaps, in dozens of other categories? Go to the library; inspect any volume of *Dissertation Abstracts* under the general heading of the area of your interest and you will be suddenly aware how intimately the world of everyday life and the world of research have become intertwined. You will see the research intimately related to the ever-expanding and exploding universe of knowledge. You may also realize, after such an experience, that all you need is to see your own area of interest in clear, sharp focus and then to enunciate the problems indigenous to it in precise, lucid terms to secure a problem area within which you might carry on your own research efforts.

Remember that research is a cyclic process. Review again the cycle of research as we presented it at the close of Chapter 1. That will be the model for all of the discussion from this point forward. Research begins with a situation from real life which raises an unanswered question in the mind of the researcher. The researcher sees that question in terms of a clearly defined research goal, formulated in terms of a precise statement of the problem. This is the genesis. With an unmistakably clear statement of the problem, research begins.

Practical Application

At this point, you are now ready for another application of the principles that we have been discussing. Turn to Project 4, Appendix B, "Practicum in Research." This project will give you an opportunity to zero in on a research area and state a research problem.

Let us now look at the characteristics of a researchable problem.

WHAT IS A RESEARCHABLE PROBLEM?

Many students have difficulty understanding the nature of a problem which qualifies it to be considered as suitable for research. This is partly because they do not understand the nature of research itself. They feel that merely "doing something" that terminates in a written "paper" is research. They are thinking primarily of activity as the prime ingredient—so long as you are *doing* something: for instance, finding a correlation, gathering data, or matching groups and comparing their achievement—that this is research. None of these, in fact, is research; and a problem built entirely around such activity is not a researchable problem. Research, as a refined aspect of the scientific method, is more than motion. It is inseparable from the individual engaged in it. It requires an inquiring mind which seeks fact and, after finding it, synthesizes the meaning of such fact into an accurate conclusion.

Let us say more about those activities that are often called research but that are not research. First, we begin with a basic rule: *When there is no mental struggle to force the facts to reveal their meaning, there is no research.* When a machine can take the place of the researcher, the process is not research. For this reason, activity which merely ends in finding the coefficient of correlation between two sets of data is not research. A computer can do that!

As we have said earlier, in a very real sense a coefficient of correlation is merely a signpost. It merely points you in the direction of meaningful relevancy. Here, for example, is a coefficient of correlation of 0.82. Thus, there is an indication that two sets of data are closely related. What is the *nature* of this relationship; what is the underlying *cause* for this relationship; if these two sets of data are related, *how* are they related? Answer these questions and you are *interpreting* what the correlation means. A machine cannot do that and, to do it, means that before you can provide any of these answers a mental struggle must take place. The mind of the researcher *must do battle with the observed fact* (in this case, the "observed" as a correlation) until the fact reveals its inner significance.

Generally, problems which can be answered either as "yes" or "no" are not suitable for research. Yes-no situations leave no room for data interpretation. They usually call for comparing the data to a standard or a norm and then making an arbitrary decision. "Is it cold outside?" You look at the thermometer—the standard or norm. It reads +20°F. A decision is made. Yes, it is cold outside.

Generally, yes-no category questions are superficial indications of considerations that lie at a much deeper level and that are the real substance of the matter. For example, whether it is cold outside at 20°F. depends upon many considerations. Are you an Eskimo? You may find it delightfully balmy. If, on the other hand, you are a Hottentot, you may find 20°F. unbearably frigid. "Is homework beneficial to children?" That is no problem for research because it misses the whole point of the matter. The heart of the matter is not whether homework is beneficial or not. If you can find good results as a consequence of homework, then it is beneficial; if you cannot identify any good results, then it is not beneficial. The case is as simple as that. The researchable issue is not *whether* homework is beneficial, but *wherein the benefit lies;* or if it is not beneficial, *why* it is not beneficial. Research goes below the mere surface questions which demand no interpretation of data. When you come to grips with the reasons for situations and the qualitative differences that distinguish one situation from another, then you are coming into the area which is dignified by the term *research.*

Likewise, "comparison" problems are not research: "The purpose of this research is to compare defections from East Germany during the decade 1950–1959 with those during the decade 1960–1969." All you have to do to "solve" that problem is to make two lists of figures. From what the problem states there need be no interpretation of the data at all, merely the presentation of it, a column showing the number of defections in one decade in contrast with another column showing those in the previous decade.

But, you contend, the problem *implied* interpretation. Not at all! The problem must state exactly what the researcher's purpose is. Inexperienced researchers often make the mistake of assuming that the problem implies more than it does. They think that because *they* had an assumption in mind, but did not state it in their articulation of the problem, that all the world will assume what they had in mind. This points up another basic rule: *State the problem so that the fact of interpretation of the data is clearly evident or so that it is so strongly implied in the wording of the problem that it is clearly obvious.*

There would have been no doubt of data interpretation had the preceding problem been stated: "The purpose of this research is to compare *in order to analyze the types of and reasons for* [There is the implication of interpretation. At this point the mind of the researcher must come to grips with the two columns of figures to determine exactly what these numerals represent.] defection from East Germany during 1950–1959 in comparison with those defections during the decade 1960–1969."

Comparisons are only mediate steps in arranging the data for presentation to the mind of the researcher so that he may observe it and, noting likenesses and differences, seek for the reasons which underlie the similar or disparate nature of the facts. Simple comparison by itself cannot, however, be the end of the research effort.

After the student has articulated what he deems to be a problem suitable for research, he might well test the feasibility of researching the problem by asking certain critical questions: Can the facts be discovered? Will I be able to secure the facts? After I secure the facts, what do I intend to do further? How do I propose to force the facts to reveal their meaning? Can a computer or a clerk do what I propose to do? (If this last question is answered in the affirmative, you had better think very carefully as to whether you have a problem for research.)

Mere activity is not enough. There must be (1) discovery of fact and (2) interpretation of that fact if your undertaking is to be dignified by the term *research.* Let us now look at some matters with respect to stating the problem. And this is, after all, the first order of business in any proposal.

The Statement of the Problem

State the problem fully and precisely. There is a prerequisite, however. Before you can state the problem, you must see it with unmistakable clarity. But once you see the problem clearly, waste no time in getting it down into as few words as possible. *Always, however, state the problem in a complete, grammatical sentence.*

There are bad habits in research practice as there are bad habits in other areas of human behavior. One of the worst of these is to allow yourself to cultivate the habit of "idea burping." Idea burping is the expression of fuzzy thinking and *inchoate* impressions evidenced by jotting down meaningless groups of words which are vague verbal fragments. Jotting down a phrase, a clause or two is merely to deceive yourself that you fully comprehend what at best you are unable to articulate except by a splutter of wordy and meaningless fragments. If you really know what your problem is, why not state it clearly? Each word should be expressive, sharp, and definitive. Your problem should be stated so well, in fact, that anyone, anywhere could read it, understand it, and react to it without benefit of your presence. Anything less than this is self-deception that you know what, in fact, you cannot express. Such deception will only cause you trouble later on.

Here, for instance, are some meaningless half-statements, mere verbal blobs that only hint at the problem but do not state it.

Welfare on children's attitudes
Palestrina and the motet
Busing of school children
Retirement plans of adults

Generally, fragments such as these evidence the fact that the researcher either cannot or will not think in terms of specifics. Although it may be irksome to you to express your thought accurately and completely, if you are one of those who thinks in terms of scraps and pieces, you had better begin now to think in terms of specific researchable goals expressed in complete, fully communicative statements.

Let us take each of the preceding half-utterances and develop them into a complete statement which indicates the specific object of the research.

- "Welfare on children's attitudes" becomes "What effect does welfare assistance given to parents have on the vocational aspirations of their teen-age children?"
- "Palestrina and the motet" becomes "The purpose of this study will be to analyze the motets of Palestrina to discover their distinctive harmonic characteristics in contrast with the same aspects of the motets of Palestrina's contemporary, William Byrd."
- "Busing of students" becomes "What factors must be evaluated and what are the relative weights of these several factors in constructing a formula for cost-estimate busing of children in a Mid-west metropolitan school system?"
- "Retirement plans of adults" becomes "The purpose of this study will be to examine the specific relationship which exists between organizational status, sense of professional satisfaction, and organizational identification of a group of well-functioning administrative and professional men who are in the sixth decade of their lives (ages 50–59) and their attitudes, role expectancies, leisure conception, and actual planning for retirement in order to determine the relative importance of each of these factors in achieving successful retirement."

One of the common faults with beginning researchers is that they do not narrow sufficiently the geographical area or the population strata of their proposed area of research. They talk about finding the solution of this or that problem "in the United States" or "among adults," seemingly never considering the fact that to get the data they will have to replicate the work of the national census or contact all "adults" within their stated parameters. It is the parameters we need to watch. We need to draw them tightly around a given population if the research project is not to get totally out of hand.

Edit Your Writing

Say precisely what you mean, then edit what you have said. Editing is eliminating useless verbiage. Choose your words precisely. To do so will clarify your writing. Take the preceding three sentences. Here they are as originally written, and then edited. Notice the useless verbiage that has been eliminated by more than 38.5 per cent:

is eliminating verbiage.

~~By~~ editing, ~~we mean getting rid of~~ useless ~~verbal baggage:~~ ~~inexact,~~

Choose your words precisely.

~~inexpressive, and needless words.~~ ~~Frequently one or two well-chosen~~

To do so, clarify your writing.

~~words~~ will ~~sharpen the thought.~~

Note also that by reducing the verbiage by more than one third we have made the expression of the thought more vital. Compare the two versions carefully and you will see what editing means.

Many students have difficulty in reading what they have written. They do not read precisely the words they have written, nor do they criticize them objectively. So long as they have the idea in their own minds, they think that any words which approximate the expression of that thought are adequate to convey it to others. Such is not the case.

You need to be rigorous with the words you write. Punctuation is important, and you should exploit it to the utmost. A colon will, for instance, indicate that what follows is an explanation in detail of the generalized statement that preceded it. Learn also to use the comma correctly. It adds precision to your writing. Similarly, the semicolon, the dash, quotation marks, italics, parentheses, and brackets are all tools in clarifying language.

Any good dictionary will usually have a section dealing with correct punctuation. Most handbooks of English usage will give you help in writing clear, concise, and effective sentences and help you to combine those sentences into unified and coherent paragraphs.

Cliches, colloquialisms, slang, jargon, and the gibberish of any group or profession usually obscure a person's thought. The patois of the lazy mind is the irresponsible use of respectable jargon. Those who employ it irresponsibly do so usually because they feel that it impresses or that it adds importance to their thought.

The thought's the thing. And when it is most clear, it is most often clothed in simple words: concrete nouns and expressive verbs. Every student would do well to study the principles of clear, lucid expression set forth by the readability experts. They have much of importance to say to people who have trouble in setting their thoughts on paper.

In general, however, some basic guidelines may help you:

1. Express the idea with the least number of words possible.
2. Use a thesaurus; it will help you find the precise word.
3. Economize on syllables. In general, if it expresses the thought equally well, a one-syllable word is preferred over a two-syllable word, a two-syllable one over a three-, and so forth. Keep the syllable count as low as possible.
4. Keep the sentence length short. Vary the length, of course, but break up those long, contorted sentences into shorter and more succinct verbal units. They are better understood.
5. Look well at each thought as it stands on paper. Do the words say exactly what you wish them to say? Read carefully, phrase by phrase. Inspect the prepositions. See if one word will carry the burden of two or more. If so, use the one word.
6. Be alert to the placement of phrases and clauses. Misplaced, these can create havoc with the thought. Take, for example:

   FOR SALE: A piano with beautifully carved mahogany legs by a woman that has arthritis and cannot play anymore.

   Misplace the modifiers, and what do you get:

   FOR SALE: A piano that has arthritis and cannot play anymore, by a woman with beautifully carved mahogany legs.

Practical Application

Turn now to Appendix B, p. 223, Project 4, Part 2, where you will have an opportunity to state your problem for research and to apply to it the several criteria governing an acceptable problem.

THE SUBPROBLEMS

Every researcher soon realizes that within the main problem are logical subcomponents, which we call *subproblems.* By being solved separately these subproblems resolve the main problem piecemeal. By looking at the main problem through its subproblems, the researcher frequently gets a more global view of the problem. Think of a problem, therefore, in terms of its component subproblems. Rather than make a frontal attack upon the entire problem, divide and conquer it in smaller segments.

Characteristics of Subproblems

Because some researchers may not be entirely familiar with the nature and the purpose of subproblems, we should discuss them briefly, outlining their characteristics.

- *Each subproblem should be a completely researchable unit.* A subproblem should be able to stand independently. It should constitute one of the several subareas of the larger research undertaking, and each subproblem might be researched as a separate subproject within the larger research goal. The solutions of the subproblems, taken together, combine to resolve the main problem of research. It is necessary, therefore, that each subproblem be stated clearly and succinctly. Often, a subproblem is stated in the form of a question. The advantage of stating subproblems interrogatively is that a question tends to focus the researcher's attention more directly upon the research target of the subproblem than does a mere declarative statement.
- *All problems are not necessarily researchable subproblems.* Every researcher must distinguish between two types of subproblems: (1) the true subproblems, whose solution will further the resolution of some part of the main problem, and (2) pseudosubproblems, which are, in fact, nothing more than arbitrary decisions that the researcher must make. These pseudosubproblems arise quite logically from the research situation, but they are problems that the researcher must resolve by deciding on a course of action to be followed as a part of the research procedure. Here are some examples of these pseudosubproblems:

> What is the best way to choose a sample?
> What instruments should be used to gather the data?
> How can the strength of a person's convictions be measured?
> How large should a representative sample be?

These are, without doubt, problems, and they must be resolved before the research project can proceed; but they are *your* problems. They call for knowledge on your part and a decision from you as to a course of action. *They are not researchable* in the sense in which we have defined research—as an application of the scientific method to the discovery of truth. These are, rather, knotty impediments that prevent you from coming to grips with the real problems for research. To resolve these problems we need to make firm decisions on procedural matters and then get on with the solution of the researchable problem itself, and its subproblems.

- *Within the subproblems interpretation of the data must be apparent.* At some point within the statement of the subproblems—as, indeed, within the main problem itself—the fact that interpretation of data will take place must be clearly evident. This may be expressed as a part of each subproblem statement, or it may occupy an entire subproblem separately.

- *The subproblems must add up to the totality of the problem.* After you have stated the subproblems, which usually number between two and five, check them against the statement of the main problem to see (1) that nothing in excess of the coverage within the main problem is included and (2) that you have no omissions, so that all significant areas of the main problem are covered by the several subproblems taken together.

- *Proliferation of subproblems is usually circumspect.* If the problem is carefully weighed, the researcher will find that he usually has in the vicinity of two to five subproblems. Sometimes the inexperienced researcher will come up with as many as ten, fifteen, or twenty subproblems. When this happens it generally means that a careful review of the problem and the subproblems should be undertaken. The researcher should study each subproblem to see whether it is truly a subproblem of the main problem or whether it falls into one or more of the following categories:

1. *The researcher has confused his personal problems with problems for research.* What he has stated as subproblems are not really subproblems, but decisions that he needs to make, procedural matters he needs to decide upon before his research can proceed.
2. *The researcher has fragmented the true subproblems.* He should ask whether it is possible to gather together two, three, four of the subproblems and to treat them logically under one subproblem heading.
3. *Frequently there is a mixture of the preceding errors.* In such cases careful study is necessary to separate procedural decisions from purely researchable goals, and then to look for "splintering" of the researchable units.

- *Beware of unrealistic goals.* Be cautious of committing yourself in the statement of both your problem and your subproblems beyond what is possible for you to achieve. Students often err in overextending themselves in terms of the geographical area which they have chosen for their research efforts. This is probably because they are afraid the "data will give out" if they restrict themselves to a realistically small area. Many state intentions in the problem or in the subproblems which are totally unrealistic. For instance, some students will write, "This study proposes to survey the science programs in the secondary schools in the United States for the purpose of. . . ." Now let's think a bit. There are 26,597 secondary schools in the United States. How do you plan to contact each of these schools? By personal visit? At most, you can probably visit no more than two schools a day. Considered another way, that's 13,298 *school* days—not counting vacations and week-ends, which, for your purposes, are lost time. That's almost sixty-six and one half school years! That's a fairly long lifetime for merely collecting the data. Maybe you're getting started a little late. This says nothing about the financial outlay of such a project. With the cost of living being what it is, $25 a day is a very conservative expense figure. For 13,298 days you should be prepared for an expenditure of $332,450.

These facts may cause you to decide upon another approach to gathering the data. You resolve to gather your data by questionnaire. Now, let's look at that approach. At 20 cents per letter—for you will enclose a stamped, addressed return envelope with each questionnaire—you will have an initial mailing bill of $5,319.40. But that is not all. You will have follow-up letters, reminders, additional questionnaires with return envelopes enclosed, and correspondence. An additional one third of the initial cost is a conservative estimate. That represents a total postage bill conservatively estimated at $7,092.53. Can you afford this amount for merely *gathering* the data?

Maybe by this time it's beginning to dawn upon you what a gigantic undertaking such a survey is. And note that we have said nothing about time, effort, and expense of processing all the data accumulated by 26,597 questionnaires, the interpreting of such data: punching the data into the computer cards, rental of computer time and programming, and the compilation of a research report, the writing of which alone in mere man-hours will represent a huge expenditure of time and effort.

A Researcher's Obligation to Mean Precisely What He Says

As a corollary to the preceding discussion, the responsible researcher is careful, in terms of what he promises in the problem and the subproblems, to mean precisely what he says. We have just been examining a researchable problem but one which is totally unfeasible from the individual researcher's standpoint. The National Education Association, the United States Office of Education, or a comparable agency might undertake such a survey and succeed in getting the data and interpreting it. But for most individuals, the task is simply beyond their capabilities.

One basic rule prevails among men of scholarly pursuit: *Absolute honesty and integrity is assumed in all the statements that a scholar makes.* We will take you at your word. We will assume that what you say in the problem is just what you mean to fulfill in the research effort. In fact, it is upon the intent stated in the problem and in the subproblems that a faculty approves the research project of a graduate student or a foundation awards a grant for sponsored research.

Because this is so, your problem is a commitment to a solemn obligation, and it should be phrased neither lightly nor irresponsibly. Once you have stated the purpose of your research in the problem, that's it! There can be no welshing, no pleading ignorance of the implications, no equivocating or avoiding the responsibility for one's own words.

You cannot, for example, when you come to a realization of the staggering magnitude of your problem, contend that you intended to take only a random sample of the secondary schools in the United States instead of all of them. Your problem stated unequivocally, "the secondary schools in the United States." Had you intended studying only some of them, you should have said so in the statement of your problem: "This study proposes to survey the science programs *in certain selected secondary schools throughout the United States* for the purpose of. . . ." This wording would have been precise and would have communicated to others exactly what you honestly intended to do.

One assumes that a researcher phrases his problem and the subproblems in full awareness of their meanings, their demands, their obligations, and one assumes that a researcher is prepared to stand solidly behind his words in terms of performance. If a researcher cannot be completely responsible for the statement of his problem and its attendant parts, one might question seriously whether he is likely to be any more responsible in his gathering and interpretation of the data.

How to Find the Subproblems

Students have difficulty sometimes in locating the subproblems within the framework of the larger problem. Here are some guidelines:

- *Begin with the problem itself.* If the problem is correctly written, you will be able to detect within it the subproblem areas which may be isolated for separate study. It is axiomatic that the totality of the subproblems must equal the totality of the problem. Therefore, because all the subproblems will add up to the problem, the first step should be to look at the problem itself with the purpose of trying to see the components that compose it.
- *Write the problem, then "box off" the subproblem areas.* Refer to p. 226 in the practicum section, where you have written your problem in its revised form. It would be well to take a clean sheet of paper and to copy your problem as you have it worded there.

Allow considerable space between the lines. Inspect what you have written carefully. Look at it with an eye to discovering within the problem the areas that should receive in-depth treatment before the problem can be resolved. Box off these areas. Within these boxes lies the genesis of your subproblems.

Let us go one step further. Enclose within *dotted lines* those specific words within the statement of the problem which indicate your intention to *interpret* the data. Every statement of a researchable problem should contain a word or a group of words which demand with respect to the amassed facts synthesis, judgment, or decision on the part of the researcher.

Contrary to popular thinking, it is not the data per se which are all-important, but what is done with the data in terms of extracting their meaning, synthesizing them into new and meaningful constellations of fact, making judgments or decisions about what all these data say. This, as we have pointed out earlier in this book, is what constitutes genuine research. The interpretation of fact is the heart of the research process.

To illustrate the preceding discussion let us take the problem cited earlier relating to the motets of Palestrina. Let us do with it exactly as we have just described:

The purpose of this study will be: to analyze the motets of
Palestrina : ① to discover their distinctive harmonic characteristics
in ③ contrast with : ② the same aspects of the motets of Palestrina's
contemporary, William Byrd.

Now write the subproblems:

Subproblem 1: In terms of harmonic structure, what are the distinctive characteristics of the motets of Giovanni Pierluigi da Palestrina?

Subproblem 2: In terms of harmonic structure, what are the distinctive characteristics of the motets of William Byrd?

Subproblem 3: What will an analysis of the harmonic characteristics of motets of Palestrina indicate when contrasted with the harmonic characteristics of the motets of William Byrd?

THE MEANING OF "THE SETTING" OF THE PROBLEM

This chapter has been entitled "The Problem and Its Setting." Up to this point we have been discussing merely the problem and its subparts. The statement of the problem establishes the goal of the research effort. But goal alone is not enough. A little reflection will prompt us to see that certain unresolved areas still remain, if we are to comprehend the meaning of the problem fully. In every research project it is important that we understand exactly what the researcher is attempting to do and what he does not intend to do. It is essential to our understanding of the problem that we know precisely the meaning of the terms he employs in stating the problem or in setting forth the subproblems. What basic assumptions does the researcher postulate as underlying substrata upon which his research will rest? What are his hypotheses? All these are important considerations and together they comprise what we have called *the setting* of the problem. In addition to the statement of the problem and its attendant subproblems, every researcher should set forth quite clearly and unequivocally the four principal areas we have just mentioned.

Components Comprising the Setting

The Delimitations. What are the precise limits of the problem area? The statement of the problem indicates what the researcher will include in the research endeavor. It is equally important to know what, within the periphery of the problem, he will not include. What are the limits of his thinking with respect to the problem? Where does the problem proper end and the periphery begin? The problem should be as carefully bounded for area identification as a parcel of land is for a real estate transfer.

The Definitions of Terms. What precisely do the terms which the researcher has used in the phrasing of the problem and the subproblems mean? For example, when we say that the purpose of the research is to analyze the harmonic characteristics of motets, what are we talking about? What are harmonic characteristics? Without knowing explicitly what a term means we cannot evaluate the research or determine whether the researcher has carried out what he stated in the problem. Terms must be defined operatively; that is, the definition must interpret the term *as it is employed in relation to the research project* in connection with which it is used.

Sometimes students rely on "dictionary definitions." Dictionary definitions are seldom either adequate or helpful. In defining a term the researcher makes that term mean whatever he wishes it to mean within the particular context in which he uses it. We must know how the researcher defines the term. We need not necessarily subscribe to such a definition, but so long as we know precisely what he means when he employs a particular term, we are able to understand the research objective more clearly.

Perhaps a word should be said about the nature of definitions. Formal definitions always contain three parts: (1) *the term* to be defined, (2) *the genera*, or the general class to which the concept being defined belongs, and (3) *the differentia*, the specific characteristics or traits which distinguish the concept being defined from all other members of the general classification. For example, *harmonic characteristics* (the term to be defined) shall mean the manner (the genera) in which tonal values are combined to produce individualized polyphonic patterns associated with the works of a particular composer (the differentia).

With regard to definitions, a word should also be said about a spurious type of definition, commonly called *defining in a circle.* The most classic example of this is perhaps Gertrude Stein's famous "a rose, is a rose, is a rose." Defined in a circle, *harmonic characteristics* would be "those characteristics which derive from the harmonic patterns found in the works of a particular composer." Circular definitions use the term to be defined in defining that term.

The Assumptions. Certain basic assumptions underlie the statement of every problem. So basic are assumptions that without them the problem could not exist. Let us illustrate what we are saying with an example. Take the Palestrina problem again.[1] We would assume, of course, that there is an identifiable as well as a characteristic difference that is recognizable between the harmonic structure of the motets of Palestrina and those of William Byrd. If we cannot assume this, then we have no problem, for it is upon this assumption that the problem rests.

Assumptions are what the researcher takes for granted. But taking things for granted may be the cause of much misunderstanding. What I may tacitly assume, you may never have thought of. If I act upon my assumption and in the final result such action makes a vast difference in the outcome, you may face a situation that you are totally unprepared to accept. To know what is assumed is, therefore, basic to a course of action. If we know the assumptions a person makes, we are then better prepared to evaluate the conclusions that result from such assumptions. To many students the stating of assumptions may be tantamount to stating the obvious, but because in research we try to leave nothing to chance

[1] See pp. 49, 54.

and try to prevent any misunderstanding, all assumptions which have a material bearing upon the problem should be openly and unreservedly set forth. To do so helps to provide a setting for appreciating the problem better.

The Hypotheses. Earlier in this text we discussed the reason for and the role of hypotheses in the research endeavor.[2] We pointed out that hypotheses are tentative postures, intelligent guesses, that a researcher makes to assist him in directing his thinking toward solving his problem. Hypotheses are necessary because (1) the researcher needs to have some point around which the research may be oriented in terms of searching for relevant data and (2) they allow us to comprehend the research project and the motives of the researcher.

We should keep in mind that hypotheses are neither proved nor disproved. To set out deliberately to prove a hypothesis is to defeat impartiality in research. It would bias the whole research procedure. The researcher would be looking only for those facts which would support his position. Difficult as it may be at times, we must let the chips of fact fall where they may. Hypotheses have nothing to do with proof. Rather, they are dependent for their *acceptance* or *rejection* upon the determination of what the facts reveal. From this standpoint, we say that hypotheses are either *supported (accepted)* or *not supported (rejected)* according to the dictates of interpreted fact. We must, therefore, refrain from judging the validity of any hypothesis until all the facts are in. The facts alone ultimately will either support or reject the hypothesis, and only after all of the facts are in and the interpretation of them has been made can we consider whether they support or reject the hypotheses. After they have been postulated, except to point in the direction of possible fact, hypotheses are revived only after the subproblem has been resolved.

As we mentioned earlier, we hypothesize in terms of the specific subproblems. For this reason a one-to-one correspondence usually exists between subproblems and their corresponding hypotheses, and we generally have as many hypotheses as we have subproblems. As such, a hypothesis becomes in a sense a target against which the data may be projected. As a point of reference, a hypothesis is to a researcher as a point of triangulation is to a surveyor: it provides a position from which he may begin to orient his exploration into the unknown and a checkpoint against which to test his findings.

In the interest of comparability it is appropriate in the proposal and in the chapter setting forth the problem in the final document that subproblems and hypotheses be placed reasonably close to each other. The sample proposal in the later pages of this text[3] will illustrate one way of presenting the hypotheses with relation to the problem and the subproblems.

Only one other matter is sometimes included in the section which provides the reader a setting for the problem, and this is a section entitled "The Importance of the Study." This section usually sets forth briefly and succinctly the reason for the study. It delineates the relevance of the study and establishes its pragmatic value.

Conclusion

Thus, we have come to the conclusion of the first major division of a research proposal. Essentially what we have described as the main items in the opening section of a proposal are equally the contents of the first chapter of a dissertation, a thesis, or a formal research paper. Before the reader goes further, in reading the final report, he wants to have clearly in mind what the problem is, what the subproblems are, what the limits of the investigation

[2] See pp. 6–7.
[3] See p. 192.

are, what the terms mean, what the researcher has assumed, what his hypotheses are, and what the importance of the study is. With this information he is now ready to review whatever literature may be relevant to the problem being investigated.

Practical Application

We have discussed many matters within this chapter which you should apply in practice to the problem which you have already isolated. Earlier in the chapter you were directed to stake out a problem area and, finally, to articulate the problem itself. Your problem should be fully stated in Appendix B, p. 226 (Project 4, Part 2). Now you are ready to go further.

Turn to the practicum in research section, Project 4, Part 3, and do as there directed in order to generate the subproblems and the other corollary items which comprise the setting of the problem.

A sample proposal with comments has also been included in Appendix A. You may wish now to study it to see how the problem and its setting are there presented in proposal form.

5 The Review of the Related Literature

UNDERSTANDING THE ROLE OF THE REVIEW

As a general rule, students do not understand the purpose of the section either in the research proposal or in a research report having to do with the review of the related literature. Its function derives from a fundamental position among researchers that the more one knows about peripheral investigations germane to one's own study, the more knowledgeably one can approach the problems indigenous to one's own area of investigation.

Such exploration and discussion occupies the section in the proposal or in the completed research report known as the *review* of the *related* literature. The italicized words are emphasized intentionally. They stress what needs stressing. In so doing, they describe precisely what the section does. Its function is to "look again" *(re+view)* at the "literature" (the reports of what others have done) in a *related* area: an area not necessarily identical with but collateral to your own area of study.

The Purpose of the Review

What, then, is the purpose of this review? It has several purposes. Primarily, it is to assist you in attacking your own problem. That is a fact that should always be remembered. In any research undertaking, your own problem is always central. Everything that you do, you do because it aids and assists in the attack upon your problem. Once you have chosen a problem everything else must be subservient to the solution of that problem. When you know what others have done, you are better prepared to attack with deeper insight and more complete knowledge your own problem for research. Briefly, the review of the related literature can provide you with the following benefits:

1. It can reveal investigations germane to your own, and it can show you how the collateral researcher handled these situations.
2. It can suggest a method or a technique of dealing with a problematic situation which may also suggest avenues of approach to the solution of similar difficulties you may be facing.

3. It can reveal to you sources of data which you may not have known existed.
4. It can reveal significant research personalities of whose research efforts you may have had no knowledge.
5. It can help you to see your own study in historical and associational perspective and in relation to earlier or more primitive attacks on the same problem.
6. It can provide you with new ideas and approaches which had not occurred to you.
7. It can assist you in evaluating your own research efforts, in comparing them with similar efforts related to yours.

For doctoral students this last advantage is of particular value. Dissertations are generally presumed to be *original* investigations into a hitherto unexplored problem area. Many a doctoral candidate who feels he has a monopoly on an unstudied claim finds when he begins to search the literature that what he thought was unoccupied territory has been so well tilled by others that it is, for his purpose, practically "farmed out." It is well to know where others have been before you and in what activities they have been engaged.

How to Begin a Search for Related Literature

Refer back to the chapter entitled "Tools of Research" (Chapter 2). Read again the section dealing with the library. There we discussed the master keys to the library and indicated ways to find your way through the numerous kinds of information found there. It may be well for you to begin with the indexes and abstracts: *Education Index, Index Medicus, Index of Science and Technology, Science Citation Index, Biological Abstracts, Chemical Abstracts, Dissertation Abstracts, Psychological Abstracts.* These and similar sources will provide you with principal current studies and related research projects. For contemporary events, do not overlook *The New York Times Index.* For a guide to the periodical literature of the nineteenth century, such works as *Poole's Guide to Periodical Literature* and the *Nineteenth Century Readers' Guide* are indispensable.

Bibliographies should not be overlooked. Perhaps one of the principal current sources is the *Bibliographic Index.* Besterman's *Bibliography of Bibliographies* and similar standard reference sources are helpful. For book location, *Books in Print,* the *Cumulative Book Index,* and the various catalogs of the Library of Congress, the British Museum, and the Bibliothèque Nationale should not be neglected.

One further informational area should not go without mention: the informational services, such as Medlars, ERIC, University Microfilms, which reduce significant research to microfilm, microfiche, or microprint and make it available to the researcher at a very nominal cost or through centers located at strategic points across the nation.

Certain suggestions may be helpful for the researcher beginning his quest for related literature.

• *Go to the library armed with data-gathering tools.* You'll need bibliography cards and a container to carry them in. This may be a filing box or an expandable envelope. Bibliography cards are valuable not only for gathering and recording the information but also for locating it again at a future date, should that be necessary. It is well to have a standard form, so that when recording a bibliographic item you will not omit any essential data. Every card should contain as a minimum the following items of information: author; title of article, if in a journal (in quotation marks); journal title (underscored); or title of the book, if the source is a book (underscored); publisher and place of publication; date; pages cited; source of bibliographic information; library where information was located; how item relates to the research problem; comment.

It may be well to duplicate as many of these cards as necessary and always to have a supply with you whenever you go to the library. Sometimes very valuable references are encountered unexpectedly. In the interest of conserving space and aiding in duplication of the necessary information on the card, twenty-pound bond paper is convenient for card making. It gives the necessary sturdiness for filing yet is thin enough to permit making multiple copies of the same note or bibliographic reference, if necessary.

A sample card might look something like this. It should measure 4 by 6 inches and have the information arranged as follows:

Serial No. ______

Author(s) ______________________________
(Last names first, first name, initial)

Title of article ______________________________

Journal title ______________________________

Volume ________ Pages ________ Month ________ Year ________

Place of publication, publisher, date (books only) ______________________________

______________________________ Edition ________

Source of bibliographic information ______________________________

Library where information is located ______________________________

Call number of book ________

How item relates to problem: ______________________________

____

Use reverse side for additional comment. (If used, check here ☐.)

- *Make as many copies of the bibliographic item as necessary.* You will probably want at least two copies of every bibliographical notation. You should set up two files. One should have the cards arranged by author's last name, alphabetically; the other should have the cards arranged serially by number. When making the original notation, carbon paper slipped under the original will make two or more copies at one writing. Bibliographies are arranged alphabetically according to the surname of the author.

In making notes, it is frequently convenient to have a single symbol for a complete source. In the upper right-hand corner of the sample card are the words *Serial No.* If as you write each item of bibliography you assign to that bibliographical source a number, upon making notes from that source on your note cards, it will save time and effort merely to indicate the page and serial number of the bibliographical source from which the note was made. A 1 in a circle, after making a note from a particular article or book, would refer the researcher to the bibliographical serial file, and on card No. 1 of that file would be the complete bibliographic information for the source of the note. Parallel card files, thus, serve distinctly different purposes, but for an extended research effort, each in its own way may be indispensably important.

Sometimes it is conceivable that for the fullest use of your data you may need to set up multiple classifications for the same source. Equip yourself with a pack of carbon paper cut to the size of the card you are using. A regular hand paper cutter may be used to cut regular 8½- by 11-inch carbon sheets to size. This carbon paper can then be used, if desirable, to have duplicates or triplicates of the same item.

Frequently it may be desirable to relate one bibliographic or substantive notation to several aspects of the problem or to file it under several headings. This is particularly true of historical data where you may wish to relate a particular bibliographical item to a chronological slot, so as to study it in relation to one or more other chronological sources, or to relate it to a particular author or other historical document. In such cases you may need three or four copies of a particular item. It is much easier to make multiple copies at one writing than to copy the same item later three or four times.

- *Be systematic and thorough.* "Make haste slowly" is a sound rule for the researcher. Too many students make careless, half-complete jottings that when referred to later, after consulting dozens of other sources, are either entirely unintelligible or are lacking in such essential information that they are practically useless. The original time in seeking out the item has been wasted. In such cases, the researcher must retrace his steps, wasting still more time. It would have been much better for him to have taken the required care and given proper attention to doing the job right in the first place. Little is gained by rushing to the extent that one fails to get either adequate or accurate information the first time around.
- *Relate your bibliographic items to your problem.* Always keep your research problem foremost in your thinking. In gathering bibliography, ask yourself constantly: How does this item of literature relate to my problem? Discover a connection between the problem and the item of literature. This will be a safeguard against the temptation of merely building a huge, haphazard bibliographic collection. On each card indicate precisely how that particular item relates to your problem. (The preceding specimen card includes space for this.) The competent researcher never forgets that everything he does serves only one purpose: to contribute to the solution of the problem.

How to Write the Section on the Related Literature

After they have amassed an impressive bibliography, many students do not know what to do with it. They have their cards arranged in order, while at the same time they are at a loss to know how to present their findings in the document they are preparing or what to do with the many citations as a result of their reading. A few simple guidelines may help.

- *Get the proper psychological orientation.* The review of the related literature section is a discussion of those efforts of others—those studies, research efforts, writings of others—that bear directly upon your own research effort. Think of the review of related literature section in your document as a discussion with a friend of what others have written in relation to what you plan to do. Regarding the literature section in this way will help you develop the proper psychological perspective: to see your own study in its proper framework and in correct focus with respect to the efforts of other researchers.

Too many students consider the related literature section as an unnecessary appendage to their real goal. On the contrary, a conscientious review of the related literature can open up to any researcher possibilities of which he was unaware.

- *Have a plan.* Too many discussions of related literature are unplanned and disorganized. They have no plan. The student lists whatever comes first to his attention without any organizational design. Before beginning to write the section of the review of the related literature, the student should outline the discussion that will follow. Perhaps one of the best guides for such an outline is the problem itself. A careful consideration of the problem should suggest relevant areas for discussion and indicate the direction that the discussion of the related literature section should take.

First, there are always the "classic" studies, the historically oriented writings which have prepared the way for your research effort. These studies are the efforts of the trailblazers of the broader area within which your problem lies. They connect your special realm of interest to the broad historical horizon from which you can gain perspective for your own efforts.

Begin your discussion of the related literature from a comprehensive perspective, like an inverted pyramid: broad end first. Then you can deal with more and more specific or more localized studies relating to your specific problem.

Refer to the sample proposal given in Appendix A. Here the author is interested in constructing a Strong Vocational Interest Blank scale for potential cartographers. Where does his discussion of the related literature start? It begins with the writings of the basic educational theorists of the nineteenth century who have dealt with this general area of the role of human interest and its relation to learning. Note his opening sentence: "The role of interests within the behavioral sciences is not new." That sentence takes you immediately into the eighteenth century and to the beginning of the nineteenth century with a discussion of the writings of Jean-Jacques Rousseau and Johann Friedrich Herbart. Note the organizational outline that the author follows in presenting the related literature dealing with his problem. (See Appendix A, pp. 195–202.) We have arranged these topics in the form of an inverted pyramid so that you will be able to see how the author of the sample proposal has done precisely what we have already discussed in terms of an overall plan.

Outline of the Review
of the Related Literature

Historical Overview (indicating the studies which underlie the whole area)
Interest Measurement as a Vocational Guidance Technique
The Measurement of Interests of Cartographers
The Strong Vocational Interest Approach
The Validity of the Approach
The Construction of a Scoring Key
Summary

Throughout your discussion of the related literature the plan of its organization should be clear. Use, as has been done in the sample proposal in Appendix A, headings and subheadings to indicate the organization of the discussion.

- *Emphasize relatedness.* Keep your reader constantly aware of the manner in which the literature you are discussing is related to your problem. Point out precisely what that relationship is. Too many discussions of related literature are nothing but a chain of pointless, isolated summaries of the writings of others.

Jones says. . .; Smith says. . .; Green says. . . . This is the format students generally use. This is also perhaps the worst form that a discussion of related literature can take. There is no discussion; there is no attempt to demonstrate the relatedness of the literature to the problem being researched.

Whenever you cite a study, make yourself account for that particular study in terms of your own problem, and be sure that you specifically point out to the reader in your discussion precisely what that relationship is. Unless you can establish such accountability, you would do well to consider whether you should include the study at all. Use a simple structural device such as a skeleton outline to assist you in establishing the relationship of the literature to the problem.

SHOWING RELATEDNESS OF THE LITERATURE TO THE RESEARCH PROJECT

Many discussions of related literature never quite make the nexus between discussion of the literature others have produced and the research one is doing. The discussion of the literature stands out as an incoherent section in the preliminary proposal or in the final report. To prevent this commonplace hiatus, the following procedure is recommended:

1. Write your problem at the top of the page, where you cannot lose sight of it. In this location you will be constantly aware of it as the central axis around which everything else revolves.
2. Dissect the problem by numbering its various subparts.
3. Divide the page into two columns by drawing a vertical line down the middle of the page, starting below the problem statement.
4. Cite each specific study in the left-hand column.
5. In the right-hand column opposite each study, note the particular subdivision of the problem to which it relates, and note also the rationale for including it in your review of the related literature.
6. Gather together all the citations that refer to a particular aspect of the problem, so that you have as many groups of studies as you have divisions of your main problem.
7. Study these groups in relation to each other, with the view of planning and organizing the discussion of the related literature.

The Summary

By following this procedure you will avoid mere bibliographical prattle under the guise of reviewing the related literature. Every discussion of literature and associated research relating to the problem under consideration should end with a brief section in the form of a summary in which the author gathers up all that has been said and interprets it in terms of his own problem.

Practical Application

You have begun to construct a proposal of your own research problem in Project 4 in the practicum section of this book. Presumably by this time you have your problem stated and the setting outlined in which the problem belongs. Now turn again to the practicum section and go further with the development of your own research proposal.

Turn to Appendix B, pp. 227–229. You are now ready to plan the "Review of the Related Literature" section of your proposal. In the practicum section to which you have been referred, you will be given specific directions as to how to proceed.

6 The Data and the Treatment of the Data

WHAT ARE DATA?

The word *data* is plural. We shall constantly be referring to data in this chapter as "they" and "them." In syntactical usage we shall employ the word with the plural form of the verb.

The word *data* (singular, *datum*) derives from the past participle of the Latin verb *dare*, "to give." They are those facts that a particular situation "gives" to any observer. We often refer to data by saying "these are the facts of the situation." The word *fact*, on the other hand, comes from the Latin word *facere*, meaning "to make"—what the situation "makes" or manifests to the observer.

The etymology provides the first clue to the nature of data: they are merely *manifestations* of the truth of a situation rather than the truth per se. Data are representative, intermediate, and elusive. But it is with data that the researcher must work.

Research seeks *through data* to discover what is true absolutely. In a sense, research is a constant pursuit after the complete *meaning* of what the researcher sees in the data. Data do not constitute Absolute Truth, but merely a behavioral manifestation of that Truth. The experienced researcher is constantly aware that what he most ardently seeks as the ultimate goal of his research, namely, Truth, is forever just beyond what is represented by his data and, hence, beyond his grasp.

The scientist probing the nature of subatomic matter is always conscious of an elusive sub-, sub-, subentity which, like the will-o'-the-wisp, lures him on yet always evades him. The mind of man yearns to look on beauty bare, to discover naked Truth, to understand the Ultimate. As a means of access to that clear perception and total understanding of Truth, man has chosen the pathway of research. Many times it has led him close to his goal: his mind has been enlightened, his knowledge increased, his understanding enlarged, but he has never been privileged to behold Truth Absolute or to grasp the Ultimate. Whenever he has looked on data intently and earnestly, he has always seen new problems arise which demand further research. Like the asymptotic curve, he always approaches but never meets the straight line of Truth.

Data, therefore, are not only elusive, but ephemeral. They are those facts which the researcher is permitted to glimpse at any one split second of time. For example, we are interested in identifying the discrete interests of cartographers with respect to the interests of men in general.[1] How do we accomplish this? We find some cartographers—a "population," we call them. These, of course, are not all the cartographers in the federal service; even if they were, the population would not remain stable even during the time that it takes us to gather our data: cartographers would be retiring and some would be beginning their careers. As those whom we question today pass out of the population tomorrow, the data shift and change. The process is as endless, varied, and infinitely complex as life itself.

How, then, will we find out anything about cartographers and their interests? We will dip down into the human pool of those individuals who "engage in the production of maps. . .charts, and related graphic materials."[2] We will ask them about their interests. Good! But can we be sure that what they tell us is "true"? It may indeed be true to the best of their knowledge at the moment of their replying to our questions. Even they may not be aware, however, that at the very instant in which they are reporting to us, their interests may be imperceptibly changing. Tomorrow their interests may not be precisely the same as they were today, and in five years they may have developed an entirely different set of interests.

The nature of data, therefore, is ephemeral. Through them at best we see through a glass darkly and catch but a fleeting glimpse of what seems to be true about the interests of cartographers as compared to those of men in general. It must be so, but it is well, nevertheless, for every researcher to recognize clearly the elusive quality of even the most "reliable," the most refined, and the most "trustworthy" data.

What we have been saying about data and their relation to Truth as well as a simplification of the entire research process may be best represented by a simple stratified diagram representing the three "realms" of research: the most profound, the deepest, the farthest-removed realm from that of the researcher is the Realm of Truth Absolute.

Between the Realm of Truth and the Realm of the Data which reflect Truth is an impenetrable barrier through which the light of Truth may shine to illuminate the data but through which the mind of man may never penetrate. Within the realm which gives to the observer[3] his only perception of truth are layers of various densities of truth-revealing fact. The data that lie in juxtaposition to the Truth are the most valid, the most illuminating, the most "Truth manifesting."[4] Because these data lie closest to Truth itself, we call these *primary data.* Those data which are more remote, less directly illuminated, more likely to be contaminated by other influences we call *secondary data.*

The third realm, the Realm of the Inquisitive Mind of the Researcher, can make contact with the Realm of the Data through only one medium: the medium of the human senses, for all data come to man through his sensory receptors. Sometimes in order to perceive the data, man must devise certain instruments which are merely the extension and amplification of his sensory attributes. Thus, hovering over but always outside of the world of the data is the questioning mind of the researcher.[5] The researcher tries to peer through the realm of empirical fact to behold the Truth beneath the fact. He is always thwarted in his quest.

[1] See Appendix A, p. 192.
[2] See Appendix A, p. 193.
[3] See the etymology of the word *data,* p. 64.
[4] See the etymology of the word *fact,* p. 64.
[5] See discussion, p. 5, pp. 7–8.

Let us represent this somewhat philosophical interpretation of the research process and the nature of data by the following illustration:

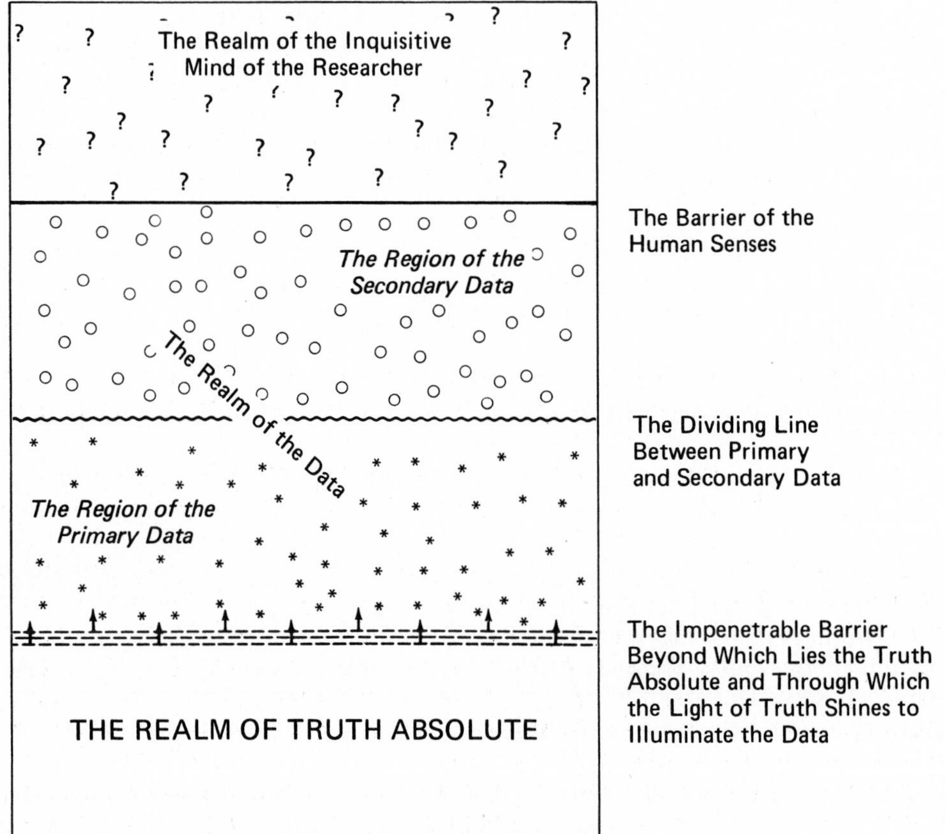

A careful inspection of the preceding diagrammatic representation of the research process reveals certain important facts with reference to the nature of data and the position of data with respect to the entire process of research. The nature of primary and secondary data has been already explained and the difference between these two types of data is clearly apparent by referring to the diagram. *Primary data* are those which lie "closest to the Truth" and, hence, reflect the likeness of the Truth with greatest fidelity. A person who actually witnesses an accident is, we say, "closer to the truth" with respect to the facts of what happened than one who merely reads about it in a newspaper.

The diagram also underscores the importance of the "barriers" which isolate the actual reality from the data and the data from the observer. The precise researcher will never forget the nature of this structure. To recall it may prevent him from making exaggerated statements or drawing unwarranted conclusions. It is the remembrance of the philosophical status quo of the several "realms" within the totality of the research process that reminds the researcher even in his most exuberant moment of discovery that no man has ever been permitted to glimpse Truth Absolute, nor can he perceive the data which reflect that Truth except through the gross and shadowy channels of man's dull senses. Such an awareness helps the researcher to be cautious and gives him a new respect for such words as *perhaps, it seems,* and *it appears to be.* The true researcher is cautious because he is wise enough to know that no man can ever be sure that what he beholds is, indeed, even a verisimilitude of the Truth.

Practical Application

Thus far we have been discussing data and the role that they play in the research process. At this juncture, therefore, it is important that you learn to think like a researcher with respect to data and their meaning, for researchers regard data differently than do most people. They look at the facts with which they are confronted more open-mindedly and they are more careful in drawing unilateral conclusions from the data with which they deal.

Turn to pp. 229–230. There you will be given an opportunity to regard certain situations with respect to data as a professional researcher may interpret them.

Criteria for Admissibility of the Data

Not all data which come to the attention of the researcher are acceptable for the researcher's use. Data can be defective, and if they are, they may affect the validity of the researcher's conclusions.

Imperfections and irregularities exist in nature, and if the researcher includes in his data those which are imperfect or irregular in quality with respect to the others, then he has no standard against which to measure any performance.

A researcher is trying to determine the effect of ultraviolet light on growing plants. But ultraviolet is a fuzzy term; it may include any radiation between 4,000 angstroms and 500 angstroms.

One of the axioms of research is that any research effort should be *replicable;* that is, it should be able to be repeated by any other researcher at any other time under precisely the same conditions. In order to regulate the precision of the conditions, therefore, certain limits must be established, certain standards set up, certain criteria prescribed which all the data must meet in order to be admitted for study. By the prescription of such standards, we can then control the type of data admitted and regulate the conditions under which the research effort is permitted to proceed. Whatever data do not meet the criteria are excluded from the study. By so doing, we ensure the integrity and uniformity of the data studied. It is much easier to do this, of course, in the physical sciences where all data are described largely in terms of quantitative values, but it is also possible within the broader disciplines of knowledge—the humanities, the social sciences, the performing arts—to develop standards and requirements to which the data must conform if they are to be admitted to the study.

But to return to the agronomist studying the effect of ultraviolet rays on growing plants, we must narrow the parameters of the data so that they will fall within certain specified limits. The agronomist must define precisely what he means by ultraviolet light. Within what angstrom range will he accept ultraviolet emission? In what intensity? With what time duration? What is meant by "ultraviolet effect on growing plants"? What effect? What growing plants? All? Some? Which?

When we can standardize the data and then admit only those data which comply with the criteria established, we can more nearly control the research effort and conclude with greater certainty what appears to be the truth of the situation. In order, therefore, to insure the integrity of the research effort, it is important that we set forth beforehand precisely what the standards are which the data must meet and that we make the consumer of the research party to these criteria. Only by so doing can both parties—the researcher and the consumer of the research—come to some understanding as to what is being studied.

THE RESEARCH METHODOLOGY

We have been discussing the limitations of the data. First we discussed the barriers through which the data must penetrate in order to reach the analytical mind of the researcher. Then we discussed the separation of data into the more desirable primary genre and the less desirable secondary kind. We have just concluded a discussion of data limitation in terms of the criteria which the data must meet in order to be admitted to the study at all. After such refinement, we are now ready to select for the treatment of the data a methodology *which will be appropriate to the nature of the data themselves.*

It is particularly important to recognize the fact that data and methodology are inextricably interdependent. For that reason the research methodology must always consider the parameters and nature of the data. *Methodology is merely an operational framework within which the facts are placed so that their meaning may be seen more clearly.* A review of any of the standard textbooks on research will reveal a broad spectrum of methodological terminology.

In reality, the whole matter of methodology is really quite simple. The research method must be appropriate to the nature of the data. Data are generally of four kinds:

1. Written records and accounts of past happenings and events (commonly called *historical* data).
2. Observations which a researcher makes directly and then subsequently describes according to his perception of the characteristics of the data or their relationships (commonly called *normative survey* or *descriptive survey* data).
3. Observations which are quantified and must, therefore, be evaluated in terms of appropriate statistical procedures (commonly called *analytical survey* or *statistical* data).
4. Observations of differences or likenesses which arise from comparison or contrast of one set of observations with another set of observations, each of which has been derived under differing conditions (commonly called *experimental* data).

These four kinds of data demand four principal research approaches—methodologies, we call them—to deal with each situation appropriately. For simplicity, we will keep a one-to-one correspondence between the categories of the preceding types of data and the methodology appropriate for each.

1. The *historical method* is appropriate to be applied to those data that are primarily documentary in nature.
2. The *descriptive survey*, or as it is sometimes called the *normative survey method*, is appropriate for data that are derived from simple observational situations.
3. The *analytical survey method* is appropriate for data that are quantitative in nature and that need statistical assistance to extract their meaning.
4. The *experimental method* is appropriate for data derived from an "experimental-control" situation in which two separate groups are involved, one of which has been conditioned by an extraneous variable, the other of which has been sealed off from the influence which has affected the first group and, hence, which may be used as a "yardstick" against which to measure the effect of the variable.

Each of these several methods has its discrete characteristics. Each, likewise, makes certain demands of the data so that the methodology may be competent to deal with the particular type of data in terms of revealing the meaning of those data and evaluating their significance. We have sketched the gross differentials for each methodology. In the next several chapters we shall consider each methodology separately, outlining not only the distinctive data characteristics in further detail but also the unique nature of the specific methodology to handle the data of each type.

Methodologies of Research Design

7 The Historical Method

HISTORICAL RESEARCH: THE MEANING OF EVENTS

The historical method is the means by which the researcher deals with the significance, the latent meaning of history. History is a phenomenon. It is a transcript of the relentless surge of events, the sequential and meaningful record of human activity. The historical method aims to assess the meaning and to read the message of the happenings in which men and events relate meaningfully to each other. The object of the historical method, therefore, is to interpret the signs of the times past and to see in what might otherwise be considered merely the happenstance of blind fortune a rationale and design.

In order to appraise accurately, however, the meaning and relationship of events, the historical researcher should always seek to get as close to the original happenings as possible in the hope of thus better reconstructing the past. To do this the historical researcher generally relies upon documentary sources, although occasionally artifacts are studied either alone or in conjunction with documentary evidence. In his search for historical truth, therefore, the researcher relies, if at all possible, upon only *primary* data. On p. 66 an explanation of the nature of primary data has been presented. The use of primary data tends to ensure the integrity of the study and strengthen its reliability. It is, therefore, generally considered to be a *sine qua non* of historical scholarship.

External Evidence and Internal Evidence

With documentary research, the matter of evidence should not be overlooked. Evidence evaluates the data in two directions and is variously known as *external evidence* or *internal evidence*, or these terms may also be referred to as *external criticism* or *internal criticism.*

We shall consider these terms briefly. *External evidence* asks of the document only one question: "Is it genuine?" External criticism, therefore, is concerned with the authenticity of the document or the artifact. The first question that a historian must ask of his document is, "Is it real, is it actually what it purports to be, or is it a counterfeit?" One needs only to recall Thomas Chatterton and the famous "Rowley Manuscripts" to realize how easy a hoax can be. That happened in the eighteenth century. In the twentieth appeared a spurious biography of a United States businessman, motion picture producer, and aviator which fooled one of the world's largest publishers and landed its author in jail! Frauds are not uncommon, nor is their acceptance unusual. One needs only to remember how thoroughly archeologists were taken in by the Piltdown Man and that Thomas J. Wise issued for years "private editions" of Victorian writings which deceived famous collectors until the fraud was exposed in 1934 by John Carter and Graham Pollard. It is extremely important, therefore, to know whether the document that one employs as the basis of his research effort is genuine. External evidence or external criticism of the document is of paramount importance to the credibility of the research.

Quite apart from the question, "Is it genuine?" which is the consideration of external criticism, is the equally important question of *internal evidence.* The question here is not one of authenticity but of *meaning.* In considering a manuscript in terms of internal evidence the researcher asks such questions as, "What does it mean?" "What was the author attempting to say?" "What thought was he trying to convey?"

Take a well-known utterance. The time is November 19, 1863. Abraham Lincoln is speaking at the dedication of a national cemetery in Gettysburg, Pennsylvania. In that brief but famous dedicatory address the President said, "But, in a larger sense, we cannot dedicate—we cannot consecrate—we cannot hallow—this ground. The brave men, living and dead, who struggled here, have consecrated it, far above our power to add or detract."

The question now is, what did Mr. Lincoln mean by "the brave men, living and dead?" Did he mean only the brave Union men? (We must remember that he was dedicating a Union cemetery.) Did he mean the brave Confederate men as well? Or did he mean brave men, indiscriminately—with no thought of North or South but merely of courage and valor? It is interesting to speculate as to just what President Lincoln did mean. To a study in depth of the Gettysburg Address or a biography of Abraham Lincoln, it is essential to know precisely what the president meant by those words.

The matter of internal evidence is not so far from us as we might at first surmise. What does the decision of a court mean? What do the words of the decision convey as to the intent and will of the court? The question comes up all the time in legal interpretation. In such instances, the primary question, which is the sole concern of internal evidence, or internal criticism, is *what do the words mean?* What is the intent? What is the message they seek to convey?

The Role of Chronology in Historical Research

The student of historical research needs to distinguish very carefully between two other concepts that are frequently confused under the general rubric of "the study of history." One of these concepts is *genuine historical research—historiography*, as it is sometimes called. It is with this that the researcher should be primarily concerned. The other concept is *chronology:* the setting down of occurrences and events in the order of their occurrence. Chronology usually is merely a listing of dates and events. It is, therefore, not research. It is not research, because mere chronology sets down events in the order in which they have occurred but it does not demand any *interpretation of the meaning* of such events, and in this respect it fails to fulfill a prime requirement of the discipline of research.

The following is chronology:

1492: Columbus discovers America.
1607: First permanent English settlement in America (Jamestown, Virginia).
1620: Pilgrims land at Plymouth Rock.
1626: The Dutch settle New Amsterdam.
1630: Puritans establish Massachusetts Bay Colony.

1634: Lord Calvert settles Maryland.
1682: William Penn founds the colony of Pennsylvania.
1733: Georgia founded.
1754-1763: The French and Indian Wars.
1775-1783: War of American Independence.
1789: George Washington inaugurated first president of the United States of America.
1792: First political parties appear in America.
Industrial revolution begins in America.

In this form the list is merely a succession of dates marking a series of happenings in the first 300 years of American history.

Moreover, format does not change genre. The mere recasting of a chronological list into paragraph form with the amenities of prose composition and appropriate documentary footnotes does not change the nature of the process nor transform pedestrian chronicle into historical research. It is still merely the reporting of happenings, the recital of events, the listing of occurrence after occurrence.

All too many students think that in writing historical research the more voluminous the document they produce, the more impressive the research effort. Reams of paper and an effusion of footnotes, they think, produce a display of historical scholarship which stamps their effort with the imprint of research. Nothing could be further from the truth. Mere compilation of historical happening is only compilation of historical happening, nothing more.

This is not to imply that chronology does not fill a very important place in historical study. It does. It is the grist of the research mill. It provides the first step in the process of data interpretation and interpretation is, as we have earlier said, the necessary element of all research.

In consequence of what we have just said, let us look analytically now at the chronological list given above. What, in fact, do these events say? What do they mean? Are they merely isolated happenings? Have they any relationship? These are questions that the historical researcher is always asking of his data. They represent the basic attitude of historical research. If we are to do historical research, we must seek not only to identify and isolate the chain of events of substantive history, important though that chronological process is, but also to understand their meaning in terms of their relation both to each other and to the problem under study.

History is unique in several of its dimensions. One of these is the *dimension of historical time;* the other is the *dimension of historical space.* Both of these dimensions are extremely important to the researcher in interpreting historical data. We will discuss first the concept of historical time, then we shall inspect the concept of historical space. Because history is inseparable from the time in which its events have happened, we should examine the preceding chronology in terms of its time orientation and relationship.

Many beginning researchers fail to become familiar with the time dimension; hence, they do not appreciate the significance that the temporal relationship gives to the data. Earlier in these pages[1] we demonstrated that the more angles from which data were regarded, the more meaningful those data became with each angular viewpoint. Historical data are no exception.

In the preceding chronological table, the time span was 300 years: 1492 to 1792. Therefore, let's do a very simple thing: draw a line 6 inches long.[2] For a 300-year span, a line of such length divides into convenient time segments the entire historical period considered:

[1] See pp. 22-23.
[2] Because of width-of-page limitations, the length of line here will be slightly shorter.

each 2-inch span represents 100 years; each inch, fifty years; each half-inch, twenty-five years; and so on. So divided, the chronological period will, then, look like this:

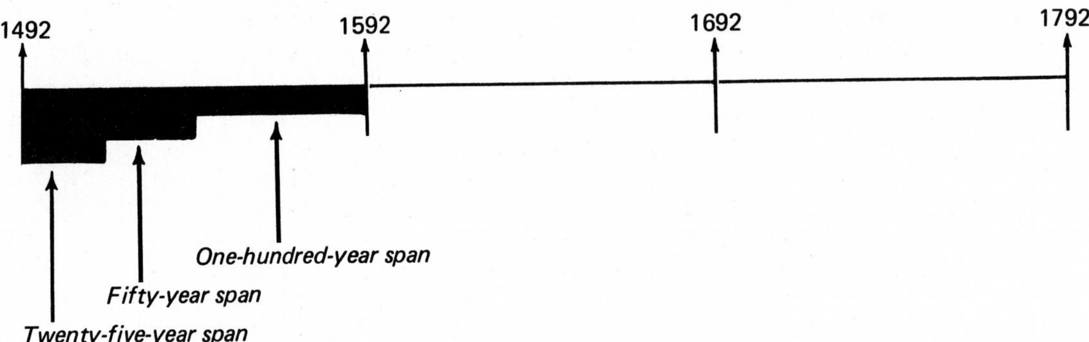

Now, within the preceding time frame, let us insert at the proper points the events listed in the chronological table on pp. 72–73. The chronology now looks like this:

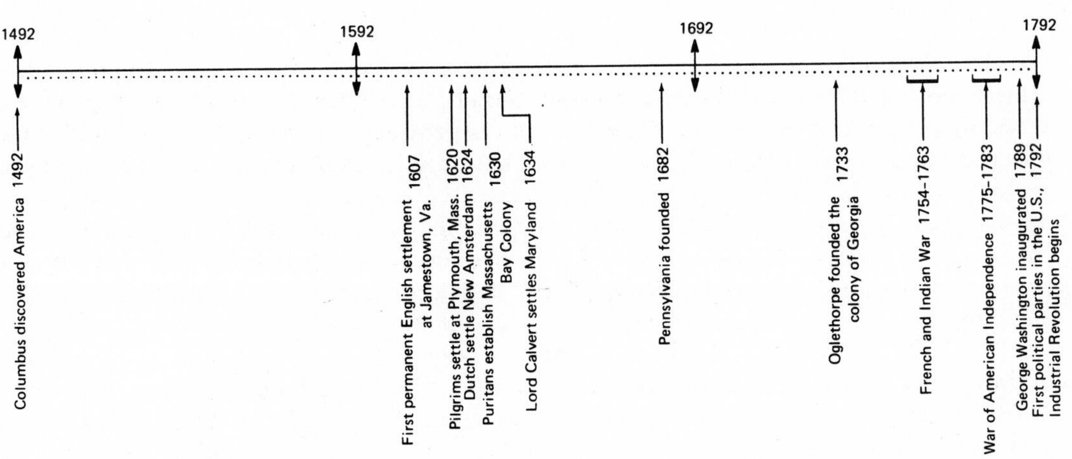

How different the chronology now appears. It is no longer merely a list of items with equidistant spaces between them. It has become, rather, a series of events placed along a continuum of time at the precise points of their relative occurrence. The dynamics of history are now becoming apparent. Note also the rhythms along the time line. An apparently sterile 115 years (1492–1607) elapse between the discovery of America and the first permanent English settlement at Jamestown, Virginia. Then, for slightly more than a quarter of a century, events happen in rapid succession, only a few years apart. Another century, 1634-1733, intervenes. In it, only one occurrence—the founding of Pennsylvania in 1682—is included in the chronology, and that happened almost at midpoint in this otherwise quiet century. The final half of the last century was again a time of renewed activity. It saw the last of the thirteen original colonies founded; two wars erupted; a new nation came into being and its first president was inaugurated; the American political system was born, and the era of industrial revolution was about to begin.

We need only a little imagination to realize that the device which we have been discussing briefly is capable of numerous variations. The historical researcher who is studying more than one set of chronological data within the same time frame may gain increased insight by arranging multiple time-line scales in slide-rule fashion. We might superimpose above the events which we have plotted on one time line another series of events—for example, the principal events in the history of England which determined the discoveries and explorations in the New World. Similarly, we could also plot the meaningful events from French or Spanish history over the same tercentenary period. We would then read the chart as we read a slide rule: one scale against the other.

Sometimes a realistic way to regard the time-distance dimension in historical perspective is to see it in reverse. As historical data stand in perspective at a distance of centuries or millennia from the researcher, they have a tendency to telescope and become unrealistically crowded upon each other. Historical time has a subtle way of becoming deceptive unless we are very alert as to its realities. A pencil and some simple subtraction will reveal a great deal which otherwise may escape our awareness. If we lay a particular historical period backward from the present, it brings dramatically into focus the slowness or the rapidity with which events moved in times past. Into the block of time that elapsed between the discovery of America and the establishment of the first permanent English settlement at Jamestown, you could pack all of American history from the presidency of Abraham Lincoln to the present moment! To reel time backward frequently puts historical events in vivid and dramatic perspective.

The Concept of Historical Space

We have been discussing history as a time phenomenon, and we have explored the role of time in seeking the interpretation of historical fact. But although events do happen at a particular moment in time, they also have an equal space dimension. In trying to understand the significance of historical fact the *where* dimension is frequently as important as the *when.*

Let us now consider the chronological list that we have been studying in relation to the *geographical locations* where the action took place. Here is the manner in which the events are related to a map of the United States.

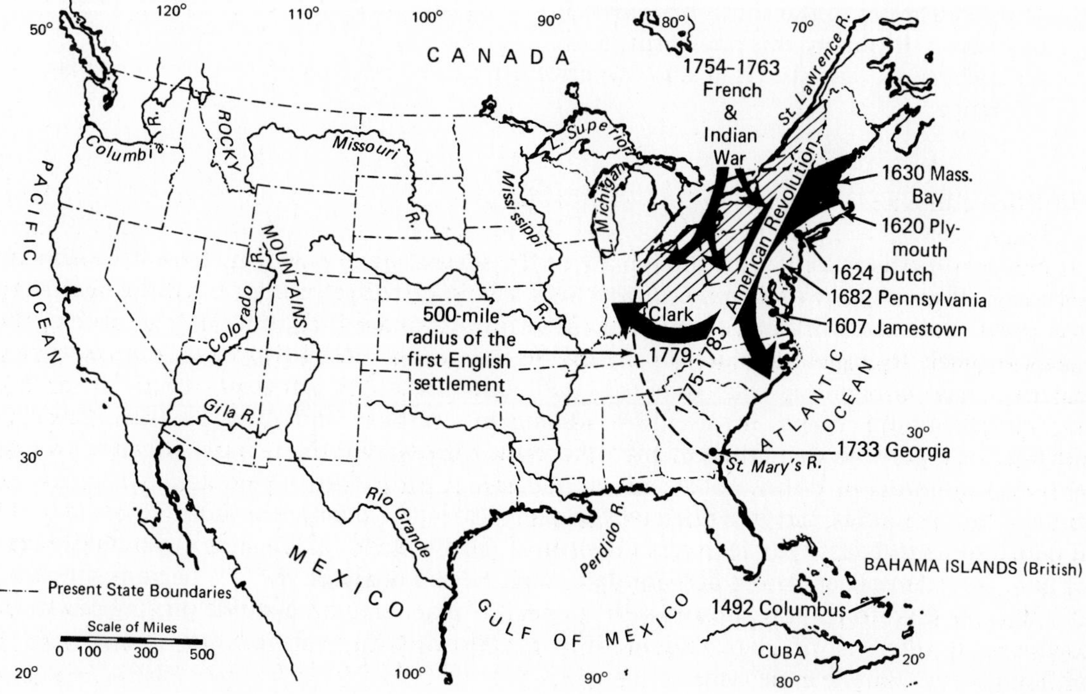

Now look back. We have arranged the same historical facts in three separate presentations: first, as a simple chronological listing; next, along a time-line continuum; and, finally, in geographical relationship to each other. Each arrangement provided you with additional insight into the meaning of the data. In each instance, we enlarged our understanding of the basic question that we ask of all data, "What do these facts *mean?*"

The geographical placement of the information reveals a number of *new* insights not apparent in either of the other two arrangements:

1. Colonization, as represented by the chronology, was not equally spread along the Atlantic coastline. It clustered north of the fortieth parallel of latitude.
2. The first English colony at Jamestown, Virginia, was pivotally located. It was just about equidistant from the northernmost as well as the southernmost point of colonization activity.
3. An arc inscribed on the map, using Jamestown as the pivotal point, will include an area in which just about all of the events of the chronology happened. Measured against the scale of miles we see that such an arc will have a radius of just about 500 miles.
4. By referring to the limits of such an arc, we see that the French and Indian War took place in the hatched area lying across the outer and northern limits of such an arc. Such a war must have probably seemed as remote to the colonists of Jamestown, Philadelphia, New York, and Boston as Vietnam and Korea seem to the air-age mind of today.
5. The War for American Independence, on the other hand, was a very intimate struggle. It swept through the colonies in a wave of events which traveled in a north-to-south direction, except for the Vincennes exploit of George Rogers Clark (1779). The hatched arrows on the map indicate the general direction and progression of events from 1775-1781.
6. The landing of Columbus on the Island of San Salvador is perhaps the only event lying outside the area of principal activity. Not only is San Salvador some 950 miles to the south of Jamestown but also removed from it by 115 years of history. Probably this one event does indeed lie outside the corpus of historical fact which we are studying and is convenient only as a point of chronological reference.

THE SYSTEMATIZING OF HISTORICAL DATA

We have perhaps said quite enough about the several ways in which historical data may be viewed. Because, however, most of the data of the historical researcher will be gathered from documents and will finally be studied in terms of hundreds or thousands of note cards, it may be well to conclude this section on the historical method by suggesting a way of gathering and controlling the data so that one reaps the greatest return from the innumerable hours spent in archives, document rooms, and libraries. In historical investigations, perhaps more than in any other type of research, the researcher can soon find himself in a morass of notes, note cards, bibliography cards, and memoranda. It is easy to read and to take notes, but it is difficult for many students to organize those notes into useful and meaningful facts for research. Historical data collecting demands a systematic plan not only for data collection but also for data retrieval and analysis. Before beginning historical research, therefore, you should have a specific plan for the acquisition, organization, storage, and retrieval of data. Some of the following suggestions may assist you in developing a systematic approach.

Note Cards and Bibliography Cards

The matter of note cards and bibliography cards should be carefully considered. Despite the widespread use of filing cards for note and bibliographical purposes, they have their disadvantages. Quantities of them take up an inordinate amount of space, and only one copy can be made of any note or bibliographical entry. The suggestion is made here that you consider instead using 20-pound paper in various colors cut to 3- by 5-, 4- by 6-, or 5- by 7-inch size. Probably for most efficient use and convenience you may wish to have certain items duplicated or printed on these sheets. Such prepared sheets will save you time and ensure that you do not overlook important information which may be essential at a later date. By mimeographing or duplicating card forms and sizes on regular 8½- by 11-inch or 8½- by 14-inch paper, they can then before use be cut to size with an ordinary hand paper cutter. On p. 60 a suggested form for a bibliography card is given. A note card might look something like this:

Main Heading Classification	Subheading	Card No. ___ One of ___ cards

Source Information: Author's last name ______________ Date of book ________ pp.______
First significant word of title ______________________________

The importance of the box in the upper right-hand corner of the card is apparent when making an extended note. For example, one knows precisely where the particular card belongs if it reads: "Card No. 2. One of 3 cards." At the bottom of the note card is a brief but exact short form of bibliographic reference. To find the complete bibliographic reference, all one has to do is to refer to his bibliography, which should be alphabetically arranged by the authors' last names.

Multiple Files and Color Coding

All notes should be taken in multiple copy—probably in triplicate or quadruplicate, depending upon your ultimate analysis of the data. Behind the suggestion of substituting 20-pound paper for cards was the thought of making multiple copies. Earlier we discussed the dimensional nature of historical data. One fact lies simultaneously in the province of time, of space, of personality, and perhaps of subject matter. Take, for example, a note on Edgar Allan Poe and his poem "Annabelle Lee." Poe wrote that poem in 1849 while living in a small cottage in Fordham in The Bronx. A student researching Poe's life in New York may wish to study this poem from several angles. He may wish to study all the poems written in 1849 for one reason or another. He may wish to study Poe's life in Fordham. He may wish to study the poems Poe wrote about his child wife, Virginia Clemm. He may wish to have a quick reference to all of the information he found on the poem "Annabelle Lee." Thus, one item of information conceivably might be studied from four separate angles. By taking four note cards (sheets) and interleaving them with carbon paper, cut to size, four copies can be made of the same note instead of one. Other notes can be made similarly. When the sheets are separated after writing the note, the headings can be added. The four cards will then look something like this:

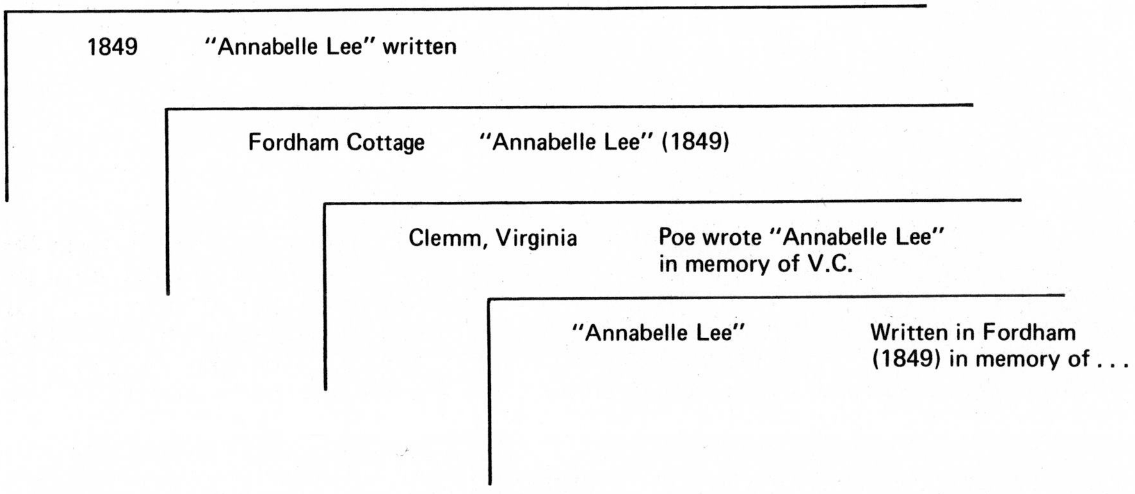

If the researcher continues to produce his cards in quadruplicate, he will have four separate files of the same data for his study. He can gather all the chronological headings together into a progressive file, year by year, of happenings. He will have a file on the Fordham period, and if he is making a more extensive study, on other locations where Poe lived. He will have a file relating to persons in Poe's life. He will have a file dealing with individual poems or separate works. For each of these areas of study, the researcher may wish to use, for ready identification, a different color of note card: white, yellow, pink, light green, and so on. If the dates are all on white cards, the color identifies the genre of data. Quick cross-referencing, interrelationships, and study of influences or of a particular genre of data is made possible by this system; and when seen in a three- or four-dimensional matrix, interpretation of historical data is greatly facilitated. One can then readily see meanings and interpretations which, in a one-card system, might easily have been missed.

Perhaps we have said enough about the historical method. We should now turn to another of the research methodologies and discuss it as a means to the discovery of truth.

Practical Application

Turn now to the practicum section (Appendix B), pp. 230–231. Here you will find a practical application of some of the aspects of the historical research method as discussed in this chapter.

8 The Descriptive Survey Method

We have been exploring one avenue to the approach of truth: the way through the documentary remains, written record, and artifacts that man has left behind him. By these means man has been able to study the events of past time and to comprehend the meaning of these events. He has been able to understand the deeds, the thoughts, and the lives of his fellow men as these have come down to him through written records and reports. From the study of these documentary remains he has been able to discern the "lessons of history."

SURVEY RESEARCH: OBSERVATION WITH INSIGHT

But all truth is not apprehended by studying past records. There are other ways, and one of these is by observing the events of the world around us. We can zero in on a target area of the complex life processes of today and observe intently what is happening there.

The method of research that simply looks with intense accuracy at the phenomena of the moment and then describes precisely what the researcher sees is called the *survey*, the *descriptive survey*, or the *normative survey* method of research.

The Meaning of Survey

The word *survey* is composed of two word elements which indicate precisely what happens in the survey process. *Survey* has the basic connotation of "the act of looking over or beyond." It has nothing to do with casual or purposeless observation.

Sur- is a derivative of the Latin word *super*, meaning "above," "over," or "beyond." The element *-vey* comes from the Latin verb *videre*, "to look" or "to see." Thus, the word *survey* means "to look over or beyond." One surveys the surface of the phenomena to discern the causal or meaningful aspects of the data which derive from those phenomena. The word *descriptive*, sometimes used in connection with this particular research methodology, also gives insight into the method. The word *descriptive* also derives from two Latin word elements: *de*, meaning "from," and *scribere*, "to write." The term, therefore, describes the essential character of the method. In employing it the researcher does two things: first, he observes with close scrutiny the population of his research parameter; second, he makes a careful record of what he observes, so that, having made his observations, he can come back to the record that he has made of them and can study that record carefully in order to discover the meaning of what he has observed.

The point should be clearly emphasized that "looking" or "seeing" is not restricted to seeing through the physical eye and by means of the optic nerve. In research, there are many ways in which we can "see beyond" that have nothing to do with physical vision. The physician "looks" at a patient's heart through a stethoscope and by means of an electrocardiogram. The educator, the psychologist, the guidance or vocational counselor "looks" at intelligence, attitudes, beliefs, or personality structure through tests, inventories, attitude scales, and other instruments. Hundreds of thousands of survey studies have been conducted in which the "looking" has been by means of a questionnaire, and in interview studies the "looking" has largely been by the ear rather than by eye.

But in each instance the observational phase has been accompanied with a recording phase, a setting down of the facts, a presentation of the data. Sometimes this takes the form of tables, charts, or graphs.

What, then, are the practical considerations in conducting a descriptive survey study? Reduced to its basic elements, the methodology is essentially simple in design. It is an approach that is used with more or less sophistication in many areas of human activity. From the citizen who canvasses his neighborhood to solicit opinions on granting a variance which permits a property owner to violate the building code of a community to the Gallup Poll, which aims to determine the attitude of people toward a national issue, surveys are commonplace in American life.

This is not to suggest, however, that because of their common occurrence that the survey is any less demanding in its design requirements or any easier for the researcher to conduct than any other method. This decidedly is not the case. In fact, the descriptive survey design makes certain specific and critical demands upon the researcher which, if not carefully respected, may place the entire research effort in jeopardy.

Characteristics of the Descriptive Survey

We shall begin by outlining the basic structure of the descriptive survey as a research method and indicating its characteristics.

1. The descriptive survey method deals with a situation that demands the *technique of observation* as the principal means of collecting the data.
2. The population for the study must be carefully chosen, clearly defined, and specifically delimited in order to set precise parameters for ensuring discreteness to the population.
3. Data in descriptive survey research are particularly susceptible to distortion through introduction of bias into the research design. Particular attention should be given to safeguard the data from the influence of bias.
4. Although the descriptive survey method relies upon observation for the acquisition of its data, those data must then be organized and presented systematically so that valid and accurate conclusions may be drawn from them.

Each of the preceding four steps will be discussed at greater length in the pages that follow. Each is important in that each deals with a critical area in survey research.

With survey studies, observation in one way or another is absolutely essential. We have already discussed briefly the meaning of observation in its wider connotation. It may be thought of as being almost synonymous with perception in the broad sense of that term, namely, of being aware of data through some means of detecting them. Many times the researcher may never see, in the conventional sense of perceiving with the eyes, the source of his data.

The Questionnaire

A commonplace instrument for observing the data beyond the physical reach of the observer is the questionnaire which, for example, may be sent to human beings who are thousands of miles away and whom the researcher will never see. In this sense, the social scientist who collects his data through the means of a questionnaire and the scientist who determines radioactive emission through the probe of a Geiger counter are in just about the same degree of remoteness from their respective sources of data. Neither sees the source from which the data originate. It is because of this impersonality associated with the questionnaire method of gathering data that we need to be governed by several practical guidelines when employing a questionnaire in gathering data.

1. *The language must be unmistakably clear in soliciting precisely what the researcher wishes to learn.* Communication is a deceptive skill. What may be crystal-clear to you may be so much meaningless jargon to another person. For example, take a very simple question: "How many cigarettes do you smoke each day?" That seems, of course, like a very clear, unambiguous question. Especially does it seem so if we accompany the question with certain choices and all the respondent has to do is to check one of the boxes:

How many cigarettes do you smoke each day? (Check appropriate box)

☐ more than 25 ☐ 25-16 ☐ 15-11 ☐ 10-6 ☐ 5-1 ☐ none

The assumption behind that question is that everyone smokes the same number of cigarettes each day. But what happens in an actual situation to an assumption of that kind? A nervous, erratic smoker gets that questionnaire. He does not fit the assumption. At the office, when the pressure is on and he is working full speed to keep on top of things, he is a chain smoker. When he gets home, on week-ends, and on his days off, he may smoke one or two cigarettes a day, or go without any cigarettes at all. How is he supposed to answer the question?

What we have just said points out one of the weaknesses of the questionnaire as a data-gathering instrument. Life is a very complex situation. There are many degrees and gradations of circumstance. For very few of us do the affairs of life fit into neat choices between yes and no or into primly graduated scales. The researcher who constructs his questionnaire all too often assumes that experience can be neatly categorized.

All questionnaires should be pretested on a small population in what is often referred to as a *pilot study.* Every researcher should at least give the questionnaire to half a dozen of his friends, or to his neighbors, to test whether there are any items that they may have difficulty in understanding or in knowing precisely what the writer of the questionnaire is seeking to find out.

Perhaps we have hinted at one of the principal causes for ambiguity and the inability of recipients to understand the questions that are asked. One of the major causes for such a situation is that the researcher has not spent enough time and care in defining the purpose for each item in his questionnaire nor has he edited each question so that it is phrased with that meticulous precision of language necessary to elicit the answer that the researcher is seeking.

2. *Questionnaires should be designed to fulfill a specific research objective.* Most questionnaires are thoughtlessly written. They bear the hallmarks of a quick, effortless attempt "to gather some data" which "may be helpful" in solving the problem. Aimless, haphazard thinking and careless, inexact expression are the most commonplace faults in questionnaire construction. This lack of design and precision of expression accounts for the small return of questionnaires when these are sent to a given population. Item by item a questionnaire should be built and quality-tested again and again for objectivity, relevance, suitability to the problem situation, and probability of favorable reception and return.

The writer of a questionnaire should never forget that he is asking of his addressee a gift of time and of effort and the favor of a reply. This hints at several important considerations in questionnaire construction. Here are some guidelines:

1. *Be courteous.* An occasional request beginning, "Would you please check . . ." will oil the wheels of cooperation and enhance your chances of having your questionnaire receive more kindly attention than one which continually pushes the questions before the respondee with only the commanding imperative which exudes an "it-is-your-duty-to-answer-the-question-for-me" attitude.

2. *Simplify.* Make the instrument as simple to read and to respond to as possible. The questionnaire should demand as little effort and time on the part of the respondent as possible. A check-item questionnaire is generally preferable to the "completion" type or one which asks the respondee to reply with an extended discussion.

3. *Think of the other fellow.* Put yourself in the place of the respondent. What would your reaction be if someone you never saw sent you a questionnaire such as you presume to impose upon another person. Look at the entire questionnaire realistically in terms of its demands on those to whom you send it. Be completely objective in the appraisal of your own questionnaire.

4. *Concentrate on the universal.* Try to address your questions to universals rather than specifics; to general problems and ideas rather than to purely local conditions and concerns; unless, of course, you are specifically making a study of local conditions and issues.

5. *Make it brief.* The questionnaire should be as brief as possible and should solicit only those data essential to the progress of the research project. This need not curtail the adequacy of the instrument, but the researcher should test every item in the questionnaire by two criteria: (a) What do I intend to do with the information I am soliciting? and (b) Is it absolutely essential to have this information?

6. *Check for consistency.* In questionnaires dealing with debatable or opinion-sensitive issues or in situations where you may suspect that the respondee may give answers that he deems prudent in certain cases, rather than what represents the truth, you may wish to incorporate a countercheck question into your list of questions at some distance from the first question; this helps to verify the consistency with which the questionnaire was answered. Take, for example, the following two questions appearing in a questionnaire as item numbers 2 and 30. This placement causes them to be widely enough separated to test their consistency. Note how they have been answered.

2. Check one of the following choices:
   ☒ In my thinking I am a liberal.
   ☐ In my thinking I am a conservative.

30. Check one of the following choices:
   ☐ I find new ideas stimulating and attractive, and I would find it challenging to be among the first to test and to try them.

   ☒ I subscribe to the position of Pope:
   "Be not the first by whom the new is tried
   Nor yet the last to lay the old aside."

The two responses do not agree with each other. In the first, the respondent indicated that he was liberal in his thinking, but later, when given the liberal and the conservative positions in another form, he indicated that his position would be more conservative than liberal.

7. *Send return postage.* Accompany your questionnaire with a self-addressed, stamped envelope for the convenience of your respondent in returning the questionnaire. To impose upon another's time and spirit of cooperation, and then to expect him to pay the postage for the return of your questionnaire is just too much to expect.

8. *Offer the results of your study to your respondent.* In return for his time and courtesy in responding to your questions, offer to send your respondent a summary of the results of your study at its completion, if your respondent wishes it. You might provide a check-space either at the beginning or at the end of your instrument where your respondent might indicate his wishes, together with his name and correct address. In questionnaires where anonymity is desirable, a separate post card may be included to supply the information.

The researcher should have clearly in mind, even before constructing the questionnaire, precisely how he intends to process the data he will get from it. Data-processing procedures will determine the form the questionnaire should take. If, for example, the data are to be card-punched and computerized, the questionnaire needs to be structured quite differently than if the data are to be handled in more conventional ways.

Questionnaires succeed as their success is planned. One researcher who conducted a particularly successful questionnaire study handled it this way:

1. After selecting her population, she sent to each of them a letter describing the potential value of the study. The letter emphasized the importance of the study to the addressee, and it invited the addressee to cooperate by answering the questionnaire.

Here is a copy of the researcher's initial letter of inquiry with marginal comments concerning some of its features.

THE AMERICAN UNIVERSITY
Massachusetts and Nebraska Aves., N.W.
Washington, D.C. 20016

The School of Nursing

August 15, 1973

Dear Alumna,

Your School of Nursing is appealing to you for help. We are not asking for funds - all we ask is a few minutes of your time.

It is to your advantage to be recognized as a graduate of a school which has an excellent reputation for the education and training of nurses to meet the realities of nursing practice. You can assist us to maintain - and to improve this reputation - by cooperating in the evaluation of the program of Nursing Education at The American University. What we would like to ask you is to give us your candid, honest opinion of the nursing program in effect when you were a student nurse in training at The American University. We have a questionnaire which we would like to send you, with your permission, and which will take no more than fifteen minutes of your time to answer.

The Lucy Webb Hayes School of Nursing at The American University is growing. With your help it can grow in professional stature and educational excellence. We are sure you will be willing to cooperate with us toward those desired goals.

As an enclosure with this letter, you will find a return post-card on which you may indicate your willingness to cooperate with us by answering the questionnaire. Thank you for the courtesy of your assistance.

Very sincerely yours,

Ruth G. Thomas

Ruth G. Thomas, R.N.

This letter was sent out by a student who was doing an evaluative study entitled: "A Study to Evaluate the Academic Program of the Lucy Webb Hayes School of Nursing at The American University."

The questionnaire was designed to gather information on one of the subproblems of the study: "How adequately do the graduates consider the program to have been in preparing them for a professional nursing career?"

Note the direct "other-fellow" appeal. The author quickly indicates this is not an appeal for money—only a few minutes of time.

The fact is strongly made that it is to the advantage of the addressee to answer the questionnaire.

Note: "with your permission!" Also, an estimate of time required helps to convince.

The positive is emphasized: we are growing; we want to grow in excellence—but we need you!

This is a splendid device for getting a commitment. The card will be reproduced later.

Note the tone. No "yours truly" here. The courteous tone is carried out to the very end of the letter.

Compare the preceding letter with the following brief note which is all too typical of the hundreds of similar ones that the author has seen proposed by his students:

> Dear Sir:
>
> I am a graduate student at XYZ University, and the enclosed questionnaire is sent to you in the hope that you will assist me in obtaining information for my Master's thesis.
>
> I should appreciate your early reply since I am attempting to get my degree this June.
>
> Yours truly,
>
> Joe Doe

This letter represents a flagrant foisting of one's own selfish demands without benefit of common courtesy as an imposition upon others. In letters of this sort may lie one of the secrets for the poor return of questionnaires when beginning researchers attempt to employ the survey method. The reaction of most readers who receive a letter like this last one is, "So what?" "Who cares?" "Why should I be concerned in doing you a favor by answering your questionnaire?" or "Get your degree the best way you can, but don't ask me to help you!"

And these reactions are not entirely without some degree of justification.

The letter is all-important. It should be carefully and thoughtfully structured, and its emphasis should stress the concerns of the person receiving it rather than emphasize the selfish interests and desires of the sender. Many students forget this; and, in so doing, unwittingly betray their own self-centeredness without perhaps intending to do so.

Let us return to the first letter, however. Mention was made there of a card which was enclosed and which gave the recipient an opportunity to express his willingness to answer the questionnaire. The card was a simple reaction form, containing the following wording:

> Dear Mrs. Thomas,
>
> [ ] Send the questionnaire. I will be happy to cooperate.
>
> [ ] I do not wish to answer the questionnaire.
>
> Comments:
>
> ______________________
>
> Name

2. Upon receipt of the card indicating willingness to cooperate, the researcher mailed the questionnaire to the respondent immediately. A log was kept of questionnaires mailed, to whom, their addresses, and date of mailing. In a desk memo date book, precisely three weeks after the mailing of the questionnaire, the respondent's name was entered as a reminder that if a reply was not received until that date a reminder letter should be sent.

3. The reminder letter was in the same vein as the initial one. It follows:

THE AMERICAN UNIVERSITY
Massachusetts and Nebraska Aves., N.W.
Washington, D.C. 20016

School of Nursing

September 5, 1973

Dear Alumna,

All of us are busier these days than we should be, and most of us have a hard time keeping abreast of those obligations which are essential and required. We know how the little extras sometimes receive our best intentions, but we also know that in reality none of us have the time which we would desire to fulfill those intentions.

From the questionnaire which reached you --we hope-- about three weeks ago, we have had no reply. Perhaps you mislaid the questionnaire, or it may have miscarried in the mail-- any one of dozens of contingencies could have happened.

In any event, we are enclosing another copy of the questionnaire. We are sure you will try to find fifteen minutes somewhere in your busy schedule to check its several items and drop it in the nearest postal box. Most of them have been returned. We'd like to get them all back. Will you help us?

Thanks. We shall appreciate your kindness.

Very sincerely yours,

Ruth G. Thomas

Ruth G. Thomas, R.N.

This letter applies phychology and human relations techniques at their best.

Note the universal and appreciative tone from the first three words of the opening sentence: "All of us . . .". The first letter began with a "you" approach. This one is much more understanding of human failure. It takes any hint of accusation out of the situation.

No need for the recipient of this letter to make excuses; we have provided two and thus disarmed the situation with the suggestion that there might be dozens more.

By enclosing a second questionnaire, come what may, she has now no excuse for ignoring you.

Note how gently the suggestion is made that she is one of the few delinquent ones.

The faith in this letter is boundless. It's pretty difficult not to comply in the face of such belief that you will do so.

The Interview Technique

Closely akin to the questionnaire method for collecting data is the *structured interview.* The interview, as a data-gathering technique, is frequently misunderstood. Most students think of it as "simply asking a person some questions" and essentially, it is just that. But it is not asking just any questions. The questions for the interview should be as carefully planned and as accurately worded as the items in the questionnaire. Interviews should be considered as strictly professional situations which demand equally professional planning and conduct on the part of the interviewer. We have seen how the questionnaire demands an integrated approach and considerable planning for its administration if it is to be a successful tool of research. This is equally true of the interview.

We have described in detail the approach of a researcher who employed the questionnaire technique in a professional and scholarly manner. Perhaps an equally effective way to illustrate the use of the interview technique may be to cite its use by another researcher who administered it in a highly professional manner. The student's problem concerned the field of international relations. It was desirable that he interview certain United Nations personnel in order to get their respective opinions concerning issues within the province of his research study. He hoped to gather his data quickly, but systematically, and planned his approach toward that end. He expected to go to New York for the series of interviews and hoped to schedule them as tightly as possible to conserve time and expense. His procedure was organized and logical. Approximately six weeks before going for the interviews, he wrote the several United Nations representatives whom he wished to see, indicating that he would be in New York on certain specific days and requesting the courtesy of an interview lasting not more than half an hour. He asked each prospective interviewee for an indication of several time slots when the interview might be scheduled. His letter explained clearly what information he was seeking and his reasons for seeking it. (Among his reasons was not that he was writing a thesis!) His reasons were mature and meaningful.

He enclosed with his letter a separate sheet containing the questions that he intended to ask during the interview in the order that he would ask them. In his letter, he suggested that if the interviewee had no objections, to tape the conference would facilitate matters, conserving time and lessening the distraction of hand-written notes. He provided a check-box for indicating whether the use of a tape recorder would be acceptable. Twenty-nine of his thirty-five interviewees had no objection to tape recording the interview. When he received his replies he set up a master chart of appointments with times and places and immediately confirmed by letter the appointment time; where there was a time conflict, he sought to resolve it by suggesting alternate times which were still open. Ten days before the interview, he mailed a reminder, together with another copy of the interview questions, just in case the interviewee had misplaced the copy previously sent. He enclosed his full interview schedule so that his interviewee might appreciate the time exigencies under which he was working.

On the day of the interview he arrived promptly. When taken in to see the person to be interviewed, he introduced himself, stated briefly that he had come in accordance with previously made arrangements, asked whether his interviewee wished a copy of the questions he had previously sent, and began with his first question. He tried to guide the interview, keeping always to his agenda of questions and seeking to preserve an easy, friendly, yet professional atmosphere. As the interview drew to a close, he thanked his interviewee for his courtesy in giving his time and went off to his next appointment.

In three and a half days he had interviewed thirty-five United Nations representatives and had over four fifths of his data on tape. Subsequently, he transcribed from the tape the substance of the interview and submitted within ten days of his visit a typed transcript to each interviewee, together with a letter thanking him for granting the interview. He asked each official interviewed to read carefully the typescript and if it was correct, to sign at the end of the copy a statement that the typescript of the interview was correct. If the official found it inexact or incorrect in any place, the interviewee was requested to correct the script or to edit it as he desired. As in all manuscript, the typescript was wide-margined and double-spaced, which permitted ample room for corrections.

In the statement acknowledging the typescript to be correct, the researcher also incorporated a "permission" clause in which he requested permission to use whatever part of the interview might provide data for his study with the full understanding that before the study was released the interview material would again be submitted to the interviewee a second time for his complete approval and permission to incorporate it into the research report. This was done, of course, prior to submitting the report as a final document for the degree. In the final document all acknowledgments were made, and the fact that the authors had inspected and approved all their quoted statements was noted. This is the only way that a researcher or an author can protect himself against accusations of falsification of the facts, libel suits, and other legal entanglements.

The steps, then, for successfully handling the interview as a technique for gathering data for one's research study are simple but very important:

1. Set up the interview well in advance.
2. Send the agenda of questions you will ask your interviewee.
3. Ask for permission to tape the conference.
4. Confirm the date immediately and send a reminder ten days before you expect to arrive.
5. Be prompt; follow the agenda; have a copy for your interviewee in case he has mislaid his.
6. Submit a typescript of the interview and get a written acknowledgment of its accuracy and permission to use the data in the research study, with subsequent submission and approval.

Tape Recording the Data

We have been discussing at some length two specific techniques of observation within the descriptive survey methodology: observing by means of the questionnaire and observing by means of the interview. But there are other ways to observe. We made the point earlier that observation need not always be a visual experience.

We observe through the ear as well as through the eye. One method of "ear observation" is described by a student who used the audio-observational approach in tape recording her data for a dissertation.[1] The student's problem for research was to categorize and to describe the classroom interaction of certain music teachers at two grade levels: the first grade and the sixth grade, and also to analyze and interpret the variation of the classroom-interaction patterns of these music teachers in the same grades and between the music teachers in grade 1 and the same music teachers in grade 6.

Here is her procedure for the collection of the data.

> The primary data, or raw data, for this study were secured by audio-tape recording the necessary class sessions of the ten teachers in the sample. The recording machine was a Wollensak Magnetic Tape Recorder, Model 7-7500.
>
> Each teacher in the sample prepared a schedule of her first-grade and sixth-grade music classes and agreed to permit the researcher to enter unannounced into the specified music classrooms prior to the beginning of each class that was to be recorded. The reason for not pre-arranging the taping sessions was to prevent any special preparation, conscious or unconscious, on the part of the teachers.
>
> The researcher entered the classroom prior to the beginning of the music class, started the tape recording machine, and left the classroom before the commencement of the music class. At the end of the class session the music teacher deactivated the tape recorder and the researcher returned to collect the tape and the equipment. This procedure was followed in order to eliminate bias in analyzing the tapes. The researcher first heard all of the tapes after having witnessed neither the teacher teaching nor the class in progress. Because of this procedure, there was unnecessary information recorded at the beginning of each tape. The analysis of the class session began with the start of instruction.
>
> Each class session was identified by the date, the time, the grade level, and the code letter of the teacher being recorded.
>
> The classroom in which music teachers taught their students varied from school to school and often varied from day to day within the same school.

[1] Alicia Leonard Pagano, "A Study of the Classroom-Interaction Patterns of Selected Music Teachers in First-Grade and Sixth-Grade General Music Classes" (unpublished doctoral dissertation, The American University, 1972), pp. 52–55.

> Sometimes the teacher entered the regular classroom of the students; and at other times, the students came to a music room or to a room designated for music on a particular day. This flexible scheduling procedure made it impossible to conceal the tape recorder from the students. Since this was true, and since students were accustomed to seeing and using audio hardware in their music classes, a decision was made to inform all of the students that their teacher and their class were being taped as a part of an educational project.
>
> If the schedule of a music teacher was changed without notice, if a music teacher was absent when the researcher came to tape, or if other circumstances prevented the recording or the coding of a tape, the researcher returned to record other sessions until a sufficient number of acceptable tapes had been collected.
>
> First-grade classes in several school systems were scheduled for a much shorter time than the sixth-grade classes. Therefore, the first-grade classes in these schools were taped during six class sessions in order to increase the total number of tallies at the first-grade level.
>
> The tape recording of the music classes with the teachers in the sample began in February and continued for a time period of eight weeks. Prior to the collection of the data, tape recordings of several music classes were obtained to provide the researcher sufficient time and materials with which to achieve observer accuracy and reliability. These tapes were not included in the data of the study.

The Flanders' System of Interaction Analysis[2] was used as the basis for the categorization and analysis of the material on the tapes. The Flanders' System contains ten categories, divided into three major divisions; these are concerned with teacher talk, student talk, and silence or confusion.

Thus, we have seen in detail how a tape-recording approach was devised and managed. What was structured for the tape-recording approach might have been used, with slight modification, with video tape and a one-way viewing panel.

The Checklist and the Sliding Scale Inventory

We shall discuss here only one additional type of observational technique, namely, the *checklist* or the *differential sliding scale checklist* or *inventory.* Even when looking at a situation, a researcher needs to look purposefully. He needs to have before him an agenda of objectives and behavioral goals toward which to direct his attention. For this reason it is well for the observer to have a list of items for which he specifically looks when observing. In its simplest form, this is a *checklist,* which is a simple means of recording: "it was observed," "it was not observed." Such a simple observational checklist is found in connection with your survey of research studies in the practicum section of this book.[3] A similar list might be compiled for any class of phenomena for which the observer wishes to record his observations in terms of frequency of occurrence.

Often, however, instead of a simple either-or choice, the researcher wishes to record varying degrees of intensity or range of frequency in the happening of certain events. These recordings may be made either by the subject himself in which he reacts to a given list of situations in terms of a graduated response or by another making the evaluation for him. This is a *differential sliding-scale checklist.* In lists of this type, a self-observational record is usually called an *inventory.* When, on the other hand, the recording is done by the researcher or an independent observer, it is frequently called a *rating scale.*

---

[2] Edmund J. Amidon and Ned A. Flanders, *The Role of the Teacher in the Classroom: A Manual for Understanding and Improving Teachers' Classroom Behavior* (Minneapolis, Minnesota: Paul S. Amidon and Associates, Incorporated, 1963).

[3] See p. 219.

The following is an example of an inventory. The author constructed it so that the reader could evaluate himself in terms of his development of certain specific habits that are critical to effective reading. The aspects of reading behavior are evaluated in terms of techniques of reading, visual factors, and emotional factors. The inventory is presented here for two reasons: (1) it is an example of the inventory approach; (2) it demonstrates the feasibility of qualifying data from an intensity-differentiated checklist. Note that the inventory explores exactly twenty-five items. By so doing, an evaluation system is based on 100 per cent full-scale performance so that by keeping a five-category weighting system, each category can then be easily expressed in terms of a percentage of strength with relation to the whole.

Reading Habit Inventory

For each of the following statements, check under Never, Rarely, Sometimes, Usually, or Always. Do not omit any of the items. Be truthful and utterly realistic. Represent your reading habits as they actually are.

	Never	*Rarely*	*Sometimes*	*Usually*	*Always*
1. When I pick up a page of print, I notice the paragraphs specifically.					
2. I read as I drive, with varying rates of speed, depending upon varying reading conditions.					
3. While reading, I find it easy to keep my mind on the material before me.					
4. After I have been reading for a while, I stop reading for a few moments and rest my eyes by looking at some distant object.					
5. I am alert to the role which punctuation plays in aiding me to get the meaning.					
6. When I pick up a piece of reading matter for the first time, I look for certain specific items which will aid me in reading the piece more efficiently.					
7. I read groups of words at one glance.					
8. I notice a distinctive style, or flavor, of the author.					
9. I enjoy reading.					
10. I can read for long periods of time without a feeling of eye fatigue or tiredness.					
11. After I read a paragraph, if required to do so, I could sum up the main idea clearly and briefly in my own words.					
12. I make a practice of skimming articles frequently.					
13. In reading a paragraph I usually try to see the organization of its thought content: I look for the main idea, and the details which support it.					
14. I do not lose my place, or skip words or lines, while reading.					
15. I am mildly conscious of grammatical structure while reading.					
16. I feel comfortable and perfectly at ease while reading.					
17. In reading larger units of writing (articles, chapters, etc.) I try to see the outline and total structure of the author's thought.					

	Never	*Rarely*	*Sometimes*	*Usually*	*Always*
18. I have little difficulty in remembering what I read.					
19. When I read, especially for any length of time, I make sure that the page before me is adequately illuminated.					
20. When I read, I am reading for some definite purpose, and I try to keep that purpose clearly in mind as I read.					
21. I read the preface of a book.					
22. In reading more difficult material, after reading a paragraph or a section, I pause to summarize in a momentary flashback the material I have just covered.					
23. While reading, I am aware of questions which arise in my own thinking about the material being read.					
24. While reading, I hold the page 15 to 20 inches from my eyes.					
25. I am aware that with practice a person can improve his reading skills, and I make a conscious effort generally toward that end.					

Count the checks in each column to obtain:	(A)					
Multiply by:	(B)	0	1	2	3	4
to obtain:	(C)		%	%	%	%

Now add the figures in row C for your final score:______%

Analysis of Your Reading Habits

Now, analyze your reading habits. What does the above Inventory mean? If you have marked it carefully and conscientiously, it should prove a helpful guide in aiding you to develop more effective reading habits than those you now have. This means that ultimately you will be a more efficient reader.

To analyze your reading habits, carefully check on the chart below, under the number of the item of the Inventory statement, the category (Always, Usually, Sometimes, Rarely, Never) as you marked it in the Inventory above. Out of the 25 items that you marked, certain of them attempted to appraise your habits associated with certain specific reading techniques. Other items attempted to evaluate the more important matters associated with ocular hygiene and visual efficiency. Finally, a few items sought to probe some of the emotional factors which may aid or hinder your total reading efficiency.

Note the line in the forms below marked, "Danger Line." As you transcribe your check marks from the Inventory above, you will find that you have checked either above or below this danger line. The check marks *below* the danger line indicate that in these matters you need to give attention to your reading habits and practices. Try to put into practice each time you read, the procedures suggested by the Inventory statements of those items which you have checked below the danger line.

1. What does the Inventory indicate as to my reading techniques? To find out, transcribe a check mark from the Inventory to the proper box in the chart following:

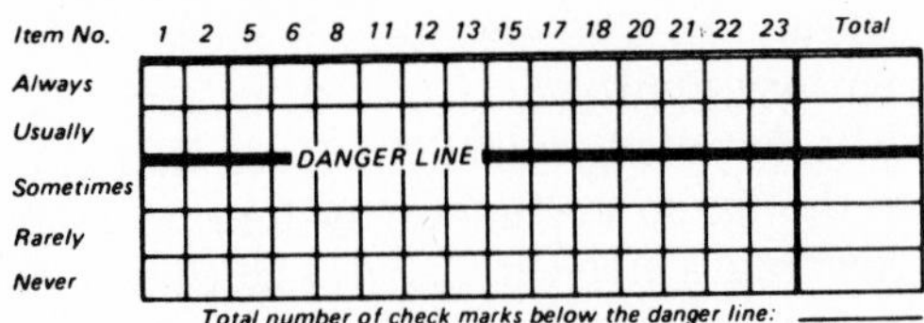

Item No.	1	2	5	6	8	11	12	13	15	17	18	20	21	22	23	Total
Always																
Usually																
DANGER LINE																
Sometimes																
Rarely																
Never																

Total number of check marks below the danger line: ______

2. What does the Inventory indicate about my visual factors in reading? Check the following chart to find out:

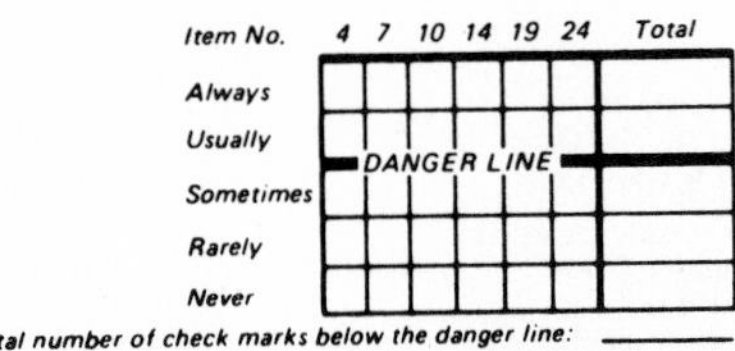

Item No.	4	7	10	14	19	24	Total
Always							
Usually							
DANGER LINE							
Sometimes							
Rarely							
Never							

Total number of check marks below the danger line: ______

3. What does the Inventory indicate about my emotional factors in reading? Check the following chart to find out:

Item No.	3	9	16	25	Total
Always					
Usually					
DANGER LINE					
Sometimes					
Rarely					
Never					

Total number of check marks below the danger line: ______

Total number of check marks in all three charts *above* the danger line: ______

Divide 25 into the *total* number of check marks you have *above* the danger line. This will give you your percentage score of *desirable* reading habits: _____%

[15] Paul D. Leedy, *Improve Your Reading: A Guide to Greater Speed, Understanding and Enjoyment* (New York: McGraw-Hill Book Co., 1956). A McGraw-Hill Paperback, pp. 40-44. Reprinted by permission of the publisher.

In contrast to the preceding which was an inventory, we present, as a means of contrast, a differential sliding-scale checklist. The purpose of the first instrument was to be self-administered. The checklist immediately following, although in subject matter very close to the first inventory, is obviously intended to be scored by an outside observer.

A Scale of Reading Attitude Based on Behavior[4]

Name of student ______________________ Grade ______ Date ______

School ______________________ Observer ______________________

Directions: Check the most appropriate of the five blanks by each item below. Only one blank by each item should be checked.

	Always Occurs	Often Occurs	Occasionally Occurs	Seldom Occurs	Never Occurs
1. The student exhibits a strong desire to come to the reading circle or to have reading instruction take place.	___	___	___	___	___
2. The student is enthusiastic and interested in participating once he comes to the reading circle or the reading class begins.	___	___	___	___	___
3. The student asks permission or raises his hand to read orally.	___	___	___	___	___
4. When called upon to read orally the student eagerly does so.	___	___	___	___	___
5. The student very willingly answers a question asked him in the reading class.	___	___	___	___	___

[4] C. Glennon Rowell, "An Attitude Scale for Reading," *The Reading Teacher,* XXV (February, 1972), 444.

	Always Occurs	Often Occurs	Occasionally Occurs	Seldom Occurs	Never Occurs
6. Contributions in the way of voluntary discussions are made by the student in the reading class.	___	___	___	___	___
7. The student expresses a desire to be read to by you or someone else, and he attentively listens while this is taking place.	___	___	___	___	___
8. The student makes an effort to read printed materials on bulletin boards, charts, or other displays having writing on them.	___	___	___	___	___
9. The student elects to read a book when the class has permission to choose a "free-time" activity.	___	___	___	___	___
10. The student expresses genuine interest in going to the school's library.	___	___	___	___	___
11. The student discusses with you (the teacher) or members of the class those items he has read from the newspaper, magazines, or similar materials.	___	___	___	___	___
12. The student voluntarily and enthusiastically discusses with others the book he has read or is reading.	___	___	___	___	___
13. The student listens attentively while other students share their reading experiences with the group.	___	___	___	___	___
14. The student expresses eagerness to read printed materials in the content areas.	___	___	___	___	___
15. The student goes beyond the textbook or usual reading assignment in searching for other materials to read.	___	___	___	___	___
16. The student contributes to group discussions that are based on reading assignments made in the content areas.	___	___	___	___	___

We have discussed at sufficient length the various observational tools and techniques generally employed in the descriptive survey study. In the last analysis, every researcher must devise the particular observational approach most appropriate for the demands of his own problem and the data with which he must deal.

SELECTING THE POPULATION

It is necessary for us now to turn to another aspect of the descriptive survey method, namely *the choosing of the population for the study*, which earlier we indicated to be the second of the four essential factors in the basic structure of the descriptive survey method.[5]

Here is a basic rule in the conduct of the descriptive survey: Nothing comes out at the end of a long and involved study which is any better than the care, the precision, the consideration, the thought that went into the basic planning of the research design and the

[5] See p. 80.

selection of the population for the purpose of the survey. *The results of a survey are no more trustworthy than the quality of the population or the representativeness of the sample.* Population parameters and sampling procedures are of paramount importance and become critical as factors in the success of the descriptive survey study.

Many students in phrasing their problems forget what we have just been saying. They announce, for example, that their goal is to "survey the legal philosophies of the attorneys of the United States and to analyze the relationship of these several philosophical positions with respect to the recent decisions of the Supreme Court of the United States."

A student who words a problem in this way has simply not thought through the meaning of his own words. "The attorneys of the United States"! The American Bar Association consists of over 147,000 attorneys, distributed over 3,536,855 square miles in the fifty states. But these are merely the first hurdles. As we look at the problem more closely, we begin to discern other, more serious difficulties. What are "philosophical attitudes"? How does one isolate these attitudes in order to study them? How do you get hold of them? How can you show a "relationship of philosophical positions" with "recent decisions of the Supreme Court"? What will this relationship look like? Will it be a statistical determination? If so, how will you quantify "philosophical positions" and "decisions"? If not, what will it be?

Earlier in these pages we discussed the necessity for considering carefully the size, the selection, and the parameters of the survey population.[6] The failure of the researcher to recognize population parameters and their demands upon the research procedures and design as well as upon his research resources is generally indicative of inexperience in the area of practical research planning and design.

Particularly with survey studies, the researcher needs to calculate all costs, of both time and money, realistically. The age of automation and computerization has given a roseate, but false sense of ease to the solution of many of the knotty problems associated with survey research. Inexperienced researchers frequently think that the computer is the magic and perfect answer to all their research difficulties. If anything poses a problem, all you need to do is to "feed the data to the computer" and out will come the resolution of all your research worries and the interpretation of the data as well. Unfortunately such is not the case. What amateur researchers sometimes fail to realize is that computers merely rearrange the data and perform mathematical and statistical operations strictly in accord with their programmed instructions. They solve no design difficulties, nor do they interpret any data. In addition, their use can be both time-consuming and expensive. There is a basic rule of the computer, known as the GIGO Law: Garbage in; garbage out! Computers are not thinking machines. Their only function is to rearrange existing data into new and potentially meaningful patterns, much as a kaleidoscope rearranges the existing bits of colored glass that were originally sealed into it and presents them to the eye of the observer in varied and fascinating designs.

But to get back to our more than 147,000 attorneys and their thoughts, it is not necessary, of course, to poll each and every one of them to get some indication of their composite thought. It may be well for us to refer to p. 7 and to review the concept of *universe*. There we defined it as a body of fact which revolves about one central question or inquiry. Here we shall define it in essentially the same manner but with particular reference to the data: *a universe of data consists of the totality of that data within certain specified parameters.* Here the "specified parameters" were that those individuals which were to be studied were "the attorneys of the United States." But a universe of data is usually too large to be studied *in toto*. Where such is the case, we have devised a method that is both logically and statistically defensible, namely, the *method of sampling.*

[6] See pp. 52–53.

We should point out that the difficulty basically arises out of the statement of the problem. If the researcher has said what he means, then he has indicated that he is proposing to survey "the attorneys"—all of them! If, on the other hand, he intends to survey only certain of the attorneys, then the statement of his problem should have accurately represented that fact by appropriate wording within the problem itself by the insertion of such qualifying—and accurately descriptive—terms as *selected*, *representative*, *typical*, *certain*, and so on. Careful researchers also say precisely what they mean. Note the difference in the meaning of the intent of the researcher between wording which says, "The purpose of this research is to survey the representative legal philosophies of a random sample of attorneys . . ." and wording such as, "The purpose of this research is to survey the legal philosophies of the attorneys of the United States . . ."

How, then, is sampling done? The answer is, "In a number of ways." Perhaps at the outset the method of sampling is not nearly as important as the purpose of sampling and a careful consideration of the parameters of the population.

Look through the wrong end of a telescope. You will see the broad world in miniature. This is precisely what the sampling procedure chosen for any particular project should seek to achieve. *The sample should be so carefully chosen that through it the researcher is able to see all the characteristics of the total population in the same relationship that he would see them were he actually to inspect the totality of the universe of data.* That may be a consummation devoutly to be wished, but samples are microcosms. In optics, unless lenses are precision made and accurately ground, one is likely to get distortion through his spyglass. Similarly, unless the sampling is carefully planned and statistically tested, distortion is likely to be present in the end result of the survey. Such distortion we call *bias;* we shall discuss this factor further in the next section. For the moment, however, we shall concern ourselves with the types, methods, and procedures of sampling.

Types, Methods, and Procedures of Sampling

One basic rule holds whenever a researcher is considering methodology in relation to data—it matters not whether this methodology concerns sampling, a statistical procedure, or any other type of operation, and that one basic rule is: *Look carefully at the nature, the characteristics, the quality of the data.* After the researcher sees this clearly, he can then more intelligently select the proper methodology for the treatment of those data.

The composition of the sample is derived by selecting the sample units from those of a much larger population. In survey studies the *manner* in which the sample units are selected is very important. Generally, the components of the sample are chosen from the population universe by a process known as *randomization.* Such a sample is a *random sample.* The two elements that are more important than any others in survey research are randomization and bias. We shall discuss randomization here. Bias we shall treat in a later section of this chapter.

Randomization means *selecting a part of the whole population in such a way that the characteristics of each of the units of the sample approximates the broad characteristics inherent in the total population.* Let's explain that. I have a beaker which contains 100 cc. of water. I have in another container a concentrated solution of 10 cc. of acid. I combine the water and the acid in proportions of 10 to 1. After thoroughly mixing the water and the acid, I should be able to extract 1 cc. from *any* part of the solution and find in that 1-cc. sample a mixture of water and acid in precisely a 10:1 proportion. Just so, if we have a conglomerate population with variables such as differences of race, wealth, education, and other factors, and *if I have a perfectly selected random sample* (a situation which is usually more theoretical than practical), I will find in the sample those same characteristics of race, wealth, education, and so forth that exist in the larger population universe.

A sample is no more representative of the total population, therefore, than the validity of the method of randomization employed in selecting it. There are, of course, many methods of random selection. We shall look at merely a few of the more common ones.

The Roulette Wheel Method. If the population is small—fifty to seventy-five individuals—each individual may be assigned a number in some orderly sequence: alphabetically by surname, by birth date (youngest to oldest or the reverse), by the respective weight of each individual, or by any other systematic arrangement. Corresponding numbers are on a roulette wheel. A spin of the wheel and its fortuitous stopping at a particular number selects the individual assigned to that number as a unit of the sample. The process of spinning the wheel and selecting the sample unit goes on until all the individuals needed to compose the sample have been chosen.

The Lottery Method. In the lottery method the population again is arranged sequentially and assigned a numerical identification. Corresponding numbers are marked on separate tabs and put into a revolving drum or closed container. The numbers are tossed so that they are thoroughly intermixed. Then one tab bearing a number is selected from the total number of tabs in the container without the selector seeing the pool. The number is recorded and *the tab is then tossed back into the tab pool.* This is an important feature of the lottery method. It ensures that every individual has the same chance of being chosen as every other individual. If, for example, we are selecting fifty units out of a population of 100 and we do not cast each tab back after it has been selected, we will have an ever-diminishing population from which to make the choices. And whereas the first choice would have one in 100 chances of being selected, the last unit chosen would have one in fifty chances of being selected or, in other words, his chances of being selected would be twice as great as those of the first individual.

In the event of the same number being drawn twice, the second drawing is ignored; the number is returned to the pool; the entire mass of numbers is tumbled again, and another drawing is made. Drawing and tumbling go on until fifty tabs have been selected purely by chance.

The Table of Random Numbers Method. The table of random numbers method is perhaps the most frequently used method for the random selection of a sample. Following is a part of a table of random numbers. We may employ this table in any manner in which we choose to use it. Generally the researcher enters the table according to some predetermined method.

Entrance into the table may, in fact, be accomplished in many ways. One fundamental principle must be kept in mind, however: *the purpose of randomness is to permit blind chance to determine the outcomes of the selection process to as great a degree as possible.* Hence, in determining a starting point for the selection of random numbers, chance must be given free reign.

Consider the following tables of random numbers. Considering the second table as a continuation of the first table, and counting from left to right, there are five blocks of random numbers in the horizontal arrangement. Vertically there are ten blocks from top to bottom of the table.

Table of Random Numbers (I)

03 47 43 73 86	36 96 47 36 61	46 98 63 71 62	33 26 16 80 45	60 11 14 10 95
97 74 24 67 62	42 81 14 57 20	42 53 32 37 32	27 07 36 07 51	24 51 79 89 73
16 76 62 27 66	56 50 26 71 07	32 90 79 78 53	13 55 38 58 59	88 97 54 14 10
12 56 85 99 26	96 96 68 27 31	05 03 72 93 15	57 12 10 14 21	88 26 49 81 76
55 59 56 35 64	38 54 82 46 22	31 62 43 09 90	06 18 44 32 53	23 83 01 30 30
16 22 77 94 39	49 54 43 54 82	17 37 93 23 78	87 35 20 96 43	84 26 34 91 64
84 42 17 53 31	57 24 55 06 88	77 04 74 47 67	21 76 33 50 25	83 92 12 06 76
63 01 63 78 59	16 95 55 67 19	98 10 50 71 75	12 86 73 58 07	44 39 52 38 79
33 21 12 34 29	78 64 56 07 82	52 42 07 44 38	15 51 00 13 42	99 66 02 79 54
57 60 86 32 44	09 47 27 96 54	49 17 46 09 62	90 52 84 77 27	08 02 73 43 28
18 18 07 92 46	44 17 16 58 09	79 83 86 19 62	06 76 50 03 10	55 23 64 05 05
26 62 38 97 75	84 16 07 44 99	83 11 46 32 24	20 14 85 88 45	10 93 72 88 71
23 42 40 64 74	82 97 77 77 81	07 45 32 14 08	32 98 94 07 72	93 85 79 10 75
62 36 28 19 95	50 92 26 11 97	00 56 76 31 38	80 22 02 53 53	86 60 42 04 53
37 85 94 35 12	83 39 50 08 30	42 34 07 96 88	54 42 06 87 98	35 85 29 48 39
70 29 17 12 13	40 33 20 38 26	13 89 51 03 74	17 76 37 13 04	07 74 21 19 30
56 62 18 37 35	96 83 50 87 75	97 12 25 93 47	70 33 24 03 54	97 77 46 44 80
99 49 57 22 77	88 42 95 45 72	16 64 36 16 00	04 43 18 66 79	94 77 24 21 90
16 08 15 04 72	33 27 14 34 09	45 59 34 68 49	12 72 07 34 45	99 27 72 95 14
31 16 93 32 43	50 27 89 87 19	20 15 37 00 49	52 85 66 60 44	38 68 88 11 80
68 34 30 13 70	55 74 30 77 40	44 22 78 84 26	04 33 46 09 52	68 07 97 06 57
74 57 25 65 76	59 29 97 68 60	71 91 38 67 54	13 58 18 24 76	15 54 55 95 52
27 42 37 86 53	48 55 90 65 72	96 57 69 36 10	96 46 92 42 45	97 60 49 04 91
00 39 68 29 61	66 37 32 20 30	77 84 57 03 29	10 45 66 04 26	11 04 96 67 24
29 94 98 94 24	68 49 69 10 82	53 75 91 93 30	34 25 20 57 27	40 48 73 51 92
16 90 82 66 59	83 62 64 11 12	67 19 00 71 74	60 47 21 29 68	02 02 37 03 31
11 27 94 75 06	06 09 19 74 66	02 94 37 34 02	76 70 90 30 86	38 45 94 30 38
35 24 10 16 20	33 32 51 26 38	79 78 45 04 91	16 92 53 56 16	02 75 50 95 98
38 23 16 86 38	42 38 97 01 50	87 75 66 81 41	40 01 74 91 62	48 51 84 08 32
31 96 25 91 47	96 44 33 49 13	34 86 82 53 91	00 52 43 48 85	27 55 26 89 62
66 67 40 67 14	64 05 71 95 86	11 05 65 09 68	76 83 20 37 90	57 16 00 11 66
14 90 84 45 11	75 73 88 05 90	52 27 41 14 86	22 98 12 22 08	07 52 74 95 80
68 05 51 18 00	33 96 02 75 19	07 60 62 93 55	59 33 82 43 90	49 37 38 44 59
20 46 78 73 90	97 51 40 14 02	04 02 33 31 08	39 54 16 49 36	47 95 93 13 30
64 19 58 97 79	15 06 15 93 20	01 90 10 75 06	40 78 78 89 62	02 67 74 17 33
05 26 93 70 60	22 35 85 15 13	92 03 51 59 77	59 56 78 06 83	52 91 05 70 74
07 97 10 88 23	09 98 42 99 64	61 71 62 99 15	06 51 29 16 93	58 05 77 09 51
68 71 86 85 85	54 87 66 47 54	73 32 08 11 12	44 95 92 63 16	29 56 24 29 48
26 99 61 65 53	58 37 78 80 70	42 10 50 67 42	32 17 55 85 74	94 44 67 16 94
14 65 52 68 75	87 59 36 22 41	26 78 63 06 55	13 08 27 01 50	15 29 39 39 43
17 53 77 58 71	71 41 61 50 72	12 41 94 96 26	44 95 27 36 99	02 96 74 30 83
90 26 59 21 19	23 52 23 33 12	96 93 02 18 39	07 02 18 36 07	25 99 32 70 23
41 23 52 55 99	31 04 49 69 96	10 47 48 45 88	13 41 43 89 20	97 17 14 49 17
60 20 50 81 69	31 99 73 68 68	35 81 33 03 76	24 30 12 48 60	18 99 10 72 34
91 25 38 05 90	94 58 28 41 36	45 37 59 03 09	90 35 57 29 12	82 62 54 65 60
34 50 57 74 37	98 80 33 00 91	09 77 93 19 82	74 94 80 04 04	45 07 31 66 49
85 22 04 39 43	73 81 53 94 79	33 62 46 86 28	08 31 54 46 31	53 94 13 38 47
09 79 13 77 48	73 82 97 22 21	05 03 27 24 83	72 89 44 05 60	35 80 39 94 88
88 75 80 18 14	22 95 75 42 49	39 32 82 22 49	02 48 07 70 37	16 04 61 67 87
90 96 23 70 00	39 00 03 06 90	55 85 78 38 36	94 37 30 69 32	90 89 00 76 33

From Ronald A. Fisher and Frank Yates, *Statistical Tables for Biological, Agricultural, and Medical Research* (New York: Hafner, 1963).

Table of Random Numbers (II)

53 74 23 99 67	61 32 28 69 84	94 62 67 86 24	98 33 41 19 95	47 53 53 38 09
63 38 06 86 54	99 00 65 26 94	09 82 90 23 07	79 62 67 80 60	75 91 12 81 19
35 30 58 21 46	06 72 17 10 94	25 21 31 75 96	49 28 24 00 49	55 65 79 78 07
63 43 36 82 69	65 51 18 37 88	61 38 44 12 45	32 92 85 88 65	54 34 81 85 35
98 25 37 55 26	01 91 82 81 46	74 71 12 94 97	24 02 71 37 07	03 92 18 66 75
02 63 21 17 69	71 50 80 89 56	38 15 70 11 48	43 40 45 86 98	00 83 26 91 03
64 55 22 21 82	48 22 28 06 00	61 54 13 43 91	82 78 12 23 29	06 66 24 12 27
85 07 26 13 89	01 10 07 82 04	59 63 69 36 03	69 11 15 83 80	13 29 54 19 28
58 54 16 24 15	51 54 44 82 00	62 61 65 04 69	38 18 65 18 97	85 72 13 49 21
34 85 27 84 87	61 48 64 56 26	90 18 48 13 26	37 70 15 42 57	65 65 80 39 07
03 92 18 27 46	57 99 16 96 56	30 33 72 85 22	84 64 38 56 98	99 01 30 98 64
62 95 30 27 59	37 75 41 66 48	86 97 80 61 45	23 53 04 01 63	45 76 08 64 27
08 45 93 15 22	60 21 75 46 91	98 77 27 85 42	28 88 61 08 84	69 62 03 42 73
07 08 55 18 40	45 44 75 13 90	24 94 96 61 02	57 55 66 83 15	73 42 37 11 61
01 85 89 95 66	51 10 19 34 88	15 84 97 19 75	12 76 39 43 78	64 63 91 08 25
72 84 71 14 35	19 11 58 49 26	50 11 17 17 76	86 31 57 20 18	95 60 78 46 75
88 78 28 16 84	13 52 53 94 53	75 45 69 30 96	73 89 65 70 31	99 17 43 48 76
45 17 75 65 57	28 40 19 72 12	25 12 74 75 67	60 40 60 81 19	24 62 01 61 16
96 76 28 12 54	22 01 11 94 25	71 96 16 16 88	68 64 36 74 45	19 59 50 88 92
43 31 67 72 30	24 02 94 08 63	38 32 36 66 02	69 36 38 25 39	48 03 45 15 22
50 44 66 44 21	66 06 58 05 62	68 15 54 35 02	42 35 48 96 32	14 52 41 52 48
22 66 22 15 86	26 63 75 41 99	58 42 36 72 24	58 37 52 18 51	03 37 18 39 11
96 24 40 14 51	23 22 30 88 57	95 67 47 29 83	94 69 40 06 07	18 16 36 78 86
31 73 91 61 19	60 20 72 93 48	98 57 07 23 69	65 95 39 69 58	56 80 30 19 44
78 60 73 99 84	43 89 94 36 45	56 69 47 07 41	90 22 91 07 12	78 35 34 08 72
84 37 90 61 56	70 10 23 98 05	85 11 34 76 60	76 48 45 34 60	01 64 18 39 96
36 67 10 08 23	98 93 35 08 86	99 29 76 29 81	33 34 91 58 93	63 14 52 32 52
07 28 59 07 48	89 64 58 89 75	83 85 62 27 89	30 14 78 56 27	86 63 59 80 02
10 15 83 87 60	79 24 31 66 56	21 48 24 06 93	91 98 94 05 49	01 47 59 38 00
55 19 68 97 65	03 73 52 16 56	00 53 55 90 27	33 42 29 38 87	22 13 88 83 34
53 81 29 13 39	35 01 20 71 34	62 33 74 82 14	53 73 19 09 03	56 54 29 56 93
51 86 32 68 92	33 98 74 66 99	40 14 71 94 58	45 94 19 38 81	14 44 99 81 07
35 91 70 29 13	80 03 54 07 27	96 94 78 32 66	50 95 52 74 33	13 80 55 62 54
37 71 67 95 13	20 02 44 95 94	64 85 04 05 72	01 32 90 76 14	53 89 74 60 41
93 66 13 83 27	92 79 64 64 72	28 54 96 53 84	48 14 52 98 94	56 07 93 89 30
02 96 08 45 65	13 05 00 41 84	93 07 54 72 59	21 45 57 09 77	19 48 56 27 44
49 83 43 48 35	82 88 33 69 96	72 36 04 19 96	47 45 15 18 60	82 11 08 95 97
84 60 71 62 46	40 80 81 30 37	34 39 23 05 38	25 15 35 71 30	88 12 57 21 77
18 17 30 88 71	44 91 14 88 47	89 23 30 63 15	56 34 20 47 89	99 82 93 24 98
79 69 10 61 78	71 32 76 95 62	87 00 22 58 62	92 54 01 75 25	43 11 71 99 31
75 93 36 57 83	56 20 14 82 11	74 21 97 90 65	96 42 68 63 86	74 54 13 26 94
38 30 92 29 03	06 28 81 39 38	62 25 06 84 63	61 29 08 93 67	04 32 92 08 09
51 29 50 10 34	31 57 75 95 80	51 97 02 74 77	76 15 48 49 44	18 55 63 77 09
21 31 38 86 24	37 79 38 86 24	37 79 81 53 74	73 24 16 10 33	70 47 14 54 36
29 01 23 87 88	58 02 39 37 67	42 10 14 20 92	16 55 23 42 45	54 96 09 11 06

Directions: Having enumerated the population (in whatever order they happen to be listed) (say, N = 582), select at random any three columns (so as to allow for all cases); say, Columns 6, 7, and 8. Reading from page 1, individuals No. 373, 467, 227, 599 . . . would be part of the sample; 635 would be ignored since no one was assigned that number. The process would be continued—going on to the next page or any other 3-digit block—until the required sample size had been obtained.

In a reduction of the first table, for illustrative purposes, we have numbered the horizontal blocks as 1, 2, 3, 4, 5; and those blocks from top downward from 1 to 0. The table, therefore looks like this:

Table of Random Numbers (I)

	(1)	(2)	(3)	(4)	(5)
	03 47 43 73 86	36 96 47 36 61	46 98 63 71 62	33 26 16 80 45	60 11 14 10 95
	97 74 24 67 62	42 81 14 57 20	42 53 32 37 32	27 07 36 07 51	24 51 79 89 73
(1)	16 76 62 27 66	56 50 26 71 07	32 90 79 78 53	13 55 38 58 59	88 97 54 14 10
	12 56 85 99 26	96 96 68 27 31	05 03 72 93 15	57 12 10 14 21	88 26 49 81 76
	55 59 56 35 64	38 54 82 46 22	31 62 43 09 90	06 18 44 32 53	23 83 01 30 30
	16 22 77 94 39	49 54 43 54 82	17 37 93 23 78	87 35 20 96 43	84 26 34 91 64
	84 42 17 53 31	57 24 55 06 88	77 04 74 47 67	21 76 33 50 25	83 92 12 06 76
(2)	63 01 63 78 59	16 95 55 67 19	98 10 50 71 75	12 86 73 58 07	44 39 52 38 79
	33 21 12 34 29	78 64 56 07 82	52 42 07 44 38	15 51 00 13 42	99 66 02 79 54
	57 60 86 32 44	09 47 27 96 54	49 17 46 09 62	90 52 84 77 27	08 02 73 43 28
	18 18 07 92 46	44 17 16 58 09	79 83 86 19 62	06 76 50 03 10	55 23 64 05 05
	26 62 38 97 75	84 16 07 44 99	83 11 46 32 24	20 14 85 88 45	10 93 72 88 71
(3)	23 42 40 64 74	82 97 77 77 81	07 45 32 14 08	32 98 94 07 72	93 85 79 10 75
	62 36 28 19 95	50 92 26 11 97	00 56 76 31 38	80 22 02 53 53	86 60 42 04 53
	37 85 94 35 12	83 39 50 08 30	42 34 07 96 88	54 42 06 87 98	35 85 29 48 39
	70 29 17 12 13	40 33 20 38 26	13 89 51 03 74	17 76 37 13 04	07 74 21 19 30
	56 62 18 37 35	96 83 50 87 75	97 12 25 93 47	70 33 24 03 54	97 77 46 44 80
(4)	99 49 57 22 77	88 42 95 45 72	16 64 36 16 00	04 43 18 66 79	94 77 24 21 90
	16 08 15 04 72	33 27 14 34 09	45 59 34 68 49	12 72 07 34 45	99 27 72 95 14
	31 16 93 32 43	50 27 89 87 19	20 15 37 00 49	52 85 66 60 44	38 68 88 11 80
	68 34 30 13 70	55 74 30 77 40	44 22 78 84 26	04 33 46 09 52	68 07 97 06 57
	74 57 25 65 76	59 29 97 68 60	71 91 38 67 54	13 58 18 24 76	15 54 55 95 52
(5)	27 42 37 86 53	48 55 90 65 72	96 57 69 36 10	96 46 92 42 45	97 60 49 04 91
	00 39 68 29 61	66 37 32 20 30	77 84 57 03 29	10 45 66 04 26	11 04 96 67 24
	29 94 98 94 24	68 49 69 10 82	53 75 91 93 30	34 25 20 57 27	40 48 73 51 92
	16 90 82 66 59	83 62 64 11 12	67 19 00 71 74	60 47 21 29 68	02 02 37 03 31
	11 27 94 75 06	06 09 19 74 66	02 94 37 34 02	76 70 90 30 86	38 45 94 30 38
(6)	35 24 10 16 20	33 32 51 26 38	79 78 45 04 91	16 92 53 56 16	02 75 50 95 98
	38 23 16 86 38	42 38 97 01 50	87 75 66 81 41	40 01 74 91 62	48 51 84 08 32
	31 96 25 91 47	96 44 33 49 13	34 86 82 53 91	00 52 43 48 85	27 55 26 89 62
	66 67 40 67 14	64 05 71 95 86	11 05 65 09 68	76 83 20 37 90	57 16 00 11 66
	14 90 84 45 11	75 73 88 05 90	52 27 41 14 86	22 98 12 22 08	07 52 74 95 80
(7)	68 05 51 18 00	33 96 02 75 19	07 60 62 93 55	59 33 82 43 90	49 37 38 44 59
	20 46 78 73 90	97 51 40 14 02	04 02 33 31 08	39 54 16 49 36	47 95 93 13 30
	64 19 58 97 79	15 06 15 93 20	01 90 10 75 06	40 78 78 89 62	02 67 74 17 33
	05 26 93 70 60	22 35 85 15 13	92 03 51 59 77	59 56 78 06 83	52 91 05 70 74
	07 97 10 88 23	09 98 42 99 64	61 71 62 99 15	06 51 29 16 93	58 05 77 09 51
(8)	68 71 86 85 85	54 87 66 47 54	73 32 08 11 12	44 95 92 63 16	29 56 24 29 48
	26 99 61 65 53	58 37 78 80 70	42 10 50 67 42	32 17 55 85 74	94 44 67 16 94
	14 65 52 68 75	87 59 36 22 41	26 78 63 06 55	13 08 27 01 50	15 29 39 39 43
	17 53 77 58 71	71 41 61 50 72	12 41 94 96 26	44 95 27 36 99	02 96 74 30 83
	90 26 59 21 19	23 52 23 33 12	96 93 02 18 39	07 02 18 36 07	25 99 32 70 23
(9)	41 23 52 55 99	31 04 49 69 96	10 47 48 45 88	13 41 43 89 20	97 17 14 49 17
	60 20 50 81 69	31 99 73 68 68	35 81 33 03 76	24 30 12 48 60	18 99 10 72 34
	91 25 38 05 90	94 58 28 41 36	45 37 59 03 09	90 35 57 29 12	82 62 54 65 60
	34 50 57 74 37	98 80 33 00 91	09 77 93 19 82	74 94 80 04 04	45 07 31 66 49
	85 22 04 39 43	73 81 53 94 79	33 62 46 86 28	08 31 54 46 31	53 94 13 38 47
(0.)	09 79 13 77 48	73 82 97 22 21	05 03 27 24 83	72 89 44 05 60	35 80 39 94 88
	88 75 80 18 14	22 95 75 42 49	39 32 82 22 49	02 48 07 70 37	16 04 61 67 87
	90 96 23 70 00	39 00 03 06 90	55 85 78 38 36	94 37 30 69 32	90 89 00 76 33

From Ronald A. Fisher and Frank Yates, *Statistical Tables for Biological, Agricultural, and Medical Research* (New York: Hafner, 1963).

The horizontal and vertical numbering of the columns gives us locational designations for determining intersecting axes and, thus, a starting point within the table. To determine the point of axial intersection and to get a starting point, you might engage in any one of several fortuitous activities. The purpose of any of these is to select two digits purely by chance. Here are some suggestions:

• *Use a telephone directory.* Open a telephone directory at random. Take the last two digits of the first number in the first column on either the left-hand or right-hand page. Let the first digit of those chosen be the designating digit of the horizontal column of the table of random numbers; the second digit will, then, indicate the number of the vertical column. The intersection of the two columns will indicate the block where you will begin within the table to select your random numbers, either in an upward or in a downward succession along the vertical column.

• *Note a vehicle registration tag.* Step outside and observe the first vehicle which passes. Note the last (or first) two digits of the registration tag. The first digit will give you the horizontal column designation; the second digit, the vertical column. Where they intersect is your place of beginning within the table.

• *Look at a dollar bill.* Note the first two digits of the serial number in the lower left- or upper right-hand corner to determine the axial locations.

• *Check the stock quotations.* Take any newspaper and turn to the stock quotation page. Take the first letter of your surname. The first stock which begins with that letter will be your predetermined stock; note its quotation for high and low. Disregard the fractional quotations. Take the first two digits in either the high or low quotation column; or if only one digit appears in each column, take the two digits together.

Having arrived at the digital block location, the next step is to determine the size of the proposed sample. If it is to be less than 100 individuals, we shall select only two-digit numbers; if it is to be less than 1,000, we shall need three digits to accommodate the sample size.

Let us go back to the total population for a moment and consider the total group from which the sample is to be drawn. It will be necessary to designate these individuals in some specific manner. It is, therefore, advantageous to arrange the individuals within the population in some systematic order (alphabetically, for example, by surname) and assign to each a serial number for identification purposes.

Now we are ready for the random selection. We shall start with the upper left-hand digits in the designated block and work first downward in the column; if there are not enough digits for the total sample demand in that direction, we will return to the starting digits and proceed upward. Having exhausted all fifty digits in any one column, move to the adjoining columns and proceed as before until the sample requirement is filled. As each digit designation comes up, select the individual in the population who has been assigned that random number. Keep so selecting until the entire sample total is reached.

The following illustration recapitulates what we have been describing. We have pulled a dollar bill from our wallet and note that the first two digits are 4 and 5. These we shall use in locating the beginning block from which we will select the first random number for the sample. For purposes of illustration, we shall assume that the total population consists of ninety individuals from which we shall select a sample group of forty. We will need random numbers of two digits each.

Here again is a reduction of the first table of random numbers, from which we have extracted the beginning block of digits which is at the intersection of the fourth horizontal block column and the fifth vertical block column:

Beginning now in the upper left-hand corner of the designated block, and remembering that there are only ninety individuals in the total population, we see that by going down the two leftmost columns of digits in the block we will choose from the total population individual number 4, and individual number 13. The next two digits—96—do not apply, because there are only ninety individuals in the population, and so we will ignore this number. Our next choices will be 10, 34, 60, 76, 16, 40, and again we will ignore the 00 as well as the next number, 76 (the first set of digits in the third block), because we already have selected that number.

Table of Random Numbers (I)

	1	2	3	4	5
	03 47 43 73 86	36 96 47 36 61	46 98 63 71 62	33 26 16 80 45	60 11 14 10 95
	97 74 24 67 62	42 81 14 57 20	42 53 32 37 32	27 07 36 07 51	24 51 79 89 73
1	16 76 62 27 66	56 50 26 71 07	32 90 79 78 53	13 55 38 58 59	88 97 54 14 10
	12 56 85 99 26	96 96 68 27 31	05 03 72 93 15	57 12 10 14 21	88 26 49 81 76
	55 59 56 35 64	38 54 82 46 22	31 62 43 09 90	06 18 44 32 53	23 83 01 30 30
	16 22 77 94 39	49 54 43 54 82	17 37 93 23 78	87 35 20 96 43	84 26 34 91 64
	84 42 17 53 31	57 24 55 06 88	77 04 74 47 67	21 76 33 50 25	83 92 12 06 76
2	63 01 63 78 59	16 95 55 67 19	98 10 50 71 75	12 86 73 58 07	44 39 52 38 79
	33 21 12 34 29	78 64 56 07 82	52 42 07 44 38	15 51 00 13 42	99 66 02 79 54
	57 60 86 32 44	09 47 27 96 54	49 17 46 09 62	90 52 84 77 27	08 02 73 43 28
	18 18 07 92 46	44 17 16 58 09	79 83 86 19 62	06 76 50 03 10	55 23 64 05 05
	26 62 38 97 75	84 16 07 44 99	83 11 46 32 24	20 14 85 88 45	10 93 72 88 71
3	23 42 40 64 74	82 97 77 77 81	07 45 32 14 08	32 98 94 07 72	93 85 79 10 75
	62 36 28 19 95	50 92 26 11 97	00 56 76 31 38	80 22 02 53 53	86 60 42 04 53
	37 85 94 35 12	83 39 50 08 30	42 34 07 96 88	54 42 06 87 98	35 85 29 48 39
	70 29 17 12 13	40 33 20 38 26	13 89 51 03 74	17 76 37 13 04	07 74 21 19 30
	56 62 18 37 35	96 83 50 87 75	97 12 25 93 47	70 33 24 03 54	97 77 46 44 80
4	99 49 57 22 77	88 42 95 45 72	16 64 36 16 00	04 43 18 66 79	94 77 24 21 90
	16 08 15 04 72	33 27 14 34 09	45 59 34 68 49	12 72 07 34 45	99 27 72 95 14
	31 16 93 32 43	50 27 89 87 19	20 15 37 00 49	52 85 66 60 44	38 68 88 11 80
	68 34 30 13 70	55 74 30 77 40	44 22 78 84 26	04 33 46 09 52	68 07 97 06 57
	74 57 25 65 76	59 29 97 68 60	71 91 38 67 54	13 58 18 24 76	15 54 55 95 52
5	27 42 37 86 53	48 55 90 65 72	96 57 69 36 10	96 46 92 42 45	97 60 49 04 91
	00 39 68 29 61	66 37 32 20 30	77 84 57 03 29	10 45 66 04 26	11 04 96 67 24
	29 94 98 94 24	68 49 69 10 82	53 75 91 93 30	34 25 20 57 27	40 48 73 51 92
	16 90 82 66 59	83 62 64 11 12	67 19 00 71 74	60 47 21 29 68	02 02 37 03 31
	11 27 94 75 06	06 09 19 74 66	02 94 37 34 02	76 70 90 30 86	38 45 94 30 38
6	35 24 10 16 20	33 32 51 26 38	79 78 45 04 91	16 92 53 56 16	02 75 50 95 98
	38 23 16 86 38	42 38 97 01 50	87 75 66 81 41	40 01 74 91 62	48 51 84 08 32
	31 96 25 91 47	96 44 33 49 13	34 86 82 53 91	00 52 43 48 85	27 55 26 89 62
	66 67 40 67 14	64 05 71 95 86	11 05 65 09 68	76 83 20 37 90	57 16 00 11 66
	14 90 84 45 11	75 73 88 05 90	52 27 41 14 86	22 98 12 22 08	07 52 74 95 80
7	68 05 51 18 00	33 96 02 75 19	07 60 62 93 55	59 33 82 43 90	49 37 38 44 59
	20 46 78 73 90	97 51 40 14 02	04 02 33 31 08	39 54 16 49 36	47 95 93 13 30
	64 19 58 97 79	15 06 15 93 20	01 90 10 75 06	40 78 78 89 62	02 67 74 17 33
	05 26 93 70 60	22 35 85 15 13	92 03 51 59 77	59 56 78 06 83	52 91 05 70 74
	07 97 10 88 23	09 98 42 99 64	61 71 62 99 15	06 51 29 16 93	58 05 77 09 51
8	68 71 86 85 85	54 87 66 47 54	73 32 08 11 12	44 95 92 63 16	29 56 24 29 48
	26 99 61 65 53	58 37 78 80 70	42 10 50 67 42	32 17 55 85 74	94 44 67 16 94
	14 65 52 68 75	87 59 36 22 41	26 78 63 06 55	13 08 27 01 50	15 29 39 39 43
	17 53 77 58 71	71 41 61 50 72	12 41 94 96 26	44 95 27 36 99	02 96 74 30 83
	90 26 59 21 19	23 52 23 33 12	96 93 02 18 39	07 02 18 36 07	25 99 32 70 23
9	41 23 52 55 99	31 04 49 69 96	10 47 48 45 88	13 41 43 89 20	97 17 14 49 17
	60 20 50 81 69	31 99 73 68 68	35 81 33 03 76	24 30 12 48 60	18 99 10 72 34
	91 25 38 05 90	94 58 28 41 36	45 37 59 03 09	90 35 57 29 12	82 62 54 65 60
	34 50 57 74 37	98 80 33 00 91	09 77 93 19 82	74 94 80 04 04	45 07 31 66 49
	85 22 04 39 43	73 81 53 94 79	33 62 46 86 28	08 31 54 46 31	53 94 13 38 47
0	09 79 13 77 48	73 82 97 22 21	05 03 27 24 83	72 89 44 05 60	35 80 39 94 88
	88 75 80 18 14	22 95 75 42 49	39 32 82 22 49	02 48 07 70 37	16 04 61 67 87
	90 96 23 70 00	39 00 03 06 90	55 85 78 38 36	94 37 30 69 32	90 89 00 76 33

04 33 46 09 52
13 58 18 24 76
96 46 92 42 45
10 45 65 04 26
34 25 20 57 27

60 47 21 29 68
76 70 90 30 86
16 92 53 56 16
40 01 74 91 62
00 52 43 48 85

From Ronald A. Fisher and Frank Yates, *Statistical Tables for Biological, Agricultural, and Medical Research* (New York: Hafner, 1963).

We have perhaps said enough with respect to the use of a table of random numbers; but because randomization is so often effected by the use of just such a table, the foregoing discussion is probably justified.

Two other matters will, however, come to the mind of the practical researcher: (1) How large a sample do I need? and (2) What is the probability of error by taking a *sample* of the population as opposed to utilizing the *entire* population?

The Size of the Sample

Let's consider the first question. One basic rule is: *The larger the sample, the better.* But such a generalized rule is not too helpful to a researcher who has a practical decision to make with respect to a specific research situation. Somewhat more definite guidelines may, therefore, be formulated.

Sample size depends largely on the degree to which the sample population approximates the characteristics and qualities resident in the general population. Take homogeneity, for instance. How homogeneous or heterogeneous is the composition of the general population? This will indicate some identity of these same characteristics in the sample. Obviously, if the population is markedly heterogeneous, a larger sample will be needed than if the population is more nearly homogeneous. Thus, the researcher should consider three factors particularly in making any decision as to sample size:

1. The degree of precision required between the sample population and the general population.
2. The variability factor of the population. (This is commonly expressed statistically as the standard deviation.)
3. The method of sampling employed. (We shall discuss briefly sampling design later in these pages.)

For those who may wish to determine the size of the sample in terms of a statistical approach, the following formula estimates the representativeness of the sample on certain critical parameters at an acceptance level of probability:

$$N = \left(\frac{z}{e}\right)^2 (p)(1 - p)$$

Where

N = the size of the sample
z = the standard score corresponding to a given confidence level
e = the proportion of sampling error in a given situation
p = the estimated proportion or incidence of cases in the population.

In considering the second question, namely, the probability of error by taking a sample of the population as opposed to utilizing the total population, we must consider how far the individual sample means deviate from the mean value for the total population. This is usually determined statistically through a determination of the *standard error of the mean.* Statistically, this is determined as follows:

$$SE_{\overline{X}} = \frac{s}{\sqrt{N}}$$

Where

$SE_{\overline{X}}$ = the standard error of the mean
s = the standard deviation of the sample
N = the number of cases in the sample

This method of determining the standard error of the mean is true for both large and small samples. The sampling distribution of means is very nearly normal for $N \leqslant 30$, even when the population may be nonnormal.

Sampling Designs

One final consideration should be discussed under the general heading of the population and its selection for study in descriptive survey research, and that is the various sampling designs commonly employed in normative survey studies.

In the descriptive survey method, the problem for the researcher is to select from the general population a sample population which will be both logically and statistically defensible. The first step in selecting any sampling design is to analyze carefully the *integral characteristics of the population;* and in view of these, then to select the sampling technique *most appropriate for the population type.*

Here are some general characteristics of populations:

1. The population may be generally a homogeneous mass of separate units.
2. The population may contain definite strata of discretely different units.
3. The population may contain definite strata but each stratum may differ from every other stratum by a proportionate ratio of its separate stratified units.
4. The population may consist of clusters whose cluster characteristics are similar but whose unit characteristics are as heterogeneous as possible.

It may be well to present in chart form the various features of each of the various sampling techniques.

Population Characteristics and Sampling Techniques Appropriate for Each Population Type

Population Characteristic	Example of Population Type	Appropriate Sampling Technique
I Population is generally a homogeneous mass of individual units.	A quantity of flower seeds of a particular variety from which random samples are selected for testing as to their germination quality.	Simple random sampling
II Population consists of definite strata, each of which is distinctly different, but the units within the stratum as homogeneous as possible.	A particular town whose total population consists of three types (strata) of citizens: white, European-background type; black, African-background type; and Mexicano-Indian-background type.	Simple stratified sampling
III Population contains definite strata with differing characteristics and each strata has a proportionate ratio in terms of numbers of members to every other strata.	A community in which the total population consisted of individuals whose religious affiliations were found to be Catholic, 25 per cent; Protestant, 50 per cent; Jewish, 15 per cent; nonaffiliated, 10 per cent.	Proportional stratified sampling
IV Population consists of clusters whose cluster characteristics are similar yet whose unit characteristics are as heterogeneous as possible.	A survey of the nation's twenty leading air terminals by soliciting reactions from travelers who use them. (All air terminals are similar in atmosphere, purpose, design, etc., yet the passengers who use them differ widely in individual characteristics: age, sex, national origin, philosophies and beliefs, socioeconomic status, and so forth.)	Cluster sampling

All sampling procedures demand certain levels of "processing" of the sample. In all cases, the following three operational levels are indigenous to the process of sampling:

1. An identification of the population, an analysis of its structure, and an assessment of its characteristics.
2. The randomization process and the selection of the sample population from the total population.
3. The extraction of the data from the sample population.

In certain populations, particularly where their composition consists of disparate elements in proportional ratios, an equalization process is necessary in addition to the three processes just indicated. The equalization process ensures proper balance among all the elements in the population in proportion to their relative strength or significance.

Schematically, we may represent each of the sampling procedures as follows:

Simple Random Sampling. Simple randomized sampling is the least sophisticated of all sampling procedures. It consists of having a population whose texture is either homogeneous or homogeneously conglomerate. The derivation of the sample is by means of a simple randomization process. Schematically, the process of simple random sampling would look something like this:

SIMPLE RANDOM SAMPLING DESIGN

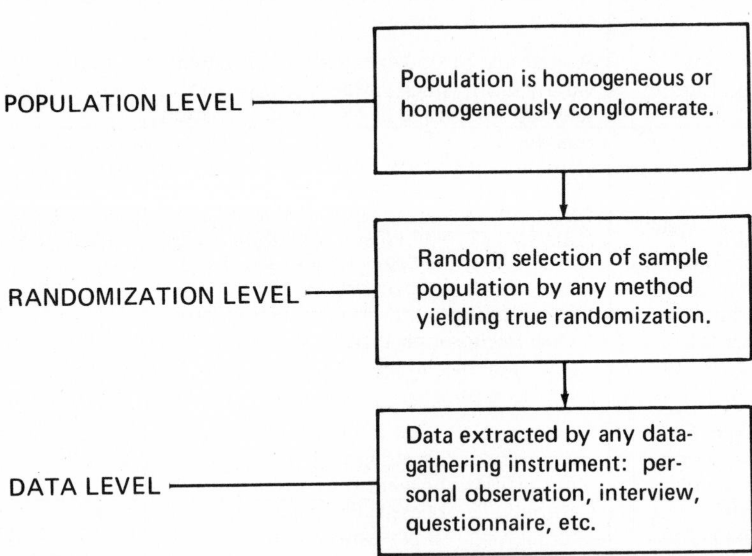

Stratified Random Sampling. In the stratified random-sampling design, certain differences between this design and the simpler method are at once apparent. The population, instead of a homogeneous or conglomerate mass, is composed of layers (strata) of discretely different types of individual units. Think of grades 4, 5, and 6 in a public school. This is a stratified population. Generally, the stratification layers are usually somewhat equal—a schoolroom has just so much seating capacity. If we were to sample a population of fourth-, fifth-, and sixth-grade children of a particular school, we should probably take equal samples from each of the three grades. Our sampling design would look, then, like the following diagram, with the addition of one more level, the "Equalization Level," at which point we would be careful to see that the sample was indeed representative of the entire population.

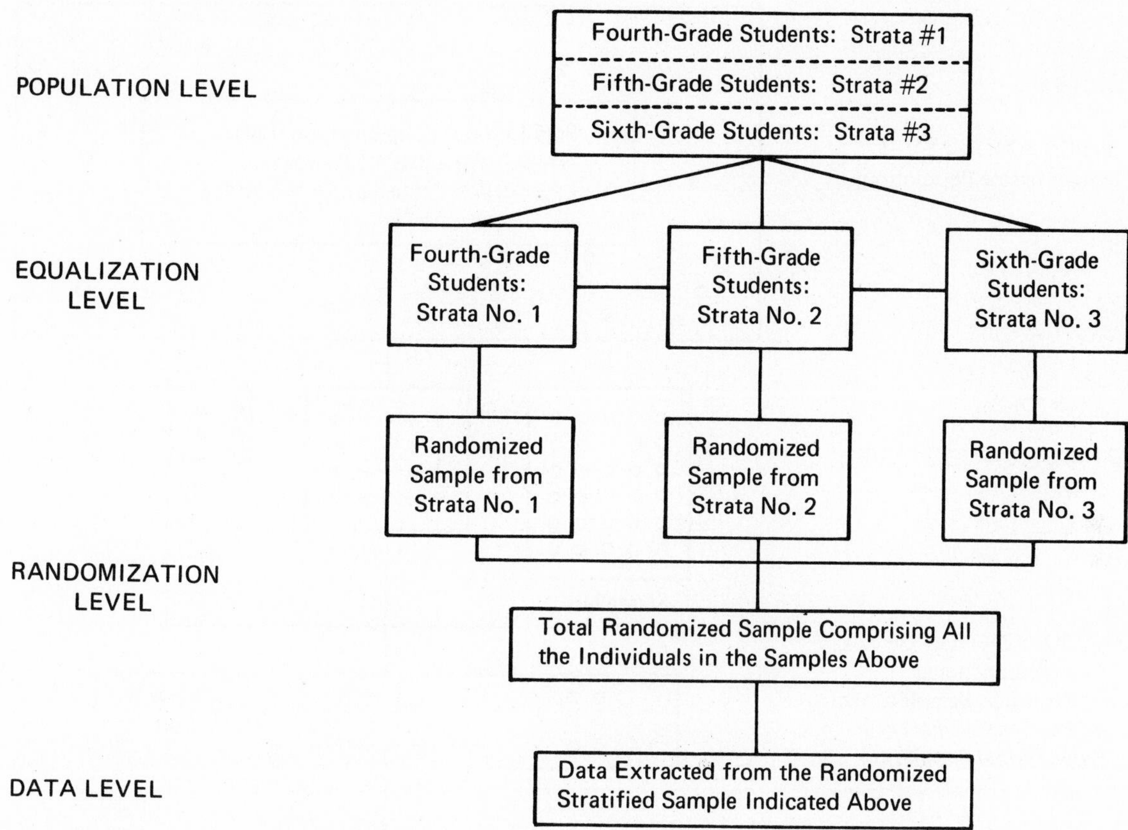

Proportional Stratified Sampling. We have just looked at the simple stratified sampling design. In it, all the strata in the population were essentially equal in size. But now we come to a population which is markedly different. Consider how vastly different are the strata of religious groups within a community which has, for example, 3,000 Protestants, 2,000 Catholics, and 1,000 Jews. Let us postulate a survey situation. We have a local newspaper which publishes a religious section dealing with interfaith church news, religious events, and syndicated articles of interest to the religious community in general. The editor wishes to determine certain facts from his readership.

It is now obvious that instead of an orderly stratification, as in the previous population, here the population is a conglomerate, religiously heterogeneous, proportional mixture in the ratio strength of 3 to 2 to 1. Unlike the three public school grades in which the separate homogeneous strata were arranged one above the other, in this population you have an *integral mixture of separate disparate units in conglomerate relationship.*

The first problem, therefore, is to effect a separation of the several discrete elements in the total population and from each of the individual groups, then, to select a random sample proportionately representative of the numerical strength of each of the components within the entire conglomerate structure.

The proportional stratified sampling design may, therefore, be represented schematically as represented by the diagram on the next page.

Cluster or Area Sampling. We shall now consider another type of sampling. Up to this point the population structure has been either homogeneous or composed of layers of different units, but now we come to a different type of population make-up. Cluster sampling is convenient, and indeed administratively necessary sometimes, in large-area studies. Sometimes it is unfeasible to attempt to make up a list of every person living within

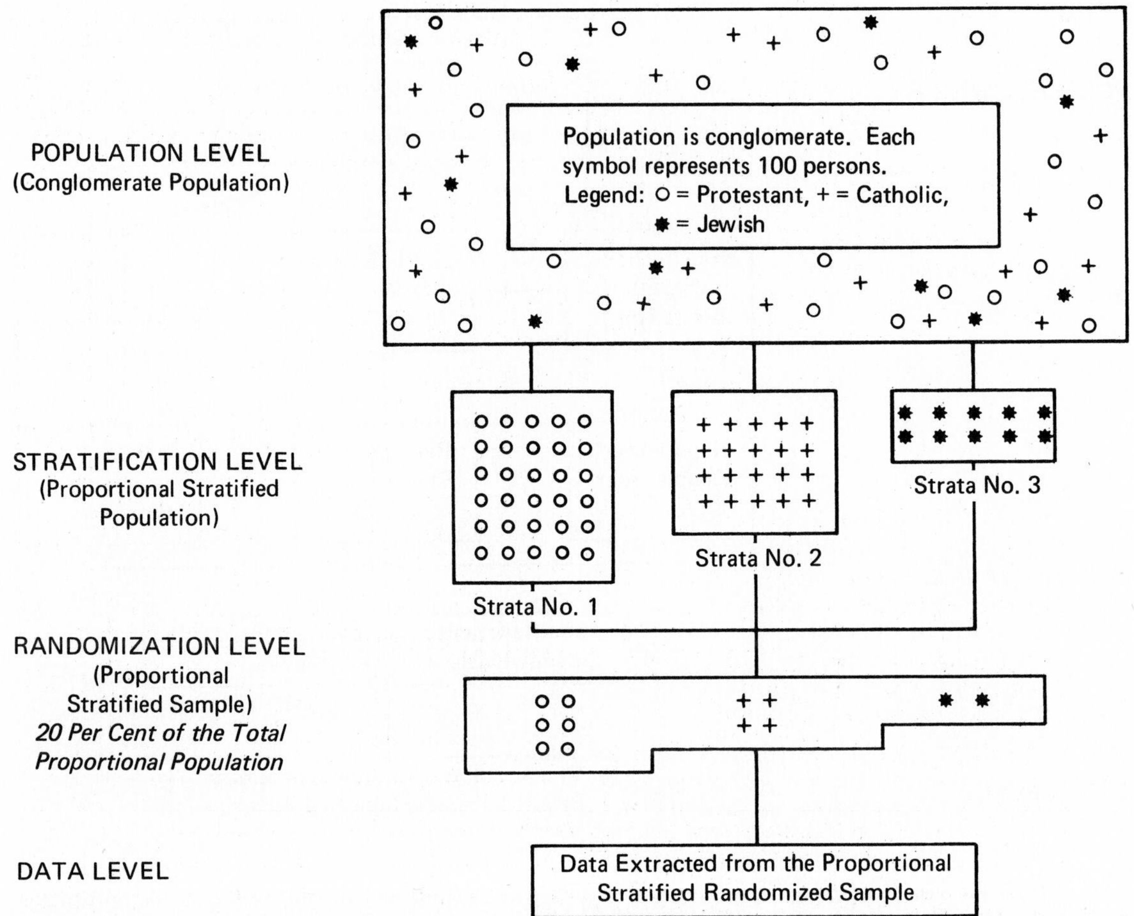

a particular area and from that list to select a sample for study through normal randomization procedures. In lieu of that, we may secure a map of the area showing political or other types of subdivision. We may then subdivide an expansive area into smaller units: a city, for example, may be subdivided into precincts, clusters of city blocks, school boundary areas, or any other convenient subdivision pattern; a state may be divided into counties, townships, or some other definable subdivision. In cluster sampling, it is important that each cluster be as similar to the other clusters as possible and yet that within the clusters the individuals be heterogeneous.

From all the clusters a random selection of specific clusters is made as the nucleus from which the sample population is ultimately derived, again by random selection. Let us take the previous situation which we used to illustrate the proportional stratified sampling of the religious groups within a community. Let us assume that the community is a large city that we have divided into twelve areas or clusters. The design, schematically represented, would be like the diagram on the opposite page.

Systematic Sampling. Systematic sampling is the final major type of sampling design we will discuss in this chapter. Obviously, there are other ways of sampling, and variants of the basic designs that we have discussed. Any good text devoted to survey design or sampling theory will discuss them all. The reason for the elaboration which has been here given in terms of the basic types is that in research planning and design where one is doing a descriptive survey study the weak links in the chain are usually found at two or three

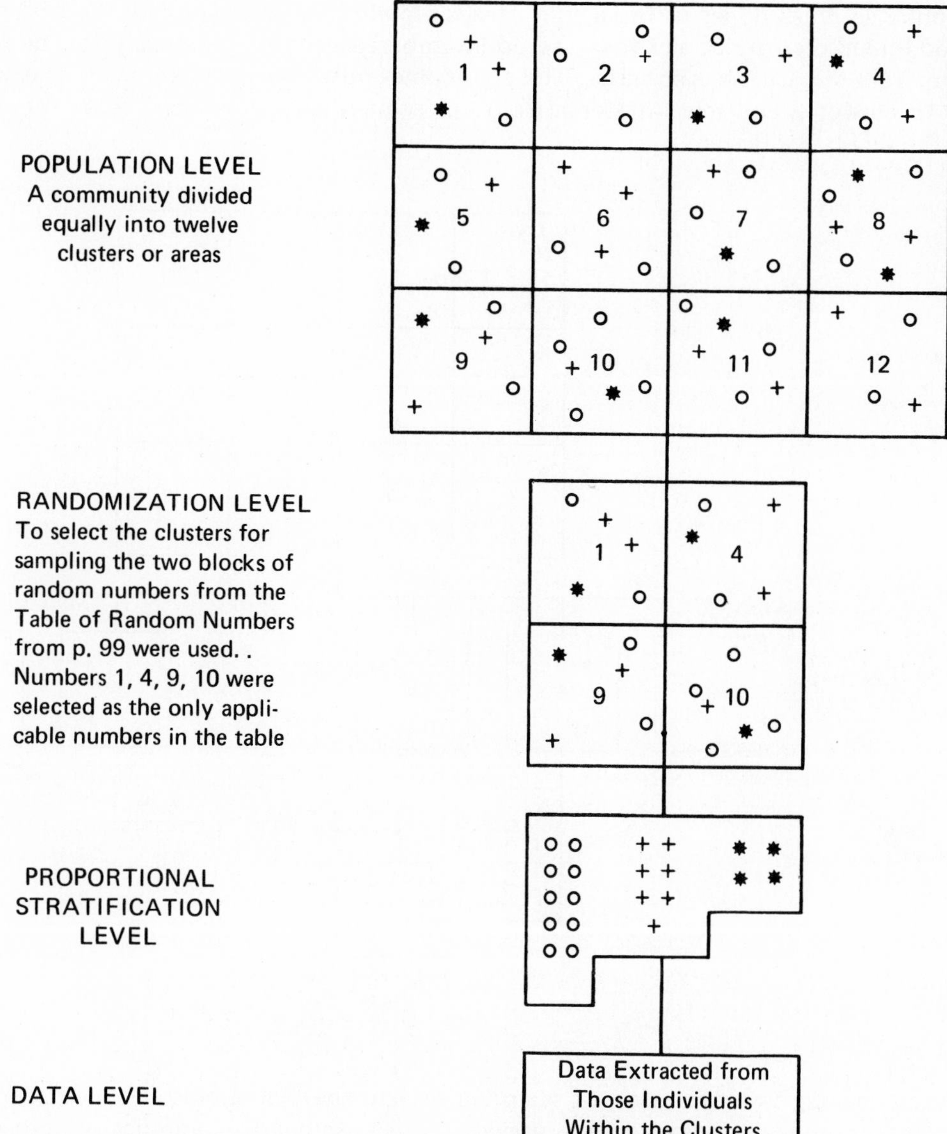

points: randomization, sampling design, and with the introduction of bias into the system. The discussion of bias will be our next consideration.

Systematic sampling is precisely what the name implies: the selection of certain items in a series according to a predetermined sequence. The origin of the sequence must be controlled by chance. Where one is selecting names from a list, in order to achieve randomicity, perhaps the first name to be selected should be the item number of the name corresponding to the first random number in a table of random numbers which falls under a certain specified limit—10, for example. In that case, should we again consult the portion of our table presented on p. 99, we should begin with the fourth name of the list. Should we be interested in selecting as an interval the next random number under 20, directly under 04 is 13. We should then begin with the fourth name on the list and, from that point onward, select every thirteenth name on the list.

Let us take the cluster diagram that we have just presented. Because there are only twelve cells in the population, to get started in systematic sampling, with either the odd- or even-numbered clusters, let us flip a coin. Heads dictate that we begin with the first number in the odd-numbered series and take the odd-numbered cells systematically for the random selection. Tails dictate the even series. The coin comes down tails, which means that we shall start with cluster 2 and select systematically, or sequentially, clusters 4, 6, 8, 10, and 12. Here is the schematic design.

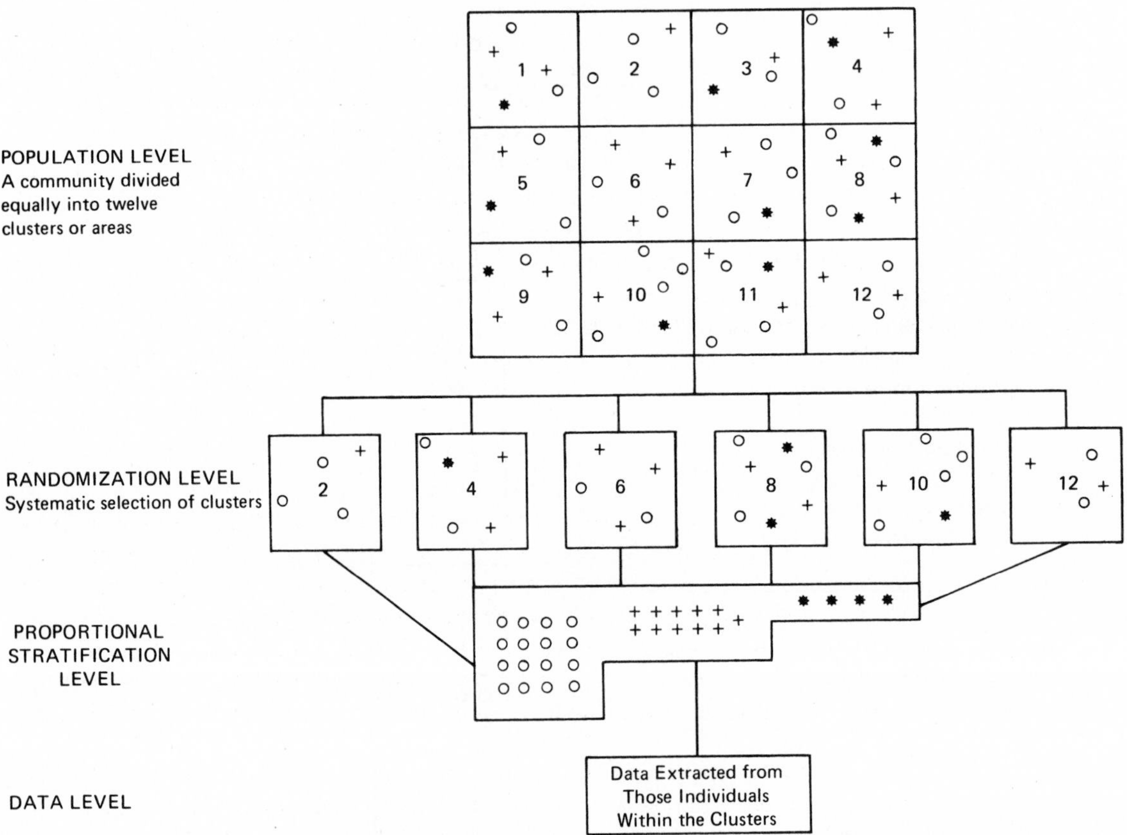

Before leaving this discussion of sampling design, the fact should be underscored that the design diagrams as presented on previous pages emphasize graphically the intrinsic nature of each design structure and show the student the distinctive characteristics of each sampling approach. Each has its particular utility in a specific situation, the parameters of which we have outlined in connection with each genre of sampling design.

In choosing a sampling design, you should not choose blindly or willy-nilly. The design should be, in a sense, *a tool of research,* and this tool should be chosen with full recognition of the task at hand and its discrete demands on the sampling procedure. A careful study of the diagrams, a consideration of your own population characteristics will aid you in selecting the sampling design that is best structured for parameters of the data and that meets the particular requirements of the population universe.

BIAS IN THE RESEARCH DESIGN

We turn now to the matter of bias in the research design. In enumerating the basic characteristics of the descriptive survey method, we indicated that the researcher needed to be particularly alert for the presence of bias in descriptive or normative survey studies: *Data in descriptive survey research are particularly susceptible to distortion through introduction of bias into the research design. Particular attention should be given, therefore, to safeguard the data from the influence of bias.*[7]

Bias is, of course, indigenous to all research, but because it can infect the descriptive survey more easily than most other methodological genres and because it is sometimes difficult for the researcher to detect, we have chosen to discuss it here. We may define *bias* as "any influence, condition, or set of conditions, which, singly or together, cause distortion or aberration of the data from those which may have been obtained under the conditions of pure chance; furthermore, bias is any influence which may have disturbed the randomicity by which the choice of a sample population has been selected."

Data are, in many respects, delicate and sensitive to extraneous influences. We talk about the solid truth, the hard fact, yet every researcher learns that data are neither so hard nor so solid as the hackneyed phrase might suggest. Data are highly susceptible to distortion. Bias is frequently minute and imperceptible in its infiltration into the research system and may be easily overlooked by even the most sensitive and careful researcher. Bias attacks the integrity of the fact. It is particularly vicious when it enters surreptitiously into the research system and its presence and influence go undetected. It will render suspect even the most carefully planned research effort.

How Bias Enters the Research Effort

The best way to appreciate bias is to see it at work. To understand precisely how bias does influence the data, let us take several instances and inspect them carefully. A researcher decides to use a city telephone directory as a source for selecting a random sample. The sample will be obviously biased, for it does not represent the entire spectrum of the general population. The lower economic strata of the population will not be adequately represented because many of this strata are unable to afford a telephone. The affluent also will not be adequately represented, for many of them have unlisted telephones. Hence, the sample will be drawn largely from a middle-strata population.

Questionnaire-type studies frequently also fall victim to bias infiltration, often without the awareness of the researcher. In questionnaire studies the researcher is frequently more concerned about the percentage of the return of his questionnaire than about the bias influence which may be exerted by those subjects who do not return his questionnaire.

Let us take a very simple situation. A questionnaire is sent to 100 citizens, asking, "Have you ever been summoned by the Internal Revenue Service to justify your income tax return?" Seventy out of 100 questionnaires are returned. Thirty-five of these reply that they have been summoned; thirty-five indicate that they have never been summoned. The researcher might include, therefore, that 50 per cent of the respondents had never been summoned, and that 50 per cent had received summonses. He may even make generalizations on this basis concerning the whole population. But this may be a very misleading conclusion. He is basing his assumption on the similarity of the population in *other* respects from an *outward appraisal:* they look like average citizens. What the researcher has overlooked is the inward motivation that may have influenced 30 per cent of his respondents to fail to return their questionnaires.

Being summoned to defend one's income tax return can be considered a reflection on one's integrity. For that reason the nonrespondents may not have wanted to indicate that they had been summoned, and hence they may merely have ignored the whole matter. The bias growing out of an attempt to preserve one's integrity may have operated to distort the

[7] See p. 80.

truth of the situation. Instead of seeming equally divided, a 35 and 65 per cent proportion may be more realistic figures.

Bias may also creep in in many other seemingly innocuous ways. In interviewing, one's personality may affect the responses of the interviewee. Two teachers, having been trained exactly alike, teaching classes whose composition is as nearly alike as it is possible to make it, may in a comparable study of their teaching, although applying the same methods and teaching the same subject matter, be grossly influenced by bias which has seeped into the system from a number of points:

- The personality of each teacher is different.
- Each class, no matter how carefully paired, is composed of individuals each of whom is different.
- The inner group dynamics are different with each group.
- Surroundings, modulated by such delicate influences as gradations of light, temperature, noise level, and other imperceptible factors alter individual reactions to a situation.
- The discussion pattern may well vary from class to class.
- The preconditioning factors of home environment may reach into the classroom situation and affect individual student behavior and reaction within the class situation.

In each of the preceding situations typical of the normal classroom—and we might go on to cite many more similar conditioning factors—we have influences, conditions, or sets of conditions which may cause distortion of the data.[8] When this happens, bias has affected the data arising out of the situation being studied.

Acknowledgment of the Presence of Bias

As it is almost impossible for man to live in this world without contacting micro-organisms, so, in the research environment, the researcher cannot avoid having his data influenced and contaminated by bias of one sort or another. What is inexcusable, however, is for the researcher not to acknowledge the likelihood of biased data or to fail to recognize the possibility of bias in the study. To interpret the data and to formulate conclusions without acknowledging the effect that bias may have had either in causing distortion of the data or in conditioning the outcome of the research is to demonstrate naiveté and an immature approach to serious research.

Those with greatest maturity in research planning and design demonstrate their integrity by admitting without reserve that bias is omnipresent and may very well have influenced their study. The most fearless among them will point out precisely how bias may have infiltrated the research design. With this knowledge we may then appraise the research realistically and judge its merits honestly. Nothing is gained by ignoring what all of us know may exist. Bias for the researcher, like the presence of germs for the surgeon, is next to impossible to avoid. We must learn to live with it but at the same time to guard against infective destruction.

Some students, however, strive so hard to make the data support their hypotheses that in so doing they deny the realities inherent in the research situation. Nothing is thereby gained. In research we cannot force the facts to support anything. The facts must speak for themselves, and if they are tainted with bias, that too we must accept as a condition to be minimized insofar as possible, and if it cannot be totally eradicated, to be faced as inevitable in most research, particularly in descriptive survey studies. To pretend that you are unaware

[8] See definition of *bias*, p. 107.

of bias, or in the face of data that are plainly biased, that your facts are pure and unsullied by any extraneous influence whatsoever (and there are multitudes of studies that give such impressions) is either scholarly hypocrisy or inexcusable ignorance.[9]

THE PRESENTATION AND INTERPRETATION OF THE DATA IN THE DESCRIPTIVE SURVEY STUDY

Data are of no value merely as data. In this discussion of descriptive survey research thus far, we have been discussing principally the acquisition of fact: how to winnow the data from the general population by appropriate sampling techniques, how to protect against their infection by bias. We have been thinking of the process of accumulation only; and while amassing of data is certainly a necessary aspect of research and one of the cardinal tenets of the scientific method, it is not the end for which the process of research was instituted. The purpose of research is to solve problems. It is to accomplish that purpose that we amass data. Let us review some fundamental principles.

Survey Research Is More Than Activity

It may be well for you at this juncture to review what has been already said in Chapters 1 and 4 of this book. Throughout these two chapters you were constantly reminded of two basic principles of research:

1. The purpose of research is to seek the answer to a problem in the light of the facts that relate to that problem.
2. Although the facts relative to the problem must be assembled for study and inspection, *the extraction of meaning from the accumulated data*—what we have called *the interpretation of the data*—is all-important.

As we have said earlier, "The *mind* of the researcher *must do battle with the observed fact until the fact reveals its meaning* with respect to the problem."[10] Research is essentially a way of thinking; it is a manner of regarding accumulated fact so that a collection of data becomes articulate to the mind of the researcher in terms of what the data mean.[11]

The descriptive survey method is, however, a very "busy" method from the standpoint of the researcher. It demands perhaps more activity than the other methodologies. It is probably the most complex of all the research methodologies. In the light of the problem, the researcher must decide upon a population, study it, choose the method of sampling it, determine how randomicity will be guaranteed, send questionnaires or conduct interviews, or observe the data directly, record and systematize the fact gleaned through the survey, and perhaps do more that we have failed to mention. All this is enough to keep any researcher busy. The activity associated with descriptive research methodology is complex, time-consuming, and distracting. With all this motion going on around him, it would not seem unreasonable if the researcher lost sight of the nuances of the problem and those of the subproblems. But it is precisely the problem and the subproblems that are the reason for all the rest of the activity. All activity is subordinate to the research itself, and the activity must sooner or later come to rest in an interpretation of the data and a conclusion of the

[9] Note on p. 87 the openness with which the researcher recognizes the likelihood of bias entering the study and not only acknowledges the fact but provides a technique for minimizing its effect: "This procedure was followed in order to eliminate bias in analyzing the tapes."

[10] See p. 47.

[11] See p. 4.

problem being investigated. Inexperienced researchers forget this. Activity for activity's sake is seductive; it gives them a sense of well-being to have amassed great quantities of data. Like Midas looking at his hoard of gold, they lose sight of the demands that the problem makes upon the data. They feel that all they need to do is to present the raw data in a series of displays and summaries—graphs, charts, tables—which will demonstrate their acquisitive skills beyond doubt.

In planning the research, in preparing the proposal, or in writing the research report, inexperienced researchers come to the point where it is necessary to answer the question, "How will the data be interpreted?" Let us take a typical situation and lift a page from a proposal in order to see how many students attempt to resolve the situation. This is a page from a proposal "to analyze the attitudes of professional employees toward certain aspects of management policy and to evaluate the relationship between these attitudes and the responsibility of management to articulate such policy for its employees."

The particular subproblem under consideration is, "What does analysis of the attitudes of employees toward management policy for salary increases and merit pay reveal?" Here is the way in which the student has handled this situation.

Treatment of Each Specific Subproblem

Restatement of Subproblem 1. The first subproblem is to determine through an analysis of employee responses the attitudes of employees toward certain aspects of management policy for salary increases and merit pay.

The Data Needed

The data needed to resolve this subproblem are those employee responses to questions concerning salary increases and merit pay.

Where the Data Are Located

The data are located in the employee responses to questions 3, 7, and 13 of the questionnaire, "Survey of Employee Attitudes Toward Management."

How the Data Will Be Secured

The data will be secured by accurately tabulating all of the responses of employees to the above questions on the questionnaire.

How the Data Will Be Interpreted

From the responses of the questions a table will be constructed similar to the following structural model. It will indicate the employee attitudes, their frequency, and the percentage of these attitudes to the total attitude response to each question.

Attitude	Frequency	Percentage
Totals		

A graph will then be constructed to show which attitudes have received the greatest number of reactions and those which have had the least number of reactions. The median and the mean will also be found for the total group as a basis for comparison.

Now let us look at that page again. Consider first the wording of the subproblem. It seeks "to determine through an *analysis* of employee responses the attitudes of employees . . ." Now read the section "How the Data Will Be Interpreted." What has the researcher really done? Has he *interpreted* (shown what the data means) any of the data? No. He has merely *tabulated and graphed* the data. He has merely rearranged it and presented it in another form. It remains as "raw" as it originally was in the questionnaire. Finally, the researcher informs us that he intends to find two points of central tendency for the data. Why?

If at this juncture the researcher returns to the subproblem and reads it carefully, he should see immediately that what he has suggested doing to the data will never produce an *analysis of employee responses* but merely an *amassing, a tabulating, a conversion* of employee responses into another form. Granted, what he has done may be the first step in preparing the data for analysis, but no analysis has been effected.

If after codification of the data, the researcher had then considered it analytically, he would have indicated that he would resolve the responses into various gradational categories. Corresponding to these categories, he would classify the responses into those supportive of and those opposed to management policies. He would indicate what these responses meant in terms of the subproblem and the larger problem situation. He would integrate the data into a formalized conclusion warranted by the facts. If he had done all this, then any reader could see clearly how he intended to *interpret* the data.

Guidelines with Respect to Data in the Descriptive Survey Study

We have said enough about the example. But from the foregoing discussion some basic guidelines for handling the data may be helpful.

1. *Be systematic in describing the treatment of the data.* In the proposal especially indicate a logical, systematic sequence of the steps necessary to solve each subproblem separately. A suggested format may be a repetition of the subproblem as it was originally stated following the problem at the beginning of the proposal. This restatement of each subproblem might stand boldly at the beginning of each section of the "Treatment of the Data for Each Specific Subproblem." Directly following the restatement of the subproblem being discussed, it may be well then to

- *State clearly the data needed.* Under an appropriate heading, "The Data Needed," indicate specifically the data you will need for the resolution of the subproblem being investigated. Do not engage in generalities. The sample page just presented was excellent with respect to the precise data that were needed. It specified that the responses to questions 3, 7, and 13 were needed for the resolution of the subproblem.
- *State precisely where the data are located.* With respect to the sample page under consideration this section is largely a repetition of the preceding statement; in other studies, however, where a student may need a certain kind of records, he should know precisely before beginning his investigation the exact location where these records are kept. Too many students begin research projects assuming that records are available only to learn too late that either no records exist or that, if they do exist, they are in an inaccessible location. To face the question frankly, "Where are the data located?" and to answer such a question in writing in terms of a specific addressable location may clear the air at the beginning of one's research effort.
- *State exactly how the data will be secured.* Again, with the sample page given, little difficulty presented itself at this point. But suppose the data are the letters of a famous person in the possession of his family. You may know precisely where the letters are kept. The next question is, how will you get them for your research purposes? Perhaps in cases like this the name and address of the individual should be given under whose aegis the data

are preserved; a statement should be included to the effect that this custodian of the data has consented for you to use them for research purposes. This should be clearly stated in the proposal so that your sponsor, your academic committee, the funding agency, or whoever may be interested in reading your proposal before the research is begun may see clearly that you have provided for all contingencies against failure to secure the data, which is a very common misfortune with many students who undertake research projects without sufficient preliminary ground work.

• *State fully and unequivocally precisely how the data will be interpreted.* This is the weakest link in most research thinking. Trust, faith, and hope are all too often substituted for clear thinking and hardheaded planning. This is by far the most difficult section of the whole proposal to write, and because it is so demanding, it is all too frequently given either slighted attention or it is answered in such vague and generalized language that the statement is worthless from a practical research planning and design standpoint. A basic test for the treatment of the data is the following: *The plan for the treatment of the data should be so unequivocal and specific that another person seeing only your proposal could carry out your research project by means of that document alone.* Every contingency should be anticipated; every methodological problem should be resolved. The section entitled "How the Data Will Be Interpreted" is the key to research success or failure, and it should be presented with utmost care and precision.

Every step in the interpretation of the data should be fully spelled out. Too many students assume this is unnecessary. They prefer to cut corners. They assume that others know what they mean, and so it is unnecessary to express it. All these assumptions are false. Too many students try to do in one tenth of a page what they should take ten pages to do. Spelling out the treatment and interpretation of the data is a tedious, time-consuming, lengthy process. To attempt to relegate the treatment of data to the broad sweep, the quick and careless approach is almost invariably to court disaster.

Certain procedural guidelines may, therefore, be given with respect to setting forth the treatment and interpretation of the data.

a. *Ask yourself continually what it is you are doing.* Make a careful distinction in your own mind between *arraying* the data and *interpreting* the data. To present the data in the form of tables, graphs, charts, maps, and so forth is simply to repackage the data in different form so that it may be seen to greater advantage.
b. *If you employ a statistical approach, give a rationale for it.* It is pointless to tell us you will derive the mean and standard deviation and to stop there. Why do you need these statistical values? How will they help you to derive meaning from the data? Is this statistical approach *indispensable* in understanding what the facts mean? What are your formulas? Why did you choose these formulas? Where did you get them? (Footnote your source, and give the symbol equivalents.)
c. *Where does manipulation of the data cease and your own thinking become absolutely essential in deriving meaning from fact?* There is this point in every project that is true research. Without synthesizing meaning from raw fact, there can be no interpretation of data. Unless you can indicate the precise point where you assume control of the data—aside from computers, graphics, tabulations, and so forth—and unless you can describe what role you will play in processing the data mentally, you should be very circumspect in calling whatever you have done interpretation of the data. You may have computerized the data, transformed them, found their statistical characteristics, repackaged them, and redisplayed them, but after all of this only the genius

of human insight can declare what these dead facts mean. Insight into the meaning of ephemeral phenomenology and impersonal fact is what we mean by the interpretation of the data. Such insight takes what is otherwise common fact grubbing and gives it the stature of research.

2. *The whole research process is cyclical.* That the entire research process is cyclical was one of the basic propositions with which this book began. Because we have been considering a subunit of research design—namely, the treatment of the data with respect to each subproblem—we find that the principle of circularity applies here equally as well as it does with the overall plan. The difference is, however, that here it is only a shrunken orbit of the greater circular process. From the point of beginning, each step should progress logically and stepwise until the process comes full circle at the point of beginning again.

Test the circularity and, likewise, the validity of your treatment of the data by the "If-Test" technique. It goes like this:

THE IF-TEST TECHNIQUE

1. Here is the subproblem, the point of beginning. (State it completely.)
2. If I have this subproblem, what data do I need?
3. If I need these data, where are they located?
4. If they are located there, how can I get them?
5. If I can get them, what do I intend to do with them?
6. If I do that with the data will the result of doing it answer my subproblem?
7. If that answers my subproblem, then what hypothesis was I testing based on that subproblem?
8. If that was my hypothesis, what will the facts show with respect to it?
9. If the data supported my hypothesis, I guessed correctly.
10. If the data do not support the hypothesis, I have learned something that I did not even suspect to be the case.

3. *Be sure the data will support your conclusions.* Unfounded enthusiasm is one of the hazards you will need to guard against. One of the marks of the immature researcher is that, bewildered by the many data he must handle or dazzled by a newly emerging concept of which he has just become aware, he makes extravagant claims or reaches enthusiastic conclusions that are not warranted by the data. Although research is indeed an exciting quest, the researcher must learn—particularly the one who is doing a descriptive survey study—that though his data frequently lie close to the vibrant pulse of life, he cannot permit this to influence his objective judgment of their message. Archimedes running through the streets of Athens screaming, "I have found it!" is perfectly justified after he is sure that he *has* found it. It was only after the Athenian bath tub ran over that he reached his conclusion. Too much research contains unfounded conclusions unwarranted by the data and based upon shaky statistical procedures or extravagant extrapolation of the observed facts. The writer of a doctoral dissertation must ultimately defend that dissertation; he must justify his conclusions, not on the basis of what he hopes might be the case, but *on the basis of the solid fact and hard data which he has presented as the basis for his conclusions.* Nothing less will suffice. Research, particularly the descriptive survey study, should rest solidly and completely upon its own factual foundation. Look the facts in the face. Report precisely what those facts say. That is good research; that is also excellent descriptive survey reporting.

Practical Application

At the conclusion of this discussion, you should turn to Appendix B, p. 231, where you will find a practical application of some of the matters discussed in this chapter. This section of the practicum in research will be particularly important if you are engaged in a descriptive-survey type of research study.

9 The Analytical Survey Method

The previous chapter has been devoted to a discussion of observational type studies in which the researcher describes what he has observed or what by minimal probing he may uncover as a describable characteristic. If he employs statistics in the purely descriptive survey study, his techniques are very often those of the first-layer, older-order statistics which reveal the points of central tendency, the variability, and the degree of interrelationship between the variables in the data. He relies upon those statistical approaches that we usually consider as belonging to the province of descriptive statistics.

In the descriptive survey, the data may have more of a tendency to be verbal. Descriptive studies deal with questionnaire data, interview data, and simple observational information. School surveys, case studies, community surveys, opinion polls, documentary surveys are all typical studies to be found in the descriptive survey category. We may characterize the inner quality of the data in the descriptive or normative survey, therefore, as being verbal or quasiverbal in character.

NATURE OF DATA IN ANALYTICAL STUDIES

We come now to a research methodology that demands a different type of data. In the analytical survey approach, our purpose is not so much to attempt to describe what the data are trying to tell us as it is to take data that are essentially quantitative in nature (numerical data) and to analyze these data by means of appropriate statistical tools so that we may infer from them certain meanings which lie hidden within them, or at least to discern the presence of potentials and dynamic forces which lie within those data that may suggest possibilities of further investigation. In the analytical survey we are concerned primarily with problems of estimation and situations demanding the testing of a statistically based hypothesis. The statistical methods employed are those techniques that are most often referred to as belonging to the domain of *inferential statistics.*

We have stressed earlier the necessity of considering the data in terms of their basic qualities and essential nature, of seeing their distinguishing characteristics before adopting a particular methodological approach for any research project. The data determine the research method; the method never precedes a careful consideration of the basic quality of the data.

On p. 68 we indicated the analytical survey method as being appropriate for those data that are inherently quantitative in nature and need statistical assistance to extract their meaning. Let us now look briefly at the essential nature of quantitative data. First, they are measurable. Measurement of data is expressed by means of various scales of value. We generally recognize four basic scalar categories for classifying analytical-survey data:

1. *The nominal scale* is the grossest of the differentiational scales. It merely expresses categorical classifications—e.g., boys, girls.
2. *The ordinal scale* is the scale next in refinement, indicating a measurement of the *degree* of difference—e.g., more boys, more girls; twice as many boys as girls.
3. *The interval scale* is a scale for which a *unit of measurement* has been established—e.g., "Tom is 3 *inches* [indicating three standard measurement *units*] taller than Kathy."
4. *The ratio scale* is a scale in which the values are measured from an absolute or arbitrary designated zero point. The ratio scale measures multiples of one value over another. Examples: "This solution of H_2SO_4 has twice the acid content of that one." "The temperature measures 25° Centigrade."

It is important to keep these four qualitative aspects of the data firmly in mind because later in the discussion of this chapter we shall show that on the basis of the measurement characteristics of the data, we select the most appropriate statistical treatment for those data.

Data also have two other characteristics. Data may be either *discrete* or *continuous.* Discrete data are those which arise from the process of counting. The number of apples in a bushel, the number of eggs in a basket, the number of people in a city are all examples of discrete data. Continuous data arise from a measurement process which is a part of a continuum, such as length, width, time, and age values. These data merge into an unbroken flow of units, a continuum of values.

So much, then, for the characteristics of data. Let us now review certain considerations with respect to statistics.

STATISTICS

Statistics as a part of the science of mathematics goes back to earliest times. The word comes from the word for *state,* and it was as a function of the business of the state that statistics first arose. Originally, statistics was a system of counting employed by the early states and kingdoms to account for their resources. It was used to count people. Moses was commanded to account for the children of Israel and, in fact, the Book of Numbers in the Bible is precisely that, a census of the Israelites. Ancient Egypt, as early as 3050 B.C., Babylonia, and the Romans all used statistical data for levying taxes and assessing their military strength. Perhaps the earliest and most famous statistical compilation among English-speaking peoples is the famous Domesday Book, dating from A.D. 1086, in which William the Conqueror directed that a complete record be made of the lands, resources, and population of early England.

The *Oxford Universal Dictionary* indicates the old as well as the more recent meaning of the word *statistics:*

> In early use, that branch of political science dealing with the collection, classification, and discussion of facts bearing on the condition of the state or the

community. In recent use, the department of study that has for its object the collection or arrangement of numerical facts or data, whether relating to human affairs or to natural phenomena.[1]

The Divisions of Statistics

Statistics as an academic discipline has made great advances within recent years. At this point we should indicate broadly the divisions of statistics and indicate the purpose and function of each division of statistical study, particularly the role of inferential statistics in dealing with the problems indigenous to analytical survey studies. The map of the statistical landscape looks something like this:

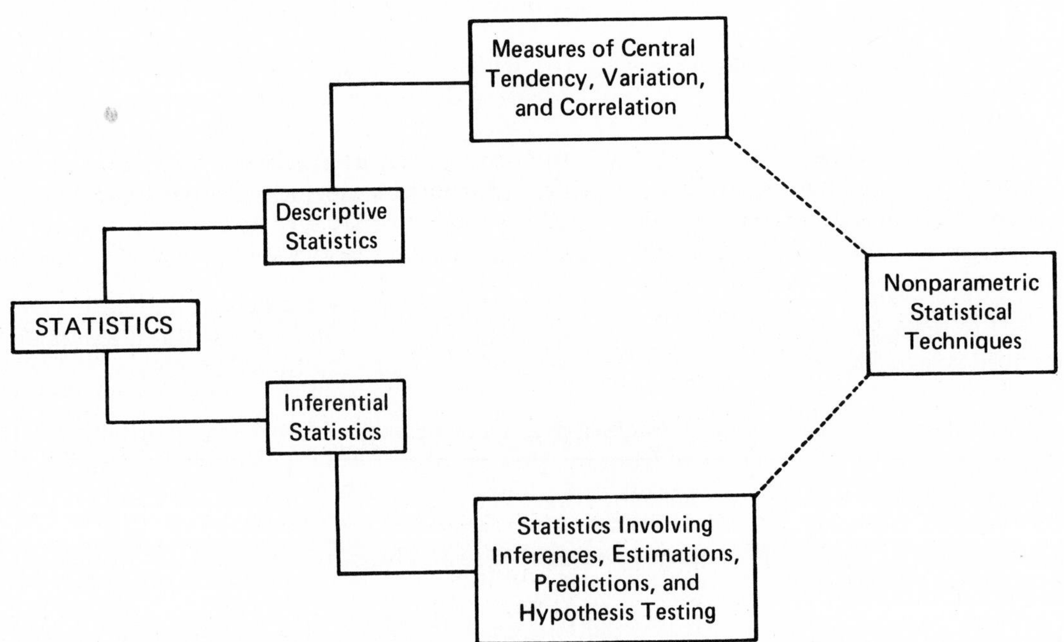

The preceding topographical plan of the statistical landscape should be viewed with some tolerance. The more one knows about research (which is another way of saying that the more one knows about life and the nature of its factual matrix) the less is one sure that anything as closely associated with life processes, such as statistics is, can be neatly isolated. Although the determination of the mean is generally thought of as lying in the domain of descriptive statistics, the testing of an assumption with respect to the population mean as postulated from the sample is conceded to be a problem in the area of statistical inference.

Researchers, especially those whose mathematical backgrounds are somewhat weak, regard statisticians in much the same way as the general populace regarded the alchemists of medieval times—wizards who wield their unnatural powers by means of a strange mystique enshrouded in a jargon of statistics and of statistical notation. The researcher who neither understands the logic nor appreciates the expressive power of statistics is awed by it.

As we have said in an earlier chapter, we do not presume in this text to make any attempt at teaching statistics for research purposes. Any library will furnish adequate volumes to this end. What we shall attempt to do here is to try to clear away some of the underbrush that so often confuses and impedes the progress of the student because he

[1] *The Oxford Universal Dictionary on Historical Principles*, 3rd ed., edited by C. T. Onions (Oxford: The Clarendon Press, 1955), p. 2007.

becomes bewildered in an area whose overall plan he does not understand and whose potential for solving his research problems he does not appreciate. We shall try, therefore, to clarify only a few basic concepts and principles with respect to the application of statistics to the demands of the analytical survey method. We shall attempt to give the student some awareness of the role of statistics in terms of function, possibilities, potential, and inherent limitations in dealing with those problems indigenous to analytic survey research.

Statistics divides in two ways: first in terms of its *functional* aspects—namely, statistics whose function is to describe the data—and statistics whose function is inferential with respect to the data. Also statistics divides *qualitatively* into parametric and nonparametric tools. Before we discuss either of these areas, however, it is necessary to clarify what a parameter is.

Parameters and Their Relation to Statistics

A *parameter* is a function, a characteristic, a quality of the population which in *concept* is a constant but whose *value* is variable. This may seem a somewhat confusing definition. Let's clarify it. Consider a circle. One of the parameters, or characteristics, of a circle is its radius. It has a functional relationship to the circle. In concept it is a constant; it is always the same for every circle: it is the distance from the center of the circle to the perimeter. In value it constantly varies, depending upon the size of the circle. Large circles have long radii; small circles have short radii. The *value*—that is, the length of the radius as measured in so many linear units (centimeters, inches, feet)—is different for each circle size. Thinking of a parameter in this way, we see that each circle has a number of parameters: circumference, area, diameter. We define these parameters in terms of concepts which are constants: the diameter is always twice the radius; the circumference is always $2r\pi$; the area, always πr^2.

Parameters are always characteristics of a *population*, a *universe* as it is sometimes called. When we have a similar characteristic of a sample, we call the "sample parameter" a *statistic*. A statistic is not to be confused, therefore, with statistics, which is the science that deals with the collection, classification, mathematical analysis, and testing, of facts, usually for research purposes. In fact, there is a difference in the symbol representing the basic characteristics which are common to both the population and to the sample or samples drawn from it.

Here is a table which shows the conventional symbols employed in statistical notation in each case.

CONVENTIONAL STATISTICAL NOTATION FOR VARIOUS PARAMETERS

The Factor Being Designated	The Symbol Employed for Designating the Factor	
	In the Case of a Population	In the Case of a Statistic
The Mean	μ	$\bar{X}$ M_g M_h*
The Standard Deviation	σ	s
Proportion or Probability	P	p
Uncertainty in	H	H
Number or Total	N	n

*M_g = Geometric Mean, M_h = Harmonic Mean

But now we return to our discussion of the difference between parametric and nonparametric statistics. *Parametric statistics* assumes that most populations have at least *one* parameter. The parameter that is perhaps the most pervasive and generally encountered in all of nature's manifestations is the great Gaussian curve of normal frequency distribution. That seems to be as universal as any phenomenon that man has observed. The nature and characteristics of this curve we discussed briefly in Chapter 2.

Take any fortuitous happening and analyze its distribution pattern: the corn production in the state of Iowa, for instance, for any given year. If we could survey the per acre yield of *every single* farmer in Iowa (literally, the *total* population, the *universe* of cornfields and corn farmers in Iowa) we would find that probably a few farmers will have had a remarkably poor yield of corn per acre, for no discernible reason except "that's the way it happened." Quite to the contrary, a few other farmers for an equally unaccountable reason will have had excessively heavy yields of corn from their fields. Generally, however, most farmers will report a middle-of-the-road yield, sloping gradually in either the direction of the greater or the lesser yield categories from what constitutes the "average" return per acre. Thus, the normal curve will describe Iowa corn production.

Walk into any clothing store and the inventory of men's suit sizes and women's dress sizes will again confirm the normal distribution curve phenomenon. Test all the children in a given school system. Their IQ scores will describe a Gaussian curve. Watch an approaching thunderstorm and an occasional flash of lightning will herald the coming of the storm. Soon the flashes will occur more frequently; at the height of the storm they will reach a peak of number of flashes per minute; gradually with the passing of the storm they will subside; and the normal curve is again confirmed. Dip into nature again and again and again and probably you will find the characteristic of normal distribution, the parameter of the Gaussian curve, occurring repeatedly. We could think of thousands of situations only to conclude that nature behaves generally according to rule of the normal frequency curve.

Because the curve is such a seemingly valid representation of the general distributional characteristics indigenous to populations, statisticians consider it a *basic parameter* which fits most life situations and, hence, which may be used as a norm against which to measure population data generally.

They also realize that random samples from populations display *generally* the same characteristics as the parent population from which they were selected. There are, of course, slight deviations in every sample: Samples are not facsimiles of the parent population. But these deviations, if the sample has been selected with adequate randomicity so that it is truly a representative sample, are presumably not of such magnitude as to be *significantly* different from the population from which the sample was drawn.

The several means of the various samples do, however, form a frequency distribution of their own, and that frequency distribution has its own mean. In other words, the mean of each sample is slightly at variance from the mean of the population from which the sample was drawn. It is axiomatic, however, that the larger the sample, the more the sample mean approximates the population mean. But the distribution of the several sample means gives us a variance phenomenon which is known as the *standard error of the mean*, and it is represented statistically as

$$SE_{\overline{X}} = \frac{\sigma}{\sqrt{N}}$$

But because

> this formula involves the population standard deviation, σ [and the purpose of using the sample was because of the fact that we could not use the population

because of its size], which is ordinarily known only to God, we poor mortals must estimate it from our knowledge of the *sample* standard deviation by the formula[2]

$$\tilde{\sigma} = s\sqrt{\frac{N}{N-1}}$$

and

$$\sigma_{\bar{x}} = \frac{\sigma}{\sqrt{N}}$$

so, substituting the estimated $\tilde{\sigma}$ for the true σ, we have

$$\tilde{\sigma}_{\bar{x}} = \frac{\tilde{\sigma}}{\sqrt{N}} = \frac{s}{1} \cdot \frac{\sqrt{N}}{\sqrt{N-1}} \cdot \frac{1}{\sqrt{N}} = \frac{s}{\sqrt{N-1}}$$

$$\tilde{\sigma}_{\bar{x}} = \frac{s}{\sqrt{N-1}}$$

By statistical means, therefore, we can estimate the standard deviation of the population with reasonable accuracy, even when the population is so large that a total survey of it is unfeasible. Two very important statements will assist us in inferring something about the population mean:

> 1. *If the population from which the samples are drawn is normal, the sampling distribution of the mean will be normal. The mean of the sampling distribution will be* μ, *the population mean, and the standard deviation of the sampling distribution will be* $\sigma/\sqrt{N}$.
>
> 2. *If the population from which the samples are drawn is not normal, the sampling distribution of the mean will become more and more normal as the number of cases in the sample gets larger and larger. The mean of the sampling distribution will be* μ, *and its standard deviation will be* $\sigma/\sqrt{N}$. [3]

Although statistics may indeed assist in the estimation of parameters in the population when the size of the population prohibits complete surveying of every individual, two important considerations must be recognized:

1. Statistical prediction and estimates are no more accurate than the fidelity with which the parameters of the sample mirror those of the total population.
2. Statistical procedures must be those that are appropriate to the character of the data being analyzed. Nothing substitutes for a careful and intelligent appraisal of the characteristics and a matching of statistical procedures to the discrete characteristics of the data.

Data and Their Characteristics

Not only do all data have certain clearly recognized characteristics, which we shall discuss in a moment, but every statistical approach has its own specific requirements in terms of the type of data appropriate for the demands of that particular statistical procedure. A glance at the table following, which charts the domain of statistical methodology, will show the necessity of knowing something of the nature of the data.

[2] Virginia L. Senders, *Measurement and Statistics* (New York: Oxford University Press), p. 467. Comments within brackets and italics are those of the author.

[3] Ibid.

Diagram Showing the Classification
and Different Types of Data

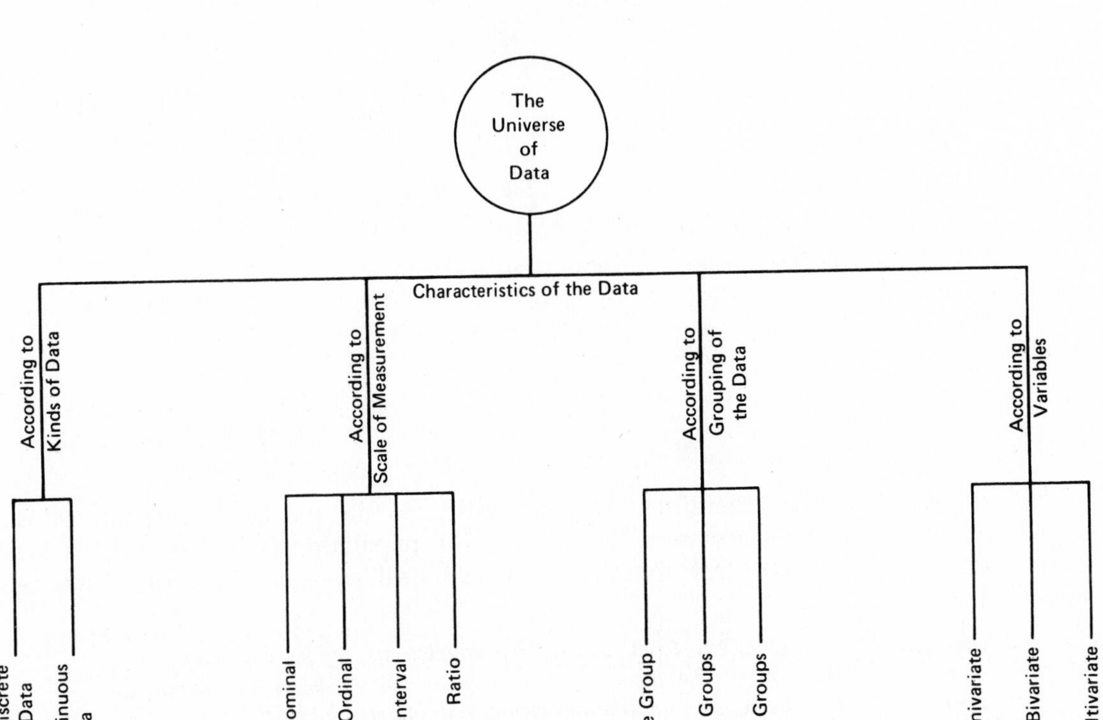

Data may assume characteristics according to four varieties of circumstance and may be classified in four ways according to

1. The type or kind of data.

   a. *Discrete data:* those data existing independently of each other. Examples: Individuals, bacteria, apples, nationalities.

   b. *Continuous data:* those data which together form a continuum. Examples: Millibars, degrees of temperature, chronological age.

2. The scale of measurement of the data.

   a. *Nominal data:* those data which have been distinguished from all other data by assigning them a name. Examples: Pine tree *(Pinus)*, supernova, inner-city children, farmers.

   b. *Ordinal data:* those data which have been assigned an order of sequence. Examples: days of the week, faculty rank in a university, inches on a foot rule, rank on a percentile scale.

   c. *Interval data:* those data which are measured in terms of difference in standard units between one object and another. Examples: A board 3 feet longer than another, an I.Q. of thirty points more than his brother's I.Q., course of alteration of 27°.

   d. *Ratio data:* data which indicate that one item is so many times as large as, as bright as, more powerful than another are measured on the ratio scale. Some statisticians indicate that the ratio scale must originate from the zero point of value. Examples: the degrees of a circular compass, a percentage scale, measurement of a vacuum in terms of torrs, voltage or amperage of electrical current.

3. The number of groups from which the data arise.

   a. *One-group data:* data which arise from a single group of subjects. This type of data is often encountered in pretest, post-test investigations of variables in one group of individuals.

   b. *Two-group data:* data which arise from a study of two groups or populations such as is the typical format in experimental studies involving a control-group and an experimental-group design.

   c. *Many-groups data:* data which arise from multigroup populations in which contrasting variables are studied against several varying group contexts.

4. Variables.

   a. *Univariate data:* data which involve merely one variable within a population. Such studies are of the simplest type and belong to the older order of research. All variables are held constant except the one being studied.

   b. *Bivariate data:* data which, as the name suggests, contain two variables. Studies such as those which measure the relative achievement in two areas, such as English and mathematics for each individual within a certain population, are of this type.

   c, *Multivariate data:* data which contain within them a number of variables which are usually isolated and studied by the multivariate analysis technique.

The terminology of statistics may be somewhat confusing. Statisticians frequently do not agree on the uniform use of either terms or symbols, and often variant formulas are given for identical operations. Consider, for example, the following. These are all formulas whose aim is to accomplish one statistical goal—to find the standard deviation:

$$SD_x = \sqrt{\frac{\sum_{i=1}^{n} x_i^2}{n}}$$

From Sheldon G. Levy, *Inferential Statistics in the Behavioral Sciences* (New York: Holt, Rinehart and Winston, Inc., 1968), p. 22.

$$S_x = \sqrt{\frac{\Sigma f(X - \bar{X})^2}{n - 1}}$$

From Allen L. Edwards, *Statistical Methods,* Second edition (New York: Holt, Rinehart and Winston, Inc., 1967), p. 33.

$$s = \sqrt{\frac{\Sigma x^2}{N}}$$

From Virginia L. Senders, *Measurement and Statistics* (New York: Oxford University Press, 1958), p. 168.

$$S_x = \sqrt{\frac{N\Sigma X^2 - (\Sigma X)^2}{N(N-1)}}$$

From Max D. Englehart, *Methods of Educational Research* (Chicago: Rand McNally and Company, 1972), p. 213.

These four formulas are *apparently* different. To the eyes of the statistician, they all say the same thing. To the bewildered mind of the student, each variant form merely adds to his confusion. Among the symbols which indicated the standard deviation, in a brief sampling of textbooks we came up with the following six variant forms from six different texts: s_x, s, S, SD, SD_x, S_x. If, therefore, you are not too adept at mathematical reasoning nor too familiar with the overall statistical terrain, it may be better for you to meet your quantitative problems with a more functional approach.

In considering the employment of any methodological techniques, but particularly with respect to managing data by means of the analytical methods afforded by statistics, it is always important to look first at the nature and characteristics of the data, and secondly at the ability of the statistical technique to handle the particular data under consideration.

The following chart, showing the classification of statistical techniques, will help you to decide in terms of the information just given with respect to the data what statistical treatment is best for the particular data that you have in hand. Any of the statistical approaches not familiar to you may be found by referring to any standard text on statistical methods.

CLASSIFICATION OF STATISTICAL TECHNIQUES AND GUIDE TO THEIR USE

Number of Groups	Type of Analysis	Purpose	Type of Data: Categorical *	Type of Data: Rank-order †	Type of Data: Measured ††
ONE	Univariate	Description	(1) One-way tables; bar, pie diagrams; modal class; conversion to proportions	(7) Array; ranking; cumulative frequencies and proportions	(13) Frequency distribution; histogram frequency polygon; ogive; percentiles; averages; measures of variability, skewness, and kurtosis
ONE	Univariate	Inference	(2) Binomial test; chi-square goodness-of-fit test	(8) Kolmogorov-Smirnov goodness-of-fit test	(14) Normal curve theory; z and t tests; chi-square variance test
ONE	Bivariate	Description	(3) Two-way tables; comparative diagrams; conditional and marginal proportions	(9) Bivariate arrays; rank-order correlation coefficient	(15) Scatter diagrams; prediction equations; Pearson correlation coefficient; standard error of estimate
ONE	Bivariate	Inference	(4) Chi-square tests of independence and experimental homogeneity	(10) Testing significance of rank-order correlation coefficient	(16) Bivariate normal distribution; testing significance of Pearson coefficient
TWO OR MORE	Univariate	Description	(5) See cell 3	(11) Comparative tables and cumulative proportions	(17) See cell 13
TWO OR MORE	Univariate	Inference	(6) See cell 4	(12) Kolmogorov-Smirnov two-sample test; Mann-Whitney U test	(18) F test of homogeneity of variance; analysis of variance

* Data that result from the application of a *nominal* scale of measurement.
† Data that result from the application of an *ordinal* scale of measurement.
††Data deriving from either an *interval or ratio* scale of measurement.
Reprinted by permission from C. M. Dayton and C. L. Stunkard, *Statistics for Problem Solving* (New York: McGraw-Hill Book Co., 1971), p. 10.

As we stated earlier, the purpose of this text is not to teach you the statistics needed for your research purposes. Rather, the purpose of this text is to try to make the tools of statistics understandable in terms of the practical methodological problems that the researcher faces.

Many a student has faced the predicament, after having had a course in statistics, of not knowing precisely "where to begin" or what statistical techniques are most appropriate for his own particular research situation. He cannot see the statistical forest for the close-up view that he has had of the individual trees. Some terms he recalls having heard discussed in class, but he has no idea under what circumstances these statistical techniques might be applied to his own research needs. Such terms as *geometric mean, harmonic mean, one-tailed test, chi square test of goodness of fit,* and *phi coefficient* are all vaguely familiar. But he does now know how to use them.

Let us recall that in Chapter 2 we simplified the statistical landscape by dividing it into four component areas.[4]

STATISTICS DESCRIBE DATA

Statistics may help you in the following four ways:

1. *It may point you to the center of the mass of data.* It may help you to find the balance point, the fulcrum. It may suggest to you what is typical. It may answer for you the question, "What is the best prediction?"

2. *It may suggest to you how diversified the data are.* It may tell you the breadth or narrowness of your facts. It may reveal how disparate and scattered are the data of your study. It may help you to answer the question, "How bad is my prediction?"

3. *It may reveal to you how closely or how distantly related your facts may be.* It can tell you how the data in one area relate to the data in another area. It can suggest to you the degree to which your prediction can be improved by knowledge of an area related to that on which your prediction is based.

4. *It may indicate to you the degree to which the facts might have occurred by mere chance, or the probability of their having been influenced by some force other than pure happenstance.* It can help you to test the "winds of fortune" and their countercurrents and to assay the force of each upon your facts. It can assist you in groping in a world beyond your facts in order to locate certain parameter landmarks: for example, the mean and the variability.

We shall be dealing with the functions that we have just stated. And we shall consider these functions in the light of a series of questions:

1. What general picture do the data convey?
2. What is the best prediction?
3. How bad is that prediction?
4. How much can prediction be improved by knowledge of another variable?
5. How does an individual compare with the group?
6. Even though we cannot see them, how can we locate parameters "out there" from the facts which we have "here and now"?
7. What is the probability that some other influence, aside from mere chance, has been at work on the data?

[4] See p. 24.

In answer to each of these questions we shall give you a chart of statistical procedures which will guide you to the specific statistical techniques which will help you to interpret your data by proper statistical means. We shall preface each chart with a brief discussion of the question which it will assist you to answer. This, then, will be the format of the next several pages: A question of broad significance, a discussion of that question in terms of its implications for the practical researcher, then a presentation of a table presenting a compilation of techniques, each classified according to the basic types of data discussed earlier in this chapter.

Look Closely at the Data

Nothing takes the place of looking carefully, inquiringly, critically—even naively—at the data. Data are the raw materials of your research effort. Inspect them carefully. Classify them according to type. Are these data nominal, ordinal, interval, or ratio? From how many angles can you view these data? In how many ways can the data be arranged and from what various viewpoints can you contemplate them?

Before considering any further statistical treatment, every researcher needs to become *thoroughly* familiar with his data. All too few are. You need to doodle with the data; try them out in every conceivable arrangement, short of a statistical formula. See what various arrangement patterns the data will fit before beginning to think in terms of means, deviations, correlations, and the like.

Data in a table look different from the way they do in a graph. They assume an added dimension when arranged in some configurational order: ascending, descending, nominal, alphabetical, and so on.

Too many beginning researchers do not take time to explore their data thoroughly. Nowhere in the whole research process is inexperience so evident as when a researcher is so impatient to get into some involved statistical treatment of his data that he rushes into statistical sophistication before he has played with his data enough to get acquainted with them and sense their nature, their configurations, their most elemental organization. Every researcher must ultimately learn that the treatment of the data starts with primitive simplicity, with open mind and ingenuity of imagination to see as much as can be seen without benefit of computational complexity.

Let's take a very simple example to see what we can do with it. Here are the reading achievement scores of eleven children: Ruth, 96; Robert, 60; Chuck, 68; Margaret, 88; Tom, 56; Mary, 92; Ralph, 64; Bill, 72; Alice, 80; Adam, 76; Jennie, 84. Now let's try as many arrangements of those scores as possible to see just how much information we can wring out of them before subjecting them to what is generally considered statistical treatment. Some of the data information may not be of any use to us in terms of our research problem. No matter. The important point is that the professional researcher discovers everything possible about the data. He leaves no stone unturned. He overlooks no lurking significances because his investigations do not seem to be uncovering big yields of meaningful information.

First, what will an alphabetical arrangement of those student's names reveal. Let's see. Remember, we're on the lookout for any meaning of whatever kind or type that we can extract from the mass of data which we presented in the preceding paragraphs.

Adam	76	Mary	92
Alice	80	Ralph	64
Bill	72	Robert	60
Chuck	68	Ruth	96
Jennie	84	Tom	56
Margaret	88		

In columnar form, the array may not be too much more meaningful, but we do have a chance to isolate individuals and grades more clearly. We have, of course, listed the data by a *nominal* arrangement pattern. Let's view this nominal arrangement in another way. We shall see these eleven boys and girls lined up in a straight row; now let's see what happens. (They are still arranged in alphabetical order.)

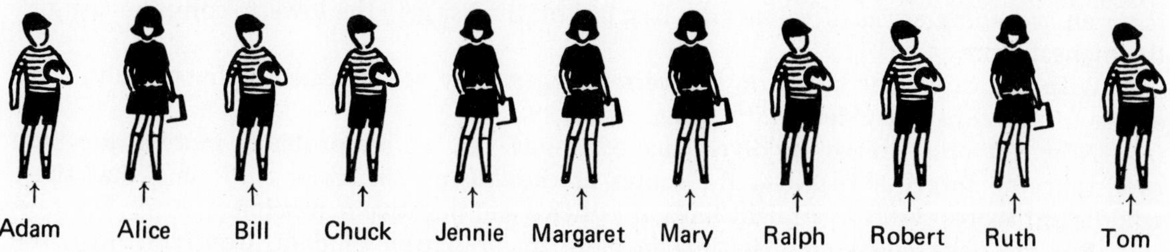

Now we can begin to discern a *ratio* pattern in these eleven children that was not so clearly apparent when we merely had names in a list. We have a symmetrical pattern, starting from either end:

one boy—one girl	1 : 1
one girl—two boys	1 : 2
two boys—three girls	2 : 3
three girls—two boys	3 : 2
two boys—one girl	2 : 1
one girl—one boy	1 : 1

Let us now rearrange the composition of the group, dividing them into the girls in one group and the boys in the other group. The data will, then, appear as follows:

Girls		Boys	
Alice	80	Adam	76
Jennie	84	Bill	72
Margaret	88	Chuck	68
Mary	92	Ralph	64
Ruth	96	Robert	60
		Tom	56

Represented graphically this diverse trend is even more striking.

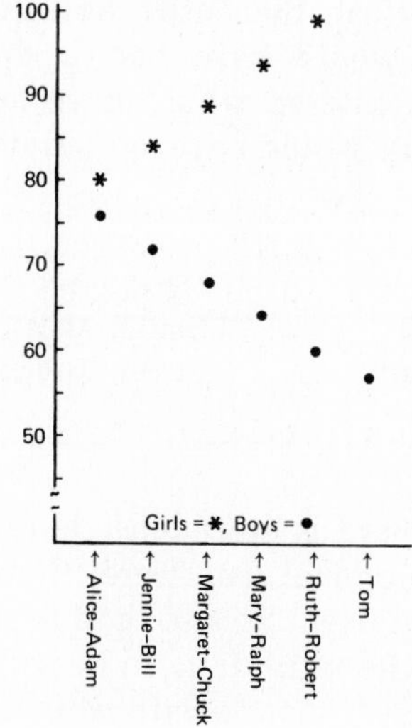

What do we see? Well, what we see may have no importance whatsoever in terms of meaning for this project, but because it represents phenomena that are active within the data, *it is important that we see it.* That is the precise point we are making: the researcher should be aware of phenomena that are active within the matrix of the data whether those phenomena are important to his purpose, as he sees it at the moment, or not.

We see that as the girls are arranged with their names in alphabetical order their scores form an *ascending* series of values: the first girl on the list gets the lowest score; the last girl, the highest score.

With the boys, the situation is reversed: when they are arranged alphabetically, their scores form a constantly *descending* series of values.

Now not only do we see divergence of trends, but we are probably more aware than ever that the intervals between the scores are *equidistant in scalar value* and that these equidistant scores result in straight lines of positive and negative regression.

But we have spent enough time in mere manipulation of data. Consider, now, the original data as we presented them; here are the reading achievement scores of eleven children: Ruth, 96; Robert, 60; Chuck, 68; Margaret, 88; Tom, 56; Mary, 92; Ralph, 64; Bill, 72; Alice, 80; Adam, 76; Jennie, 84. These scores were meaningless in the form in which they were presented. But as we began to inspect them we discovered some relationships; we became aware of certain facts that were not at first apparent. Again, we are not evaluating the importance or significance of these findings but merely pointing out that they are, indeed, inherent in the data and that competence in research begins when the researcher regards his data with such acuity that he sees all their meaning, whether that meaning is significant for his purpose or not.

As we have begun to work with the data, certain basic principles have begun to emerge which we should probably note at this point. Note that where two factors are concerned, one of them becomes dominant and governs the meaning which emerges from the data. In the inspection that we have just completed, the meaning that was derived from the data emerged primarily because we used an alphabetized list of given names of the students. By arranging the data in other ways, different meanings would probably have come to the surface. This practice suggests a new consideration and a fundamental guideline for looking at the data: *Whatever the researcher does with the data to prepare it for further inspection or interpretation will affect the meaning those data reveal, so that every researcher should be able to defend his procedure with a clear and logical rationale.*

The point is that in the preceding procedure we had no rationale whatever for arranging the data according to the given names of the children. Had we used the last names, which would have been equally logical, the entire boy-girl ratio would have gone to the wind. If we had done that, we would have had a simple one-to-one ratio, because, alphabetized, the surnames of the children would have arranged themselves in a boy-girl, boy-girl, boy-girl sequence and the list would have looked like this:

Angel, Ralph	George, Ruth	Oglethorpe, Chuck	Thomas, Margaret
Brown, Jennie	Murray, Bill	Smith, Alice	Vaughan, Adam
Daniels, Tom	Nichols, Mary	Street, Robert	

From *a research standpoint* there is no defensible rationale for using Christian name over surname or the reverse. The nominal data were, therefore, not critical to the research purpose. The ordinal data may have been. So also, and probably with more likelihood, may have been the interval, or perhaps the ratio data. In inspecting the data, therefore, we must always keep clearly in mind the *primary* goal toward which the research is directed.

Considering the interval and ratio data, however, we may have our curiosity piqued about several revelations that seem to have surfaced:

1. Why are all the scores of the girls higher than those of the boys?
2. Why are all the scores of the boys lower than the lowest score for the girls?
3. Why are the intervals between each of the scores, both for the girls and the boys, equidistant?

Looking at the situation, we may be inclined to draw a hasty conclusion, such as *Girls read better than boys.* Again, we are not looking at the data; we are not thinking correctly. Much research goes wrong at this juncture. Reading ability is a complex factor. The data do not say that girls read better than boys. What the data do say is that *on a particular test* given to eleven children—five girls and six boys—the scores of the girls were *in this particular testing situation* higher than those of the boys and that each score was precisely equidistant in terms of a point scale from every other score for both boys and girls. Furthermore, the apparent excellence of the girls over the boys was limited to test performance in those skills and aptitudes measured specifically by this test.

Honesty and precision dictate that all the conditions in the total situation be considered and that we make generalizations only as these are in strict accordance with the facts that represent the situation as it actually is. The time-operant-condition relationship is a very unstable one. The same test given to another eleven children, as similar to the first group as we can possibly pair them, the next day—or the next hour, for that matter—may produce vastly different data.

The following chart may suggest some ways in which the various categories of data may be studied.

	QUESTION
SCALE	1. What general picture do the data convey? Answer: Frequency Distributions.
NOMINAL	*Bar graphs:* only the relative heights of the bars have mathematical significance.
ORDINAL	Discrete data: *Bar graphs:* order and heights of bars have mathematical significance. Continuous data: *Histograms:* order and heights of bars have mathematical significance, and adjacent bars must be contiguous. *Frequency polygons:* horizontal distances between points are arbitrary. *Cumulative frequency and cumulative percentage graphs:* horizontal distances between points are arbitrary.
INTERVAL	Discrete data: *Bar graphs:* heights, order, widths, and spacing of bars have mathematical significance. Area inside bars is proportional to number of cases. Continuous data: *Histograms:* as for bar graphs; adjacent bars must be contiguous. *Frequency polygons:* horizontal spacing of points has mathematical significance, and area under curve is proportional to number of cases. *Cumulative frequency and cumulative percentage graphs:* horizontal spacing of points has mathematical significance. The shape of the distribution is meaningful. *Skewness* and *kurtosis* can be described. Theoretical distributions (e.g., normal) can be approximated by obtained data.
RATIO	*Bar graphs* *Histograms* *Frequency polygons* *Cum. freq. and cum. percentage graphs* *Skewness and kurtosis* *Theoretical distributions* } as for interval scale. *Transformed measurements* can be used to approximate a theoretical distribution from obtained data.

From *Measurement and Statistics: A Basic Text Emphasizing Behavioral Science,* by Virginia L. Senders.

The Matter of Means

We have elsewhere in this text[5] discussed briefly the measures of central tendency and their meaning. Senders, however, regards the matter of central tendency from a somewhat different standpoint. She considers it from the angle of optimal chance: What is the best prediction?[6]

In the normal curve, the greatest mound of data always occurs at the point of central tendency. Take an example. You are driving down the street. Suddenly you come upon a crowd of people forming in contour a human normal-curve configuration. Where the crowd is deepest, where the crest of the curve and the greatest convergence of the greatest mass of people are, that is probably where the cause lies for the massing of the crowd. It may be a street fight, an accident, a man giving away wooden nickels, but whatever the occasion, your best guess lies at the point where the human-mass median, or the mean, or the mode is likely to be located. Similarly, wherever the point of convergence of data is located, that is the most likely point to find what most probably occurs in the data. We speak of the average American, the average student, the average wage earner when we refer to those Americans, those students, those workers that we are most likely to find by a random picking of any American, student, or worker. We are considering, therefore, the matter of greatest probability, the highest incidence of correct guess. We are betting on the average as being the most likely event to occur in a broad spectrum of possibilities.

You will notice that the points of central tendency—the mean, the median, and the mode—a discussion of which is found in every textbook on research or statistics, are mentioned in the following chart. You will find also other points of central tendency that are seldom mentioned in textbooks but that the competent researcher should know about if he is to fit the statistical tool to the contour and characteristics of his data. These are the *geometric mean*, the *harmonic mean*, and the *contraharmonic mean.* We shall discuss each of these briefly.

The *geometric mean* is employed when the researcher wishes to find the point of central tendency of a growth phenomenon. We must again look at the data configuration. If the data are in the configurational pattern of a normal or "humped" curve, then the arithmetic mean is appropriate. The curve of growth is quite different, however. If growth were represented by the normal curve, an individual who begins from two cells might grow to a point of maximum development and then begin to wither away until he degenerates to a two-celled state again. But growth does not behave like that. Individuals do not grow like that, nor towns and cities, nor any other kind of growth phenomena. The growth curve for these events is the normal ogive curve, the "S" or its variants: the Gompertz curve, the modified exponential curve, or the logistic curve. Growth is a function of geometric progression. One may recall a certain Thomas Robert Malthus, an English clergyman and economist, who was the first to warn the human race of the fact of population explosion. His *An Essay on the Principle of Population as It Affects the Future Improvement of Society. . .* was the first serious discussion of the effects of growth mathematics. He contended that population, when unchecked, increases in a geometrical ratio: 2, 4, 8, 16, 32, 64, 128. . ., whereas subsistence increases only in an arithmetic ratio: 2, 4, 6, 8, 10, 12, 14. And Malthus also saw that the eventual flattening of the growth curve was determined by the arithmetic progression factor, subsistence.

Hence a growth curve appears as follows:

[5] See p. 24 and *passim.*
[6] Senders, op. cit., p. 329.

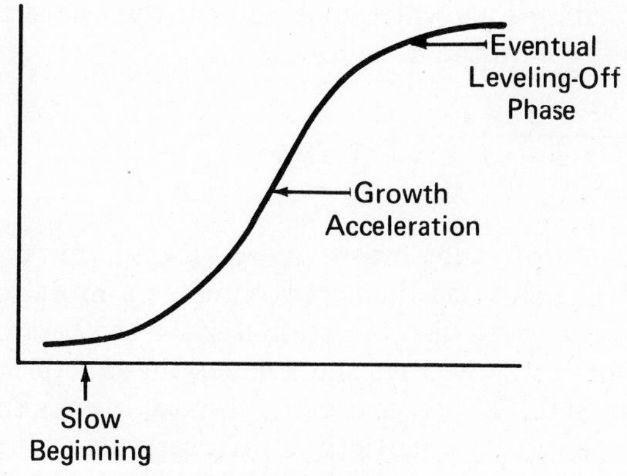

Typical Growth Curve

Biologists, physicists, ecologists, economists all encounter the growth and decay phenomena in one form or another. They all witness the same typical aspects of growth: a slow beginning—a few settlers in an uninhabited region, a few bacteria on a culture; then after a period of time, rapid expansion—the "boom" period of city growth, the rapid multiplication of microorganisms; the leveling-off period—the land becomes scarce, the city "sprawl" is contained by geographical and economic factors; or the bacteria have populated the entire culture.

Examples of situations where the application of the geometric mean is appropriate are the following:

1. In biological growth situations.
2. In population growth situations.
3. In increment of money at compound interest.
4. In averaging ratios or percentages.
5. In decay or simple decelerative situations.

We usually calculate the geometric mean in practice by the aid of logarithms.

$$\text{G.M.} = \sqrt[n]{X_1 \cdot X_2 \cdot X_3 \cdot X_4 \cdot X_5 \ldots X_n} =$$

$$\log \text{G.M.} = \frac{\log X_1 + \log X_2 + \log X_3 + \log X_4 \ldots \log X_n}{N} =$$

$$G.M. = \frac{\Sigma \log X}{N}$$

The *harmonic mean* is employed for data derived from fluctuating situations. You drive a car from one point to another. If you had a graphical record of your speed, it would resemble the profile of a series of major and minor peaks in a mountain range. Leaving the point of origin, you accelerate to a speed of 20 miles per hour for a given time; then you climb to 35 miles per hour; then, being impeded by a truck in a no-passing zone, you drop to 10 miles per hour and follow the truck. With a chance to pass it, you accelerate to 50 miles per hour. And so, fluctuating in speed, you finally reach your destination. You want to find your average speed. The harmonic mean will help you. Any fluctuating phenomenon may call for the employment of the harmonic mean. A good elementary discussion of both the geometric mean and the harmonic mean can be found in Wert,[7] and an article by

[7] J. E. Wert, *Educational Statistics* (New York: McGraw-Hill Book Company, 1938), pp. 63-80.

Ferger[8] gives advice as to conditions which may call for the use of the harmonic mean.

The harmonic mean is computed as follows:

$$\text{H.M.} = \frac{1}{\frac{1}{N}\left(\frac{1}{X_1} + \frac{1}{X_2} + \frac{1}{X_3} + \frac{1}{X_4} \cdots \frac{1}{X_n}\right)} = \frac{1}{\frac{1}{N}\Sigma\frac{1}{X}} = \frac{N}{\Sigma\frac{1}{X}}$$

One further statistic of the mean, very useful in certain instances, is the *contraharmonic mean.* It is a statistic that approximates a more realistic mean in situations where a few individuals contribute disproportionately to the total number of cases. Take an instance: a college attempts to show that the average income of its graduates, twenty years after graduation, is about $50,000 per year per graduate. It cites the income (the *arithmetic* average income!) of the men in its twentieth anniversary class. It does not reveal, however, that one of these graduates is an oil tycoon with an income of $1.75 million a year; another is a corporation president whose total income from salary, stocks, and other sources totals $875,000 per year; another is president of a land speculation and realty firm whose income is upward of $500,000 per year; and a fourth is a corporation lawyer with earnings of $375,000 per year. The rest of the graduates are white-collar "professionals" whose incomes range between $10,000 and $20,000 per year. These comprise most of the class. Badly skewed curves may alert us to consider in such instances the possibility that the contraharmonic mean may be the more appropriate measure to use in determining the point of central tendency.

We can employ the contraharmonic mean in only those instances where each X in the following formula is itself a frequency expressed in terms of a *number* of this or that: the *number* of dollars, the *number* of arrests, the *number* of accidents.

The formula for deriving the contraharmonic mean is as follows:

$$\text{C.M.} = \frac{\Sigma fX^2}{\Sigma fX}$$

Perhaps the following chart[9] will show the measures of central tendency and their several uses together with the various categories of data with which each is appropriate.

SCALE	QUESTION
	What is the best prediction? Answer: Measures of central tendency.
NOMINAL	*Mode:* the mode is the numeral representing the category with the highest frequency of occurrence. It is the prediction most likely to be right.
ORDINAL	*Mode:* as for nominal scale. Appropriate for discrete data only. *Median:* the point above and below which lie 50 per cent of the cases. It is the prediction that is just as likely to be too high as too low. It is more stable than the mode.

Table continued on next page.

---

[8] Wirth F. Ferger, *Journal of the American Statistical Association,* XXVI (March, 1931), 36-40.
[9] Senders, op. cit., p. 330. Reprinted by permission.

INTERVAL	*Mode:* as for ordinal scale. *Median:* as for ordinal scale. The prediction that minimizes average error. *Mean:* $\bar{X} = \frac{\sum X}{N}$: The prediction that makes the sum of the errors zero, and makes the sum of the squares of the errors a minimum. More stable than the median.
RATIO	*Mode:*, *Median:*, *Mean:* as for interval scale. *Geometric mean:* $GM = \sqrt[N]{X_1 \cdot X_2 \ldots \cdot X_N}$ *Harmonic mean:* $HM = \frac{N}{\sum \frac{1}{X}}$ *Contraharmonic mean:* $CM = \frac{\sum fX^2}{\sum fX}$ (Geometric, harmonic and contraharmonic means:) Statistics for special situations.

From *Measurement and Statistics: A Basic Text Emphasizing Behavioral Science,* by Virginia L. Senders. Copyright © 1958 by Oxford University Press, Inc. Reprinted by permission.

The Message of Curves and Deviations

We have just been discussing the question of "What is the best guess?" Now we turn to the opposite question, "What are the worst odds?" Both questions are important, especially for the researcher who is willing to look at the data impartially and dispassionately. Some researchers would like to look at the first question and forget the latter one. If you feel like that, it means that you need to cultivate a more unemotional response to the cold fact.

If, as we have just been discussing, the probability index of the correct guess rises with the tendency of the data to cluster about the point of central tendency, then it is, conversely, true that the farther the data are dispersed from the central pivotal axis, the greater the margin of predictive error becomes. Consider these two curves:

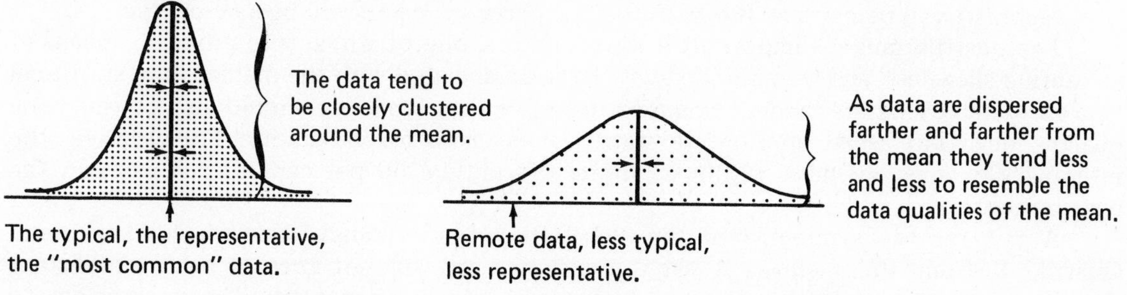
The data tend to be closely clustered around the mean.
The typical, the representative, the "most common" data.
As data are dispersed farther and farther from the mean they tend less and less to resemble the data qualities of the mean.
Remote data, less typical, less representative.

The data are more similar when they cluster about the mean. Scatter them and they lose some of their unity of character; they are more diverse in nature. As they recede from the mean, they lose more and more of the quality which makes them typical. It is easy for us to talk about one, two, or three standard deviations from the mean. That type of language keeps everything impersonal, faceless. But as there is a difference in atmosphere of living, of culture, of life itself as one goes further and further from a metropolitan center, so data change in complexion as they recede into the second and third deviations from the mean.

Also a high, peaked curve—*leptokurtic*, as it is called—is an indication of a data accumulation which evidences more *homogeneity* than a low, flat, spreading curve—*platykurtic*, as this type is called—which hints at greater *heterogeneity* within the mass of data.

Statistics and surveying are somewhat similar. Each needs a point of origin from which to make further measurements. With surveying it is a triangulation point; with statistics it is one of the parameters of the data, usually the mean, which establishes the precise fulcrum point for the mass of the data. If we can establish the mean, then from it we can initiate further measurements of the data—the only purpose of which is to learn more about the data, discern their characteristics, identify their quality.

It is important to see the parameters of the data, both their centrality and their spread. Only by so assessing quantitatively, only by seeing the data in terms of number values, can the researcher know anything about those data he has amassed. Like a cartographer charting an unknown land, the researcher must "chart" his data, appreciate the meaning of the "peaks and valleys," and survey the expansiveness or narrowness of their spread. Such information aids greatly in the later process of interpreting the data. It is important to review the measures of spread, or variability, that we have already considered in earlier pages. There are several statistical measures to assist us in describing the dispersion of the data from the mean or from the median.

Perhaps the most unrefined measure is the *range*. The range merely measures the over-all spread of the data from its lowest to its highest value. This is the entire data-value spectrum. (Reference to p. 27 will illustrate the range.) The range has, however, limited usefulness as a measure of dispersion and may even be misleading if the extreme upper and lower limits are inordinately out of line with the other values of the series. Take an example. The following is the range of the number of children in six families: 18, 6, 5, 4, 3, 0. Now we might say that the families range from a childless couple to a family of eighteen children. But drop off the extremes of the array and the situation is much more realistic and typical when we say that two thirds of the families surveyed had from three to six children.

The next measure of dispersion is the *quartile deviation*. The quartile deviation divides the data into four equal parts. Quartile 1 will lie at a point where 25 per cent of the items lie within the first quadrant of the data. Quartile 2 will divide the items into two equal parts and will be identical with the median. Quartile 3 will lie at a point where 75 per cent of the values are below it.

If, instead of dividing the data into four equal parts, we divide it into ten equal parts, then each part will be a *decile;* if into 100 equal parts, each part will be a *percentile.*

The quartile range is important in several ways, one of which is to provide a means of measuring skewness, and because the quartiles are associated with the median, any statistical approach employing the median as a measure of central tendency should also consider the quartile deviation as an appropriate statistical measure for variability. Furthermore, the interquartile range includes within its limits the middle 50 per cent of the cases in the distribution.

A test for the symmetry of the distribution is the equidistance of Quartile 1 and Quartile 3 from the median. A skewed distribution will not present such equidistant symmetry. A *measure of skewness* takes advantage of this asymmetry. The measure gives a value of zero when Quartile 1 and Quartile 3 are equidistant from the median. The equation, with a lower limit of 0 and an upper limit of 1, may be stated as follows:[10]

$$Sk_q = \frac{Q_3 + Q_1 - 2Md}{Q_3 - Q_1}$$

[10] William A. Neiswanger, *Elementary Statistical Methods,* Revised Edition (New York: Macmillan Publishing Co., Inc., 1956).

We shall have more to say about measures of skewness when we discuss the matter of the standard deviation. For all practical purposes one may consider this index of skewness as comparable to a percentage index.

If we measure the dispersion of the data to the right and to the left of the mean and sum the deviations disregarding the algebraic signs, dividing the summed differences by the number of cases, we get the *average deviation.* The equation for the average deviation is

$$AD = \frac{\Sigma |x|}{N}$$

where $|x| = X - \overline{X}$, disregarding algebraic signs.

We can, of course, take the average deviation around any point of central tendency. When calculated from the median, the average deviation is less than when taken from any other point of central tendency. The equation is

$$AD_{mdn} = \frac{\Sigma (x - M_{dn})}{N}$$

The average deviation is very readily understood and for that reason has some merit. It is acceptable when no further statistical procedure is contemplated. It is a little-used value, however, and the standard deviation and variance have largely supplanted it.

The *standard deviation* is the standard measure of variability in most statistical operations. It is an expression of variability from the arithmetic mean and it is the foundation for modern statistical practice. We have discussed the several forms of its equation on p. 121.

To understand the reason for using the standard deviation, we must recall what happens numerically when we find the average deviation, which we have just been discussing. In finding the average deviation, as we subtract all the deviations of lesser value than the mean which lie on the normal curve distribution to the left of the mean, all of them become *negative* values. Thus, the values to the left of the mean (which are all negative) and those to the right of the mean (which are all positive) tend in summation to cancel out each other. This is because these values are linear. Practically, we can change this situation by ignoring it, which we suggested that you do when finding the average deviation. But this is rather dubious mathematical ethics. It is neither sound mathematics nor sound statistics to ignore what you do not like. We can, however, change negatives to positives in a perfectly acceptable mathematical manner. In algebra, if we multiply a negative value by itself, it becomes positive. Thus, by squaring all negative deviations they become positive: $-2^2 = (-2)(-2) = +4$. And then, $\sqrt{+4} = +2$. We have changed linear numbers to square numbers and then taken the square root of the square number. By changing all the linear numbers to square numbers and then summing the squared values and dividing this summation by the *number of deviation values* and, finally, taking the square root of the quotient, we have gone full circle mathematically and are back again to an average of the deviations from the mean in which all the values, regardless of what sign they bore originally, have been transformed to positive integers. It is important to note that we divide the summed squared deviations (not the summed deviations, squared!) by the total number of deviations from the mean. Finally, we take the square root of the resultant quotient, which, in turn, will give us the standard deviation. In terms of an equation, the standard deviation is

$$s = \sqrt{\frac{\Sigma x^2}{N}}$$

When we come to analyzing the data, we shall probably need another statistic based on the standard deviation. This is the statistic known as the *variance.* The variance is simply the standard deviation squared.

$$s^2 = \frac{\Sigma x^2}{N}$$

In discussing the matter of the quartile deviation, we presented a method of determining skewness in the normal distribution. We suggested at that point that another method of determining the degree of skewness in the population would be presented after we had discussed the standard deviation. In this latter method, devised by Karl Pearson, we make use of the major parameters of the normal distribution: the mean, the median, and the standard deviation. It is sometimes referred to as the *Pearsonian measure of skewness.*

The formula for the coefficient of skewness is

$$Sk = \frac{3(\overline{X} - Md)}{s}$$

where

$\overline{X}$ = the arithmetic mean
Md = the median
s = the standard deviation

For normal distributions the coefficient value is 0. It varies ±3, but a coefficient in excess of ±1 is rather unusual.

These measures of central tendency, dispersion, and skewness should provide us with sufficient means of "seeing" through the eyes of statistical analysis what the mass of data appears to be. For we have been considering data, to this point, *en masse,* looking at the parameters which are indigenous to that mass: where the center of it lies; how far it spreads; whether that spread shows distortion or skewness, as we have termed it. We have piled up, as it were, all the data and looked for the point where all those data balanced; and from that point of mass balance we have investigated ways in which we should describe the entire spread of those data and measure their deviation from the point of data mass equilibrium.

We come now to a closer look at those data. But before proceeding let us summarize in the following table what we have been discussing thus far.

	QUESTION
SCALE	What are the worst odds? Answer: Measures of dispersion.
NOMINAL	Except for verbal descriptions ("longer than") this category is inappropriate for indicating measures of dispersion.
ORDINAL	Range: $X_{max} - X_{min} + 1$. Unstable. Interquartile range: 75th percentile – 25th percentile. Semi-quartile range, Q. Half of interquartile range. Other interpercentile ranges.

Table continued on next page

INTERVAL	Range, quartile ranges, as for ordinal scale *Average deviation: AD:* $AD = \frac{\Sigma\lvert x\rvert}{N}$ *Standard deviation,* s, *and variance,* s^2: $s = \sqrt{\frac{\Sigma x^2}{N}}$ $s^2 = \frac{\Sigma x^2}{N}$ More useful in later computations than *AD.*
RATIO	Various ranges, *AD*, s *and* s^2 } as for interval scale. *Coefficient of variation, V:* $V = \frac{100s}{\bar{X}}$ Expresses variability in terms of absolute size of measured objects.

From *Measurement and Statistics: A Basic Text Emphasizing Behavioral Science,* by Virginia L. Senders. Copyright © 1958 by Oxford University Press, Inc. Reprinted by permission.

So that we do not lose perspective, we should remind ourselves at midpoint in discussing the analytical survey method that this is all merely statistical manipulation of the data. It is not research, for research demands interpretation of the data. In finding means, medians, quartiles, standard deviations, and the like, we have not interpreted the data; we have not told what the data mean in terms of the problem. We have merely tried to *see what the data looked like!* After we know what the data are and what their basic nature is, we can attempt to say what those data mean. Then we can descry whether there are forces acting upon those data which are the real culprits, causing the data to behave as they do. For example, apropos of skewness, if we toss a die 100 times and come up with a skewed distribution of fifty-three times the die comes up 5, we might suspect that the statistic is merely an *indication* that we are playing with a loaded die. But let us consider other ways of analyzing the data.

Measuring Relationships

So far we have been discussing unilateral factors: points of convergence of data dynamics, the place within the data mass which a scientist might call the data "center of gravity," the fulcrum, the measure of central tendency. We have also been discussing data spread: again, what the scientist may think of in terms of data "density" or, contrariwise, as data dispersion. This we have called deviation or variance. But the point is that these characteristics of the data are one-dimensional.

Think of a datum as you think of an atom. Within the atom lies a whole organization of forces: the central proton, the kinetic electrons, the mesons, the neutrons, the neutrinos. All of these forces, each dynamic within itself, each interacting within the structure, causes each atom to be a complex, dynamic structure. The same is true of data. Within the data are forces, dynamics, measurable trends which, when discovered and expressed as one "force" in relation to another "force," make the data more meaningful and significant.

Take, for example, growth force. This dynamic which is inherent in all living things may be expressed in terms of human beings in so many units of linear measure at some particular point in time. Jane is six years old and is 3 feet, 10 inches tall. The feet and inches are the linear measure which expresses one aspect of the growth force. But within those same data are other "dimensions" to the growth force. Another dynamic of the same data is expressed in terms of corporeal mass pulled by the force of gravity. Jane weighs so much at the particular time when she is so tall. She should weigh approximately 46 pounds.

Now we can construct a chart with one axis representing height and the other axis representing weight in terms of standard units of inches and pounds. On such a grid we can plot Jane's height and weight in terms of each other and represent both forces by a single point. Suppose we had 100 Janes. Some of them would be taller; some, shorter; some weigh more; some, less. Nevertheless, each one could be assigned a single point which would represent her composite height-weight data.

What we have been doing, of course, is correlating two variables in terms of each other. We should remember, however, that as these factors are represented on a grid, convention suggests that the independent variable be plotted along the horizontal axis; the dependent variable along the vertical axis. The independent variable is the one upon which the variations of the dependent variable seem to depend. When neither factor can be said to be the cause of or dependent upon the other, then the *variable to be predicted* should be plotted on the *Y* axis.

On pp. 28–31, we have discussed the subject of correlation. We will not, therefore, repeat here any of the discussion on those pages. We shall present here, however, a digest of the various correlational procedures which are broad enough in spectrum to cover most of the needs of the normal researcher. You will appreciate immediately upon studying the accompanying tabular digest that *the nature of the data governs the correlational procedure employed.* All too many would-be researchers begin by deciding, for instance, that they will use a Pearsonian coefficient of correlation for showing a relationship between two factors when, in fact, this correlational technique may be entirely inappropriate to the nature of the data they have at hand. The cardinal rule is, therefore: *look at the data! Determine their nature; scrutinize their quality, then select the appropriate correlational technique suited to the type of data with which you are working.*

In the following table we have characterized the several correlational techniques by the type of data required for each variable. Having taken you thus far, the rest is merely a matter of some further searching among a broad range of statistical texts for appropriate formulas and relevant discussions as to the specific application and the discrete characteristics of each statistical approach. We shall not attempt to go further into the statistical realm of correlational concerns.

Digest of Correlational Techniques

Correlational Technique	Symbol	Variable Characteristic X	Variable Characteristic Y	Comment
Parametric Correlational Techniques				
Pearson product moment correlation	r	Continuous	Continuous	The most commonly used coefficient.
Biserial correlation	r_b	Continuous	Continuous, but forced into an artificial dichotomy	Much used in item analysis. An array of grades in which some are "pass," others "fail" is an artificial dichotomy.
Point biserial correlation	r_{pb}	Continuous	True dichotomy	Example: heights and weights of boys and girls.
Tetrachoric correlation	r_t	Artificial dichotomy	Artificial dichotomy	Less reliable than Pearson r. Do not use with nominal or ordinal data.

Digest of Correlation Techniques

Correlational Technique	Symbol	Variable Characteristic X	Y	Comment
		Parametric Correlational Techniques		
The phi coefficient (fourfold coefficient)	Φ	True dichotomy	True dichotomy	Statistic is related to χ^2. Assumes variable can have values of only +1 or -1.
Widespread biserial correlation	r_{wbis}	Widespread artificial dichotomy	Continuous	Used when interested in cases at extremes of dichotomized variable.
The triserial correlation	r_{tri}	Continuous	Trichotomy	Developed by N. Jaspen. See *Psychometrika*, 1946, 11, 23-30.
Correlation ratio	η	Continuous	Continuous	Nonlinear relationship between variables. Scattergram necessary to determine linearity.
		Nonparametric Correlational Techniques		
Spearman rank-order correlation (Rank difference correlation)	ρ	Ranks	Ranks	Similar to the Pearson *r*. Particularly well suited to situations of 25-30 cases.
Kendall's coefficient of concordance	W	Used with three or more sets of ranks		Value of W varies between 0 = no agreement to 1 = perfect agreement.
Kendall's tau-correlation between ranks	τ	Ranks	Ranks	Can be used wherever ρ is appropriate but preferable to ρ when number is less than 10.
Contingency coefficient	C	Two or more categories	Two or more categories	Similar to r_t. Closely related to χ^2. Correlations similar to Pearson *r* with large sample and at least five categories for each variable.
		Special Correlational Techniques		
Partial correlation	$r_{12.3}$	Correlational method involving more than two variables.		The partial *r* is used when the relationship between two variables is influenced by a third variable.
Multiple correlation	$R_{1.234}$	One variable (criterion) vs. many variables.		Employed where two or more variables are used to predict a single variable. In the symbol subscript $R_{1.234\ldots n}$ the subscript 1 stands for the criterion variable; the 234 for the predictor variables.

INFERENTIAL STATISTICS

Leaving what many consider to come within the bailiwick of descriptive statistics, we shall turn now to the role of inferential statistics as it relates to the needs of the researcher. Inferential statistics has, of course, two principal functions:

1. To predict or estimate a population parameter from a random, or representative, sample.
2. To test *statistically based* hypotheses.

Prediction: One of the Roles of Inferential Statistics

Prediction is an area of statistics with many ramifications. We cannot venture too far into its territory. Again, statistical texts will provide you with this information. We shall, however, comment briefly concerning some general underlying concepts and principles.

Earlier we discussed prediction or estimation of values in terms of measures of central tendency. Such estimates were in relation to the normalcy of the individual to the group. The fellow who huddled closest to the pole which marked the midpoint of the distribution was most typical, more nearly "average" than those who were positioned further out in the distributional "boondocks."[11] You could take a chance in prediction that the pole-hugger type would be in the majority in any normal distribution. Because of this fact, most school administrators gamble that the great majority of students will be C students—merely "average."

But we conditioned our estimate of "goodness-of-guess" by considering it in contrast with "badness-of-guess" as indicated by the degree of dispersion or variation within the distributional whole. We also considered the predictional possibilities of the line of regression. If at age six a child is in first grade; at seven, in second grade; at eight, in third grade; at nine, in fourth grade—would we not be reasonable in estimating that this same child would graduate from high school at the twelfth grade at age eighteen, and should he go on to a four-year college, graduate from there at age twenty-two? That is prediction, or estimation, but it is again individual in nature, whether it is one person, one trait, one characteristic, or whatever. We are still in the unicorrelational ballpark.

These estimating techniques are not, however, those that we usually consider within the realm of inferential statistics. Inferential statistics is more concerned with estimating *population parameters* from *sample statistics.*[12] The population estimates that we commonly attempt to make are estimates of *parameters* with respect to frequency distributions or parts thereof, estimates with respect to the μ (central tendency of the population), the σ (variability of the population), or the proportion or probability, the P, versus the $\overline{X}$, the s and the p, respectively.

To understand precisely what we mean by estimation, let us take a simple situation. Joe is a production manager of a manufacturing corporation. He has a sample lot of connecting-rod pins. These pins fit snugly into assembly units, permitting the units to swivel within a given arc. The diameter of the pins is critical. If it is too small, the assembly unit will wobble in turning; if too large, the assembly will stick and refuse to move. Joe has received a number of complaints from customers that the pins are faulty. He wishes to estimate on the basis of the sample, how many of the units may have to be recalled for replacement of pins. The sample is presumably random and representative. From this

[11] See p. 131.

[12] The student should review carefully the distinction between a *parameter* and a *statistic.* See p. 117.

sample, Joe wishes to know relative to the hundreds of thousands of pins that have been assembled and sold on the market.

1. How many of them are within acceptable tolerance limits.
2. How widely they vary in diameter measurement.
3. What proportion of the pins produced will be acceptable in the assemblies already marketed.

His problem is to judge population parameters on the basis of the sample statistics. From the sample he can estimate the mean, the variation, and the proportion of acceptance within the population universe. These are the values that we gave as the μ, the σ, and the P.

Certain basic assumptions underlie all prediction procedures. Estimates of whatever kind assume that the sample is random and representative of the total population. Only by their being so can we have any congruity between the sample and the population universe from which the sample was chosen and, conversely, toward which the prediction will be made. The sample ideally should be a miniature microcosm of the much greater universe of the population. The more this is so, the greater the predictive accuracy of the sample. When such a situation exists, we then have statistical techniques to accomplish a projection from the statistic of the sample to the corresponding parameter of the population: from the sample mean to the population mean, from the sample variability to the population variability, from the sample probability to the population probability. Whatever we can determine with respect to a statistic of the sample, we can estimate with respect to a parameter of the population.

Point vs. Interval Estimates

In making estimates of population parameters from sample statistics, we can make estimates of two types: (1) *point estimates* and (2) *interval estimates.* A *point estimate* is a single statistic which is taken as the best indication of the corresponding population parameter. We have discussed (on pp. 118–119) the variability within samples—the error of the means of random samples from the true mean of the total population. This variability we must recognize and take into account when making any kind of estimate, particularly point estimates, where we are shooting, in fact, for a statistical "bull's-eye."

Point estimates do not leave us with any freedom, should the population parameter value vary from the sample statistic value, which it almost invariably does. Although point estimates have the virtue of being precise, precision has its own price; and the price for precision is that the point estimate will generally not exactly correspond with the true parametric value.

At best, an estimate is a statistical flight into the unknown. The prediction of population parameters is at best a matter of dead reckoning. It takes its sightings from a randomly selected sample and, then, with what accuracy it may, it takes into account the other conditioning factors, and on the basis of these contingencies makes its prediction. We have seen earlier (p. 119) that the accuracy in estimating the population mean depends upon (1) the size of the sample and (2) the degree of its variability.

In the example of the connecting-rod pins, had we been told that the company produced 500,000 pins, of which Joe had a sample of 1,000 with a given mean diameter and a standard deviation of .05 inch, we then would have been able to have made a parametric estimate. Although the values we had predicted may not have been precisely accurate for the total production of connecting pins, they would certainly have been better than nothing.

So much for point estimation. A much more comfortable procedure is the *interval estimate* of parameters. In this type of prediction, we specify a band within whose limits we estimate that practically all the values will lie. Such a band is commonly called the *confidence interval* because we are "confident" that between the delimitation values we have set 95 per cent of all the data values will be found. At times, depending upon the research refinement that we seek, we may set the limit at 99 per cent of confidence. Statisticians usually consider these two values as standard for confidence levels. Sometimes we phrase the same concept in terms of *level of significance.* This is looking at the concept of the confidence interval precisely in reverse.

Any factor which causes more than a 1 per cent or, in the case of a 95 per cent confidence limit, a 5 per cent variability in the data values is considered to be the result of something other than mere chance.[13] We speak of a factor as being *statistically significant* at the 5 per cent level or at the 1 per cent level of significance. In brief, what this means is that we permit a certain narrow margin of variance which we deem to be natural and the result of pure chance. Any variation *within* this statistically permissible band is not considered to be significant. Whatever exceeds the set limits, however, is considered to be the result of some determinative factor other than that of natural fortuitousness, and so the influence is considered to be a significant one. The term *significant* in the statistical sense in which we have been using it is very close to its pure etymological meaning, namely, "giving a signal" that something is operating below the surface of the statistic that needs further investigation.

We have said enough about estimation for you to appreciate its importance. To venture further would get us involved in a statistical methodology and specific operational procedures. That is not the province of this text. (For those who wish a guide to such procedures we present the following Summary Table of Point and Interval Estimates of Parameters.) The student must consult the texts of the statisticians for these matters.

There still remains the last of the functions of inferential statistics in the analytical survey method, namely, the *testing of hypotheses,* to which we now turn.

The Testing of Hypotheses

We have indicated that the province of inferential statistics was twofold: (1) to predict or estimate a population parameter from a sample statistic and (2) to test statistically based hypotheses. We have discussed the first of these functions. The present discussion is to investigate the second: the testing of statistically based hypotheses. At the very outset we should clarify the matter of terminology. The term *hypothesis* can bewilder you hopelessly unless you understand that it has two entirely different meanings in the literature of research.

The first of these two meanings restricts the word *hypothesis* to a *research-problem-oriented hypothesis.* On the other hand, the second usage of the term is limited to a *statistically oriented hypothesis.* In the first meaning, a hypothesis exists because the research problem, or the subproblems issuing from it, arouse a curiosity in the researcher's mind which, in turn, results in the positing of a *tentative* guess relative to the resolution of the problematic situation. Refer again to the example of the perplexed motorist which was given in the first chapter.[14] The hypothesis is, therefore, a reasonable conjecture, or an educated guess. Its purpose is a very practical one: it provides a tentative objective, an operational bull's-eye, a logical construct which helps the researcher look for the data. Based on the conclusions to which the data force him, the researcher must either confirm or deny the hypothesis that he has posited.

[13] See comment with reference to the die on p. 135.

[14] See pp. 6–7.

A SUMMARY TABLE OF POINT AND INTERVAL ESTIMATES OF PARAMETERS

SCALE	KIND OF MEASURE			
	Frequency distributions or parts thereof	Central Tendency	Variability	Correlation
NOMINAL	$\tilde{P} = p$ $\quad \sigma_p = \sqrt{PQ/N}$ $\frac{p - P}{\sigma_p}$ is normally distributed when $NP \geqslant 5$. Confidence bands for estimating P from p. Chi-square test for correspondence of obtained and expected frequency distributions.		$\tilde{H} = \hat{H} + 1.3863N$	$\tilde{T} = \hat{T} - \frac{(r-1)(k-1)}{1.3863N}$
ORDINAL	Confidence interval for any population percentile made in terms of sample percentiles. Kolmogorov-Smirnov confidence band for entire cumulative percentage histogram.	$\widetilde{\text{Mdn}}_{pop} = \text{Mdn}$ Confidence intervals in terms of sample percentiles.	Confidence intervals for Q_1 and Q_3 in terms of sample percentiles.	
INTERVAL AND RATIO	Chi-square and Kolmogorov-Smirnov tests can be used to determine goodness of fit of any theoretical distribution —e.g., normal.	$\tilde{\mu} = \bar{X}$, $\tilde{\sigma}_{\bar{X}} = s/\sqrt{N-1}$ $\frac{\bar{X} - \mu}{\tilde{\sigma}_{\bar{X}}}$ has t-distribution for samples from normal populations. For small samples from nonnormal populations, use Tchebychev's Inequality. Same principles for Mdn., but $\tilde{\sigma}_{Mdn} = 1.253\tilde{\sigma}_{\bar{X}}$.	$\tilde{\sigma}^2 = s^2\left(\frac{N}{N-1}\right)$ For samples from normal populations, Ns^2 has chi-square distribution with $N - 1$ degrees of freedom.	Confidence bands for estimating ρ from r. $z_r = 1.1513 \log_{10} \frac{1+r}{1-r}$ $(z_r - z_\rho)(\sqrt{N-3})$ has unit normal distribution if population is normal bivariate.

From *Measurement and Statistics: A Basic Text Emphasizing Behavioral Science*, by Virginia L. Senders. Copyright ©1958 by Oxford University Press, Inc. Reprinted by permission. (Modified at the direction of the author.)

In a sense, a problem-oriented hypothesis in research is comparable to a scaffold in construction engineering. Each has its purpose as a function of an ongoing operation: in the case of the hypothesis, it is the pursuit of the data which when inspected and interpreted will help in the solution of the problem being researched; in the case of the scaffold it is the erection of an architectural structure. The completion of the project makes both the hypothesis and the scaffold of no further use. Both are vitally necessary, though intermediary functionaries whose sole purpose is to facilitate the achievement of the ultimate goal.

When, however, one comes across the phrase *tests of hypotheses*, he is talking about an entirely different matter. Here the word *hypothesis* refers to a statistically based hypothesis, commonly known as the *null hypothesis*. The null hypothesis postulates that there is no *statistically* significant difference between phenomena which occur by pure chance and the statistically evaluated behavior of the data as they have been observed by the researcher in a survey or an experimental research design. If a difference *does* occur and the magnitude of that difference is such as to exceed the possibility of its having been caused by random error or pure chance, then we conclude that some intervening variable aside from the fortuitousness of nature is energizing the data and, in consequence, we reject the null hypothesis. It is this comparison of observed data with the expected results of normative values that we call testing the hypothesis, or perhaps, more accurately, testing the null hypothesis.

What is frequently confusing to the uninitiated researcher is that this test is nothing more than a statistical comparison of the data from two situations. One of these we consider mathematically "ideal" because it conforms to the parameters of the normal distribution. The data of the second situation we derive from life. To these latter data we apply certain statistical processes to determine whether their calculated values diverge from the mathematical ideal value enough to reject the null hypothesis. It is important to keep clearly in mind, therefore, the differentiation between the two types of hypotheses. You will usually find the null hypothesis represented in the literature by the symbol H_o.

We should also look at hypothesis testing from another point of view. From the interpretation that we have given to the word *research* early in these pages,[15] namely, "a systematic quest for undiscovered truth," through the techniques of the scientific method, the testing of the null hypothesis does not contribute much to the fulfillment of this basic aim of pure research. Also, we have indicated that statistics is merely a "tool of research," whose function in the entire research process is merely to take the data, quantify them, and inspect them in their quantified form so that, having been converted into the language of mathematics, they may reply to the researcher in terms of quantitative values and, by so doing, give some indication of the characteristics of the data and the dynamics which affect them which cannot be explored in any other manner. Statistics has its function, but that function is medial: to inspect the data by means of a tool of research whose facility is that of revealing aspects of the data of which we might not otherwise be aware. Statistics leaves us frequently with merely an indication that factors or forces either are or are not present which may be influencing the data.

In the last analysis, the testing of the null hypothesis merely confirms or denies the deeper presence of "something" that is working within the data. It is this all-important something that the genuine researcher seeks to identify and evaluate. To stop with a mere indication that "something" is there which "accounts for a significant difference" between one set of data and another set of data is to settle for a ghost, and research is not a systematic quest for ghosts. It is a search for Truth.

Statistical hypothesis testing is a decision theory and, as such, it has value for those who must make decisions on the basis of the statistical characteristics of samples. But to confuse statistical hypothesis testing with the aims of pure, basic research is imprecise thinking. For the beginning researcher the deceptiveness of the situation lies in the insinuation, through confusingly similar terminology. To discover that certain factors within the system are "statistically significant"—which statistical significance is itself established by hypothesis testing—and to think that this is tantamount to interpreting the data is to have lost sight of the meaning of research. Research and statistics are vastly different and discrete. Merely to show one set of data different in mathematical values from another set of data demonstrates that fact and nothing else. It merely proclaims statistical incongruity between two sets of data. It does not extract from those data any meaning; it does not isolate the causes that account for the statistically significant difference; it does not deal with the meaning of the data nor resolve any problem or subproblem related to the research; it does not answer *any* question except whether one value within one set of data exceeds another value within a second set of data beyond a given statistical tolerance point.

What we are saying here is what every researcher must ultimately learn—to call a spade a spade. This is not to deprecate the role or function of the science of statistics; it is merely

[15] See p. 9.

to bring both statistics and research into proper focus. They are two entirely different disciplines with different functions and separate purposes.

Every researcher must ultimately develop an intellectual acuity that looks with honest, unprejudiced candor at his procedures and at his results. With clear vision, he must appraise them intrinsically for their precise worth and character. He must learn to think without confusion clearly in terms of exactly what it is that he has done. If what he has done is mere statistical manipulation of the data so that he derives nothing more than a numerical index of a relationship or an index of a dynamic between various sets of data, then he has done merely that and nothing more. If, on the other hand, he has indeed inspected those data intently and tested them by every means at his command and has, from such procedures, derived *directly from the data* a set of underlying causes and meaningful facts, then he has *interpreted* those data and derived from them a new insight that brings him closer to the Realm of Truth. That is quite different from running the data through a statistical operation. *The one process ends in a decimal value; the other ends in insight into the meaning of the facts.* That is the critical difference between analytical statistics per se and the analytical survey method of research. The latter includes the former, but they should never be confused as to which is which.

NONPARAMETRIC STATISTICS

Before we leave the discussion of the analytical survey method, we should present briefly the nonparametric statistical methods of dealing with certain types of data. Thus far, we have been subscribing to an assumption: that all populations and the samples drawn from them demonstrate certain parameters. We have assumed that the mean and the standard deviation were the common attributes of all data. This is not universally so. Not all data are parametric in character. Nature does not invariably behave as a Gaussian curve. Take a page of print. We have a binary world. No normal distribution there. Any given point on the page is either black or white. Human beings are either male or female, alive or dead. As we have the world of the bell-shaped curve, so also do we have the world of the sharp dichotomy: the world of the either/or.

Sometimes also the data world looks more like a stairway than a bell-shaped curve; the data occur at graduated elevations—data ranked above or below data in a well-escalated arrangement. Take a graduating class. When each student is ranked in academic subjects, John ranks first in mathematics and fifteenth in English. Other students have individual rankings up and down the academic staircase. To study a ranked situation of this kind, a statistical system based upon the assumption of normal distributions, of means, and of standard deviations is simply not applicable.

Data with such characteristics as we have just been describing demand a statistical methodology which will recognize the particular characteristics of the data and provide specialized approaches which will take these singular characteristics into account. Such a methodology is found in the *nonparametric statistical techniques.* The system of nonparametric statistics makes no assertions about parameters nor about the form of the distribution underlying the data. As a general rule, nonparametric statistics are less powerful than the parametric techniques. By less powerful, we mean that, in general, they require larger samples in order to yield the same level of significance. They also are less likely to reject the null hypothesis when it should be rejected, nor do nonparametric techniques differentiate between groups as sensitively as do the parametric methods.

The Principal Nonparametric Techniques

The Chi Square Test. Perhaps the most commonly used nonparametric test is the *chi square* (χ^2) *test.* It is almost invariably used in causal comparative studies. We employ χ^2

also in instances where we have a comparison between observed and theoretical frequencies, or in testing the mathematical fit of a frequency curve to an observed frequency distribution. Chi square is applicable when we have two variables from independent samples, each of which is categorized in two ways. Chi square is also valuable in analyzing data that are expressed as frequencies rather than as measurements. Of all the nonparametric tools, χ^2 is probably the most important.

There are, however, other nonparametric approaches which have specialized application and although we cannot go into a discussion of these in detail, we can list the principal ones with brief comments as to their significance and usual applications.

The Mann-Whitney U-test. The Mann-Whitney *U*-test in nonparametric statistics is the counterpart of the *t*-test in parametric measurements. It may find use in determining whether the medians of two independent samples differ from each other to a significant degree.

The Wilcoxon Matched Pairs, Signed-Rank Test. The Wilcoxon matched pairs, signed-rank test is employed to determine whether two samples differ from each other to a significant degree when there is a relationship between the samples.

The Wilcoxon Rank Sum Test. The Wilcoxon rank sum test may be used in those nonparametric situations where measures are expressed as ranked data in order to test the hypothesis that the samples are from a common population whose distribution of the measures is the same as that of the samples.

The Kolmogorov-Smirnov Test. The Kolmogorov-Smirnov test fulfills the function of χ^2 in testing goodness of fit and of the Wilcoxon rank sum test in determining whether random samples are from the same population.

The Sign Test. The sign test is important in determining the significance of differences between two correlated samples. The "signs" of the sign test are the algebraic plus or minus values of the difference of the paired scores. Where the difference between the paired scores favors the *X* variable a plus sign is given, those favoring the *Y* variable are assigned a minus designation. The null hypothesis postulates a 0 value with the pluses equaling the minuses. To test for significance between the plus and minus signs, χ^2 can be used.

The Median Test. The median test is a sign test for two independent samples in contradistinction to two correlated samples, as is the case with the sign test.

The Spearman Rank Order Correlation. The Spearman rank order correlation, sometimes called Spearman's rho (ρ) or Spearman's rank difference correlation, is a nonparametric statistic that has its counterpart in parametric calculations in the Pearson product moment correlation.

The Kruskal-Wallis Test. The Kruskal-Wallis test is sometimes known as the Kruskal-Wallis *H* test of ranks for *k* independent samples. The *H* in the title of the test stands for null hypothesis; and the *k* (from the German *klasse*, "class") for the classes or samples. The test looks for the significance of differences among three or more groups, and it has been developed along the same general lines as the Mann-Whitney *U* test. The Kruskal-Wallis test is a one-way analysis of variance and is the nonparametric correspondent of the analysis of variance in parametric statistics. Its purpose is to determine whether *k* independent samples have been drawn from the same population.

The Kendall Coefficient of Concordance. The Kendall coefficient of concordance is also variously known as Kendall's concordance coefficient *W* or the concordance coefficient *W*. It is a technique which can be used with advantage in studies involving rankings made by independent judges. To analyze the rankings the Kendall coefficient will indicate the degree to which such judges agree in their assignment of ranks. The Kendall coefficient *W* is based on the deviation of the total of each ranking. To test the significance of *W*, we employ the null hypothesis and test it by employing the χ^2 technique.

The Corner Test. A little-known test is the corner test, whose function is to test the hypothesis that two continuous variables are independent. The test is a graphical one. The data are plotted as for a conventional correlation study. When all the data have been plotted in a matrix plot arrangement, medians are drawn for the X variable, which median will be parallel to the X axis. A Y median is also drawn through the plotted data to divide them equally in a horizontal direction. The four quadrants are then assigned the conventional plus and minus signs and, consequently, the plotted data falling within each quadrant thus become either positive or negative. Now inspect the data in the four quadrants. Draw a line to the left and a line to the right, also similar lines above and below the median lines at the extremity of the lesser of each of the respective groups of data. The test of significance will be based upon the count of the number of points lying outside the lines marking the boundaries of the lesser groups of data. If a point lies beyond one of the demarkation lines, it is given a value of 1; if it lies beyond two of these lines, it sets a value of 2. The algebraic sum of all the outlying points is the test statistic. From it is computed the degree of association and the nature of that association.[16]

The following is a summary table of both parametric and nonparametric tests applicable to testing statistical hypotheses. You may find it helpful in selecting the proper tool for the specific situation.

TESTS OF HYPOTHESES

SCALE	HYPOTHESIS							
	Two independent samples have:		Two correlated samples have:	*k* independent samples have:		*k* correlated samples have:	Two variables are:	
	Equal variability	Same central tendency or proportion	Same central tendency	Equal variabilities	Same central tendency	Same central tendency	Uncorrelated or independent	Linearly related
NOMINAL		$p_1 - p_2$ is normally distributed with $\sigma_{D_p} = \sqrt{p_a q_a \left(\frac{1}{N_1} + \frac{1}{N_2}\right)}$			Chi-square test for equality of several sample proportions.		Chi-square test of independence. Likelihood-ratio chi-square. If $T = 0$, $1.3863NT$ has chi-square distribution with $(r - 1)(k - 1)$ degrees of freedom.	
ORDINAL	Run test (also sensitive to differences in central tendency).	Run test (also sensitive to differences in variability. Median test. Rank-sums test.	Sign test		Median test Kruskal-Wallis test	Friedman test (sometimes called 'analysis of variance by ranks').	Contingency test of association. Test of hypothesis that $\rho_O = 0$.	
INTERVAL AND RATIO	F test. Assumes normality of populations.	$\tilde{\sigma}_{\bar{X}_1 - \bar{X}_2} = \tilde{\sigma}\sqrt{\frac{1}{N_1} + \frac{1}{N_2}}$ $\frac{\bar{X}_1 - \bar{X}_2}{\tilde{\sigma}_{\bar{X}_1 - \bar{X}_2}}$ has t-distribution with $N_1 + N_2 - 2$ degrees of freedom when samples are from normal populations with equal variances.	Wilcoxon Test for Paired Replicates. For large samples, or small samples from normal populations $\frac{\bar{D}}{sD/\sqrt{N-1}}$ has a t-distribution with N − 1 degrees of freedom.	Bartlett's Test for Homogeneity of Variance.	Analysis of variance. $\frac{\tilde{\sigma}^2_B}{\tilde{\sigma}^2_W}$ has F distribution if samples are from normal populations with equal variances.	Analysis of variance (two dimensional). Assumes normality and homogeneity of variance.	Test hypothesis that $\eta = 0$ by use of F ratio. Test hypothesis that $\rho = 0$ by use of F ratio or t-test.	Test hypothesis that $\rho = \eta$ by use of F ratio.

From *Measurement and Statistics: **A Basic** Test Emphasizing Behavioral Science*, by Virginia L. Senders. Copyright © 1958 by Oxford University Press, Inc. Reprinted by permission. (Modified at the direction of the author.)

Looking Backward

It may be well at this juncture, after what has been a somewhat long and at times involved discussion, to turn to the opening pages of this chapter to review there what has been the purpose of this discussion: "our purpose is not so much to attempt to describe what the

[16] A full explanation of the corner test is given in Albert Rickmers and Hollis N. Todd, *Statistics: An Introduction* (New York: McGraw-Hill Book Company, 1967), pp. 403-405.

data are trying to tell us as it is to take data that are essentially quantitative—(numerical data) and to analyze those data by means of appropriate statistical tools so that we may infer from them certain meanings which lie hidden within them, or at least to discern the presence of potentials and dynamic forces which lie within those data that may suggest further investigation for the researcher."[17]

It may also be helpful to review again the map of the statistical landscape, presented earlier in the chapter.[18] Both of these review exercises may help you to see what this chapter has been all about. It may bring into focus the tool of statistics as this handmaiden of the mathematics has become an ancillary servant of research.

Practical Application

> *We derive a clear understanding of statistics and statistical procedures by seeing these in actual practice and by encountering them in the literature. To give you an opportunity to see more clearly some of the matters we have been discussing here, turn to Project 9, p. 234, of the practicum section. There you will be given an opportunity to learn more about statistical aspects of research.*

[17]See p. 114.
[18]See p. 116.

10 The Experimental Method

GENERAL CONSIDERATIONS

The experimental method is the last major methodological approach in research that we will consider. This methodology goes by various names: the experimental method, the cause and effect method, the pretest–posttest control group design, the laboratory method. By whatever name, the basic idea behind the methodological approach is to attempt to account for the influence of a factor or, as in the case of complex designs, of multiple factors conditioning a given situation. In its simplest form, the experimental method attempts to control the research situation, except for certain input variables which then become suspect as the cause of whatever change has taken place within the investigative design.

Underlying Concepts

The matter of *control* is, in fact, so basic to the methodology that we frequently refer to this means of searching for truth as the *control group–experimental group design.* At the outset, we assume that the forces and dynamics within both groups are equistatic. We begin with *matched groups.* These groups are randomly selected and paired so that, insofar as possible within the limits of the crude evaluative instruments that we have available, especially in the social and humanistic sciences, each group will resemble the other in as many characteristics as possible and, certainly, with respect to those qualities that are critical to the experiment. Mathematically, we may represent the equivalent status of these groups at the beginning of the experiment as

$$\text{Experimental group} = \text{Control group}$$

And although we assume that both groups have at the beginning of the experiment identical characteristics, identical values, and identical status, perfect identity is more theoretical than real. In recognition of this fact, therefore, we employ the phrase *matched groups*, or we say that they are "groups matched on the basis of x, y, and z." The x, y, and z are the qualitative parameters which provide the basis for matching.

Perhaps a glance backward will bring into contrast the distinctive nature of the experimental method. Reviewing the various research methodologies we see that each has its own discrete characteristics, that each provides a unique way to handle the data which fall within its methodological boundaries: the historical method deals with the study of documents; the descriptive survey, with the study of observations; the analytical survey, with the investigation of data dynamics and the interrelationships of these dynamics through appropriate statistical techniques. We shall now look at the experimental method and see its distinctive characteristics.

The Characteristics of the Experimental Method

The experimental method deals with the phenomenon of *cause and effect.* We assess the cause and effect dynamics within a closed system of controlled conditions. Essentially, the basic structure of this methodology is simple. We have two situations. We assess each to establish comparability. Then we attempt to alter one of these by introducing into it an extraneous dynamic. We re-evaluate each situation after the intervening attempt at alteration. Whatever change is noticed is presumed to have been caused by the extraneous variable. Basically this is the method practiced in research laboratories and is known as the experimental method.

But we must clarify the difference between an *experiment* and the *experimental method.* They are not the same. An illustration will suffice to establish the distinction. Consider a problem that arose in the laboratory of Thomas Edison in the early days of the electric light. Edison had given his engineers the well-known tapering and rounded bulb for them to calculate its cubic volume. They brought to play on the problem all their mathematical knowledge. When they reported to Edison, each of them had a different answer. Edison then went into his laboratory, drew a container of water, measured its volume, immersed an incandescent bulb in it, and snipped off the pointed glass end. The water rushed into the bulb because it was a vacuum, filling the bulb completely. Edison measured the difference between the water in the container after filling the bulb and subtracted that volume from the water in the container originally; the difference was the cubic capacity of the bulb. That was an *experiment.* It was not *research,* nor was Edison's method *the experimental method of research.* It lacked interpretation of data.

Experimental research needs to be planned. We call this planning the *designing of the experiment.* In experimental research, however, the word *design* has two distinct meanings. Because of this fact, the inexperienced researcher may frequently be confused. In one sense, the word *design* refers to *the propriety of the statistical analysis necessary to prepare the data for interpretation.* Frequently a student comes to his professor, who advises him that he needs the assistance of a statistician to help him with the "design" of his research. What *design* means here is usually that the proper statistical techniques for analyzing the quantitative data that the student has at hand must be properly selected and utilized in accordance with the nature of those data. The meaning of the term in this sense is strictly beyond the province of this text. Many statistical textbooks on experimental design are available, and the student should refer to them. The meaning of the term as it is employed in a purely research connotation refers, of course, to *the total architectural plan, the tectonic structure of the research framework.* This goes far beyond the mere selection of statistical tools to process data.

We shall explore design in this sense further in this chapter. Where the term *experimental design* is used, it will mean, of course, the architectonics and planning of the entire experimental approach to a research problem. The statistical aspects are only one phase in that total approach and prepare the data merely so that the researcher may be in better position to assess its meaning and interpret its significance.

TYPES OF EXPERIMENTAL DESIGNS

Experimental designs have been variously categorized by different writers in the field of research. Perhaps the simplest of these is the dichotomized classification of Wise, Nordberg, and Reitz[1] in which they classify all experimental designs into two types: (1) *functional designs* or (2) *factorial designs.* The difference between these two design types is whether the researcher is able to control the independent variable at will (the *functional design*) or whether he is *not* able to control the independent variable (the *factorial design*) during the course of the experiment. Earlier we indicated that the matter of control was fundamental to the experimental method. So basic is it, indeed, that its presence determines the *nature* of the variable. If the investigator has control over the variable and is able to manipulate it or change it at will, then we say that the variable is an *independent variable.* If, on the other hand, the investigator has no control over the variable and it occurs as the result of the influence of the independent variable, then that variable is the *dependent variable.*

Take a very simple situation. The investigator has a potentiometer connected to a voltage source and by means of it, by merely turning a knob, he is able to *control* the voltage that passes through it. The potentiometer is in turn connected to a voltmeter. The deflection of the indicator hand on the face of that voltmeter *depends* upon the voltage potential which is controlled by the investigator and is, thus, the *dependent* variable.

We do, however, experiment with factors and forces over which we have no control whatsoever. A person's reaction time, his intelligence quotient, his age—no investigator can control these factors.

A more conventional categorization of experimental designs has been made by others. Perhaps the most complete categorization has been made by Campbell and Stanley.[2] They divide experimental studies into four general types: (1) *pre-experimental designs,* (2) *true experimental designs,* (3) *quasiexperimental designs,* and (4) *correlational and ex post facto designs.* We shall look at each of these briefly.

Pre-Experimental Designs

The One-Shot Case Study. In the one-shot case study a conventional symbolism will be employed. When a group, an individual, or an object are exposed to an experimental variable, the letter *X* will be used. The letter *O* will indicate an observation or measurement of the data.

The one-shot case study may be represented by the following symbolic formula

Design I: $X \rightarrow O$

This is the simplest and most naïve experimental procedure. This is the method behind many superstitious folklore beliefs. We see a child sitting on the damp earth in mid-April. The next day he has a sore throat and a cold. We conclude that sitting on the damp earth causes one to catch cold.

X = exposure of child to cold, damp earth → *O* = observation that the child has a cold.
(variable)

[1] John E. Wise, Robert B. Nordberg, and Donald J. Reitz, *Methods of Research in Education* (Boston: D. C. Heath and Company, 1967), pp. 133–137.

[2] Donald T. Campbell and Julian C. Stanley, "Experimental and Quasi-Experimental Designs for Research on Teaching," in N. L. Gage, ed., *Handbook of Research on Teaching* (Chicago: Rand McNally and Company, 1963), pp. 171–246. Also published separately by Rand McNally and Co., 1966.

The One-Group Pretest–Posttest Design. The one-group pretest–posttest design is a type of experiment where one group has a pre-experimental evaluation, then the influence of the variable, then a postexperimental evaluation. It is represented as follows:

Design II: $O_1 \rightarrow X \rightarrow O_2$

A teacher wants to know how effective hearing a story read masterfully on a tape recorder would be in improving the reading skills of her class. She selects a likely group, gives them a standardized reading pretest, exposes them to daily taped readings, posttests them with a variant form of the same standardized test to determine how much "progress" they made because of (so she supposes) the tape recorder technique.

The Static Group Comparison. The static group comparison is a familiar control group–experimental group procedure, and it is symbolically represented as follows:

Design III:

$$\frac{X \rightarrow O_1}{- \rightarrow O_2}$$

Here is a design in which two nonrandomly selected groups are designated by the dictates of chance, one to be a control group and the other to be the experimental group. The experimental group is exposed to variable *X*; the control group is not. Control groups in the paradigms under study are represented by a __. At the close of the experiment both are evaluated and a comparison is made between the evaluation values to determine what has been the effect of factor *X*. No attempt is employed in this design to obtain or examine the pre-experimental equivalence of the comparison groups.

These three designs, although commonly employed in many research projects reported in the scholarly journals, are loose in structure and leave much to be desired in terms of factors which, not being controlled, could inject bias into the total research design.

True Experimental Designs

In contrast to the somewhat crude designs that we have discussed to this point, the true experimental designs evidence a greater degree of control and refinement and a greater insurance of both internal and external validity. These are new terms. With experimental designs, *internal validity* is the basic minimum without which any experiment is uninterpretable.[3] The question that the researcher must answer is whether the experimental treatment did indeed make a difference in the experiment.

Eternal validity asks the question as to how generalizable the experiment is. To what populations, settings, treatment variables, and measurement variables can the effect, as observed in the experiment, be generalized?[4] Of the two types of validity, internal validity is certainly the more important insofar as the integrity of the study is concerned. The following suggested designs are those that are more likely to be strong in both types of validity, which is certainly the aim of every experimental researcher.

As we emphasized so strongly in the discussion of the descriptive survey method, randomization is one of the greatest guarantees of validity. In each of the three designs that follows, randomization is a necessary and constant factor in the selection of all groups, both experimental and control. In the paradigms randomization will be indicated by the letter *R*.

[3] Ibid., p. 175.
[4] Ibid.

The Pretest-Posttest Control Group Design. The pretest-posttest control group design is, as Mouly remarks, the "old workhorse of traditional experimentation" design.[5] In it we have the experimental group carefully chosen through appropriate randomization procedures and the control group similarly selected. The experimental group is evaluated, subjected to the experimental variable, and re-evaluated. The control group is isolated from all experimental variable influences and is merely evaluated at the beginning and at the end of the experiment. A more optimal situation can be achieved if the researcher is careful to match the experimental against the control group and vice versa for identical correspondences. Certainly where matching is effected for the factor that is being studied, the design is thereby greatly strengthened. For example, if we are studying the effect of reading instruction on the IQ level of students, wisdom would dictate that for both control and experimental groups as nearly as possible members of each group should be selected in, as much as possible, a one-to-one correspondence with IQ scores.

The paradigm for the pretest-posttest control group design is as follows:

Design IV:

$$R\text{--}\left[\begin{array}{l} O_1 \rightarrow X \rightarrow O_2 \\ \\ O_3 \quad \underline{\rightarrow} \quad O_4 \end{array}\right.$$

R is the randomization process that is common to both groups. O_1 and O_2 are the two evaluations of the experimental group, before and after its exposure to the experimental variable *X*. O_3 and O_4 are the evaluations of the control group. The _ indicates that in place of the intervening variable for the experimental group, no influence was permitted to impinge upon the control group.

As Campbell and Stanley indicate, good experimental design is separable from the use of statistical tests of significance; but because this is such a common design in the experimental methodology, researchers often use incorrect statistical procedures to analyze such data. Borg and Gall[6] caution against this and recommend that the best statistical method to use is analysis of covariance, in which the posttest means are compared using the pretest means as the covariate.

The Solomon Four-Group Design. R. L. Solomon, in 1949, proposed in the *Psychological Bulletin* an "extension" of the control group design,[7] and it is a refinement on the previous design discussed. For the first time explicit consideration was given to a design which emphasized a regard for factors of external validity.

The design is obviously an "extension" of Design IV, as is seen when one analyzes the following paradigm:

Design V:

$$R\text{--}\left[\begin{array}{l} O_1 \rightarrow X \rightarrow O_2 \\ O_3 \rightarrow \_ \rightarrow O_4 \\ \qquad\;\; X \rightarrow O_5 \\ \_ \qquad \_ \quad\; O_6 \end{array}\right.\left.\begin{array}{l} \\ \\ \\ \\ \end{array}\right\} > \text{"extension"}$$

[5] George J. Mouly, *The Science of Educational Research*, second edition (New York: Van Nostrand Reinhold Company, 1970), p. 336.

[6] Walter R. Borg and Meredith D. Gall, *Educational Research: An Introduction*, second edition (New York: David McKay Company, Inc., 1971), p. 383.

[7] R. L. Solomon, "An Extension of Control Group Design," *Psychological Bulletin*, 1949, 46, 137–150.

The fact that the pretest disappears in groups 3 and 4 constitutes a distinct advantage. It enables the researcher to generalize to groups which have not received the pretest in cases where it may be suspected that the pretest has had an adverse effect on the experimental treatment. It removes a kind of hawthorne effect from the experiment. A group of subjects is pretested. The question now is, "What effect does this pretesting have?" It may provide them with additional motivation to do well under experimental conditions. It may contaminate the effect of the experimental variable. The "extension" takes care of these contingencies.

In terms of experimental designs, the Solomon four-group design is probably our most powerful experimental approach. The data are analyzed by doing an analysis of variance of the posttest scores. This rigorous bivariate structure does not require, however, considerably larger samples and demands much more energy on the part of the researcher to pursue it. Its principal value is in eliminating pretest influence, as we have previously pointed out, and where such is desirable the design is unsurpassed.

The Posttest-Only Control Group Design. We come now to the last of the generally employed true experimental designs. In the thinking of some researchers, especially those in education, psychology, and the social sciences, the phrase *pretest-posttest* has become so habitual that it is inconceivable to many of them to slough off the first half of the phrase and have anything in terms of scientific research left. Some life situations, however, defy pretesting. You cannot pretest the forces in a thunderstorm or a hurricane, you cannot pretest growing crops or growing children. These phenomena happen only once. The design here proposed may be considered as the last two groups of the Solomon four-group design—the "extension" part:

Design VI:

$$R \text{- -} \begin{cases} X \rightarrow O_1 \\ \_ \rightarrow O_2 \end{cases}$$

In order to test for significance in this design the *t* test would probably be the simplest and best. Randomness is critical in the posttest-only design and should be carefully considered as an important element in the success of employing such an approach.

Quasiexperimental Designs

Thus far, in the experimental designs we have been emphasizing the importance of randomness of group composition. Life presents certain situations occasionally where random selection and assignment is not possible. Such experiments, carried on under conditions where it is not possible to guarantee randomness must rely upon designs which are called *quasiexperimental designs.* In such designs it is imperative that the researcher be thoroughly aware of the specific variables his design fails to control and to take these into account in the interpretation of his data.

The Nonrandomized Control Group Pretest-Posttest Design. The nonrandomized control group pretest-posttest design configuration is similar to the first of the true experimental designs that we discussed, except for the lack of randomization.

Design VII:

$$O_1 \rightarrow X \rightarrow O_2$$

$$O_3 \rightarrow \_ \rightarrow O_4$$

This design is not to be confused with the pretest-posttest control group design (Design IV), in which the composition of groups is *randomly* chosen. The researcher might well consider the employment of Design VII in situations where the true experimental designs (Designs IV, V, and VI) are not feasible.

To minimize the differences that might exist between the experimental and the control groups, the researcher might attempt to match as closely as possible and on as many variables as possible the two groups in a kind of quasirandomization before the beginning of the experiment. Again, the researcher might consider, if feasible, consolidating the so-called control group and the so-called experimental group into one amalgamated group and from this supergroup dividing the total number of students into two groups by means of randomization, one of which may then be designated as the control group and the other as the experimental group. Still another way to compensate for initial differences, as suggested by Borg and Gall,[8] is by the analysis of covariance technique. Analysis of covariance reduces the effects of initial group differences statistically by making compensating adjustments of final means on the dependent variable.

The Time-Series Experiment. The time-series design consists of taking a series of evaluations and then introducing a variable or new dynamic into the system, after which another series of evaluations is made. If a substantial change results in the second series of evaluations, we may assume with reasonable experimental logic that the cause of the difference in observational results was because of the factor introduced into the system. This design has a configuration much like the following paradigm:

Design VIII: $O_1 \rightarrow O_2 \rightarrow O_3 \rightarrow O_4 \rightarrow X \rightarrow \boldsymbol{O}_5 \rightarrow \boldsymbol{O}_6 \rightarrow \boldsymbol{O}_7 \rightarrow \boldsymbol{O}_8$

In this paradigm the $\boldsymbol{O}$ indicates that these observations are different in character than those of the series before the introduction of the variable.

This is the design that was formerly widely used in the physical and biological sciences. The classic discovery of Sir Alexander Fleming of the power of *Penicillium notatum* to inhibit staphylococci is an example of this type of design. Dr. Fleming had observed *n* number of times the growth of staphylococci on a culture plate. Then, unexpectedly, a culture plate containing well-developed colonies of staphylococci was contaminated with the spores of *Penicillium notatum.* Dr. Fleming noticed that the colonies in the vicinity of the mold seemed to be undergoing dissolution: the $\boldsymbol{O}_{5,\,6,\,7,\,8}$ of the paradigm.

The weakness of this design is in the probability that a major event which may be unrecognized may enter the system along with, before, or after the introduction of the experimental variable. The effects of this extraneous factor are likely to be confounded with those of the experimental factor and the wrong attribution of the cause for the effect observed may be made.

Control Group, Time Series. A variant of the time-series design is to accompany it with a parallel set of observations, but without the introduction of the experimental factor. This design would, then, take on a configuration like the following:

Design IX:

$$O_1 \rightarrow O_2 \rightarrow O_3 \rightarrow O_4 \rightarrow X \rightarrow \boldsymbol{O}_5 \rightarrow \boldsymbol{O}_6 \rightarrow \boldsymbol{O}_7 \rightarrow \boldsymbol{O}_8$$
$$O_1 \rightarrow O_2 \rightarrow O_3 \rightarrow O_4 \rightarrow \_ \rightarrow O_5 \rightarrow O_6 \rightarrow O_7 \rightarrow O_8$$

Such a design tends to assure greater control for internal validity. The advantage of a design of this construction is that it adds one further guarantee toward internal validity in drawing conclusions with respect to the effect of the experimental factor.

Equivalent Time-Samples Design. A variant of the previous design is the equivalent time-samples design. The object of its construction is to control history in time designs. The intervening experimental factor is sometimes present, sometimes absent. Suppose we have a

[8] Borg and Gall, op. cit., p. 394.

class in astronomy. One approach is to teach astronomy through audiovisual materials; another method is to teach the subject by means of a textbook. An equivalent time-samples design of this class might look like the following:

Design X: $[X_1 \rightarrow O_1] \rightarrow [X_0 \rightarrow O_2] \rightarrow [X_1 \rightarrow O_3] \rightarrow [X_0 \rightarrow O_4]$

In this paradigm X_1 indicates the time when the audiovisual approach was used with the class and X_0 the time when the textbook approach was used. We see also that the instructional cells are such that we can compare observations such as O_1 with O_3, and O_2 with O_4.

Gilbert Sax has suggested two variants of this basic design.[9] One utilizes two variables in the study, so that the schematic of the design looks like this:

Design X_a:

$$[X_1 \rightarrow O_1] \rightarrow X_0 \rightarrow O_2 \rightarrow \{X_2 \rightarrow O_3\} \rightarrow X_0 \rightarrow O_4 \rightarrow [X_1 \rightarrow O_5] \rightarrow X_0 \rightarrow O_6 \rightarrow \{X_2 \rightarrow O_7\}$$

If pursued over a long enough time span, some multivariate comparisons might be made. For example, in the preceding sequence we could

Compare	with	To explore variable
O_1	O_5	X_1
O_2	O_6	X_0
O_3	O_7	X_2

Whereas in the preceding design Sax introduces a second variable in the equivalent time-samples design, he goes even further to suggest an equivalent materials design:

Design X_b:

$$[M_a \rightarrow X_1 \rightarrow O] \rightarrow [M_b \rightarrow X_0 \rightarrow O] \rightarrow [M_c \rightarrow X_0 \rightarrow O] \rightarrow [M_c \rightarrow X_1 \rightarrow O] \ldots$$

Sax comments on this design: "This design is exactly the same as the equivalent time-sampling design except that the different materials are introduced throughout the course of the experiment. Assuming that these materials are equivalent, experimental controls would seem to be adequate."[10]

Correlational and Ex Post Facto Designs

Correlational designs are usually attempts to establish cause-effect relationships between two sets of data. We might represent the situation by the following diagram:

$$\overrightarrow{\underleftarrow{O_a \neq O_b}}$$

Correlational studies are always particularly hazardous. So often researchers think that if they can show a positive correlation between two factors which *in their thinking they deem to be related* then they *assume* the fact of causality (i.e., that one factor is the cause of

[9] Gilbert Sax, *Empirical Foundations of Educational Research* (Englewood Cliffs, N.J.: Prentice-Hall, Inc., 1968), p. 363.

[10] Ibid.

the other). This is erroneous reasoning. The fact that one can demonstrate a statistically positive correlational relationship between two sets of data in no way implies any causality between them.

The preceding diagram indicates the possibilities within any correlational situation. We have indicated the observed data with respect to each factor as O_a and O_b. Now, given two variables of this type, with O_a as the independent variable, three conclusions might be drawn with respect to these data:

1. O_a has caused O_b: $O_a \rightarrow O_b$.
2. O_b has caused O_a: $O_a \leftarrow O_b$.
3. Some third variable is responsible for both O_a and O_b: $O_a \neq O_b$.

Perhaps some of the difficulty with the causal-comparative correlational studies has been the fact that we have failed to recognize the structure of the correlational factors with which we work. We have a tendency to simplify. Especially in a research endeavor we think of a certain effect as having *a* cause when, in fact, because of the complexity of many situations we are not dealing with *a* cause for a particular phenomenon but with a constellation of causes all of which contribute to a greater or lesser degree to the effectualization of the phenomenon. Arbitrarily selecting any two or even several factors for any given phenomenon and then attempting to ascribe the causality of the phenomenon to the limitation of our selection may be irrational and foolhardy, especially in the face of extremely complex problems whose tributaries of causality may spread far beyond anything that we may have conceived as being remotely relevant to the problem and its co-related factors.

Correlation is too simple for most of the realities of life, and its simplistic approach disarms the researcher. It is an extremely deceptive tool, and one that the researcher needs to employ with the utmost caution and with maximum wisdom.

Ex Post Facto Studies. The ex post facto study belongs to a "no-man's land" in the discipline of research. Although it is usually considered under the heading of experimentation, by its very nature it has little that is experimental about it. We indicated in the early pages of this chapter that control was the one condition that marked the experimental study and that the element of control was characteristic of the experimental method. But after an event has happened, how can it be controlled? Mouly asserts

> A relatively questionable quasi-experimental design is the *ex post facto* experiment, in which a particular characteristic of a given group is investigated with a view to identifying its antecedents. This is experimentation in reverse: instead of taking groups that are equivalent and exposing them to different treatment with a view to promoting differences to be measured, the *ex post facto* experiment begins with a given effect and seeks the experimental factor that brought it about. The obvious weakness of such an "experiment" is that we have no control over the situations that have already occurred and we can never be sure of how many other circumstances might have been involved.[11]

Strictly, because of the lack of the control element, the methodology may be somewhat difficult to classify. Yet it is a method that pursues truth and seeks the solution of a problem through the analysis of data. Science has no difficulty with such a methodology. Medicine uses it widely in its research activity. Physicians discover a pathological situation; they inaugurate their search "after the fact" and begin to sleuth into events and conditions antecedent in order to discover the cause for the illness or the disease.

[11] George J. Mouly, *The Science of Educational Research,* second edition (New York: Van Nostrand Reinhold Company, 1970), p. 340.

The research which is going on in space laboratories with respect to the moon rocks is a research which is purely ex post facto. So much "post" indeed that it is separated from the fact by millions and even billions of years. Yet no one will deny that this research is oriented to specific problems, supported by specific data, and given direction by underlying hypotheses.

If we were to represent ex post facto research, it might conform to the following sketch:

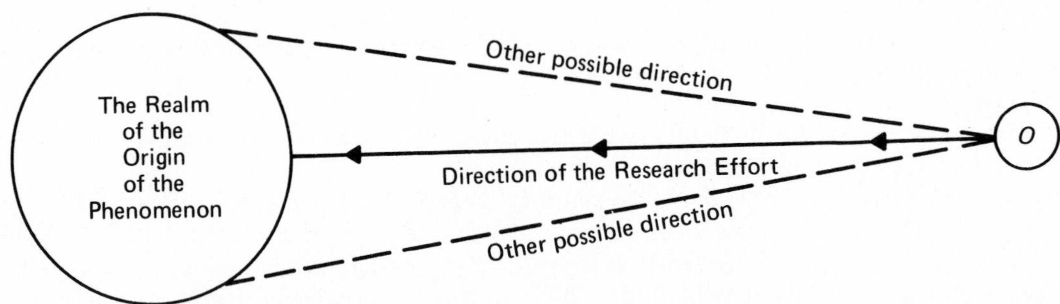

The entry of the sketch is at the far right-hand side. Here is where the researcher encounters the observed fact (*O*). That observed fact originated from a much larger area, which is the Realm of the Origin of the Phenomenon. From this point the researcher must formulate all his hypotheses and aim his research effort. Because of the disparity between the size of the observed instance and the expanse of the possibility out of which it may have arisen, it is always possible that the direction of the research effort in ex post facto studies may lead nowhere. We may seek the cause of a disease, for instance, and our efforts may come to naught. So vast is the realm of the origin of the phenomenon and so miniscule the single observed fact, that to attempt to construct a nexus of cause and effect and to extract meaning from the situation may be very difficult indeed. We are indeed doing, as Mouly has suggested, "experimentation in reverse."

Let us conclude this broad section of the book, which has dealt generally with methodology, with a word about methodologies other than those we have mentioned here that the researcher may encounter. We have suggested in this text the broad generic methodologies within which other types will be accommodated which are sometimes discussed separately and as discrete methodologies in themselves. Inspected closely, you will usually find that these minor methodologies take on definite characteristics of the broader forms.

One author, for example, indicates that predictive methods are a separate type of methodology.[12] But we have chosen to include prediction as an aspect of analytical statistics and to consider it under the analytical survey method. Others have decided to include the case study method as a discrete methodology, but because it is an approach which keeps observational details of the behavior of one or more individuals, we have felt that this approach might reasonably be included in the descriptive survey methodology.

Other writers have chosen to indicate still other methodologies: the cross-cultural method, the developmental method, the causal-comparative method, the correlational method, the statistical method, and even the philosophic method. You should not be disturbed, therefore, if you find some disagreement and some discrepancy in the organization of the discipline of research. In a very real sense it is a new discipline. It is, similarly, a chaotic discipline. We pointed out in the first chapter the multiple meanings that

[12] Ibid., pp. 357-376.

the word *research* has. It means, in fact, almost all things to all men. Little wonder then that the divisions, the discussions within the larger framework, the terminology, the basic viewpoints should differ so widely. Unsettledness is a characteristic of youth; this is true of both young people and young academic disciplines. Some writers on research do not mention *any* discrete methodologies. Many think of statistics as being synonymous with research and vice versa. Some will quarrel violently with some positions that are taken and some concepts that are articulated in this volume. This may not be too serious. It is but an indication the growing pangs of a discipline which is as yet very young and of indecisive mind.

Let us turn now to a pair of chapters devoted to some suggestions on presenting the results of research.

Practical Application

Turn to the practicum section at the back of this book. On p. 236 you will find a practical application of some of the matters we have been discussing in this chapter.

Presenting the Results of Research

11 Writing the Research Report

THE REPORT AS A COMMUNICATIVE DOCUMENT

The research report is a straightforward document that sets forth clearly and precisely what the researcher has done to resolve the problem. In structure, it is factual and logical. It makes no pretense at being a literary production. It must, however, be readable, which is another way of saying that the writer of the research report must know how to communicate clearly.

Most reports suffer from the fact that those who attempt to write them have little skill in English expression. They have not learned well the basics of sentence and paragraph structure. They know too little about English grammar and have never mastered the elements of rhetoric: the application of the principles of unity, coherence, and emphasis to the written word. Punctuation was invented to facilitate the expression of ideas, but those who know little of punctuational usage find difficulty in communicating by means of the written word. We shall say more of matters pertaining to style, format, and readability in the next chapter.

The Parts of a Research Report

The research report has a relatively simple outline. In general, it should achieve three objectives:

1. It should acquaint the reader with the research problem and explain its implications adequately enough so that all who read the research may have the same orientation to the problem being researched.
2. It should present the data fully and adequately so that the data within the report itself will substantiate all the interpretations and conclusions which the researcher draws from them.
3. It should interpret the data for the reader and present their implications for resolving the problem being researched.

We shall discuss briefly each of these matters and amplify their significance so far as they relate to writing the research report.

Acquainting the Reader with the Research Problem. The first section of the research report should have but one purpose: to create between the writer of the report and the reader of the report a meeting of minds. The reader should understand through the merits of the report itself what the writer had in mind with respect to the problem and the setting in which the problem was conceived. Much research report writing is of poor quality because the writer has not approached his task from the standpoint of covering every conceivable situation; consequently, the reader may not get the precise thought that was in the mind of the writer. We cannot assume that the reader will be aware of important facts that we have never told him.

At the outset of the report, after perhaps a few paragraphs of introductory and orientational remarks, the document should set forth clearly and unmistakably the problem that has been researched. This has presumably been done in the proposal as well as the spelling out of the other items which should comprise the first chapter of the final report. At this juncture it may be well for you to turn again to the sample proposal in Appendix A and review there the section entitled "The Problem and Its Setting."

If the problem has been divided into subproblems, these also should be stated following the statement of the problem. The object of the first section of the research document is to present for your reader in as lucid a manner as possible just what it is that you are concerned with. The reader will then be in a better position later on to understand your interpretation of the data and to judge the merits of the research effort. The research methodology should also be stated and justified.

Terms which may be ambiguous or which may be used in a specialized sense, must be defined. For a meeting of minds, it is imperative that the reader and the researcher be concerned with precisely the same definitions of the terms, the same concepts, the same ideas. Only in this way can they understand each other. In case you have forgotten what we said earlier about these matters, it may be well for you to review Chapter 4.

Delimitations should be clearly set forth. It is well for all who read the research to know precisely how much area the research endeavor occupies. Without any equivocation the lines should be drawn to demarcate exactly what areas relevant to the problem will not be studied.

The research report provides no opportunity for foggy thinking or unclear language. We should see explicitly the hypotheses that are being tested; we should know exactly what the assumptions are upon which the researcher relies. In addition, the first chapter of the research report should indicate the importance of the study to both the academic audience and to the practical world of men and affairs, and it should perhaps end with a section delineating chapter by chapter what the organization of the remainder of the study will be.

These matters might well comprise the first chapter of the research report, thesis, or dissertation. It is presumed, of course, that appropriate organization will be indicated by the use of headings, subheadings, and subsubheadings.

The chapter on the review of the related literature is also designed to acquaint the reader with the research problem as that particular problem is related to the corollary literature of the research problem area. We need at times to see a particular research endeavor against the broad background of the efforts of others in the same arena. This gives us a better understanding of the orientation of the problem to the larger general research environment. We have discussed previously the function of the review of the related literature. What has been said there is highly appropriate to the writing of the research proposal or the research report document. In this connection it may be well, therefore, for you to review Chapter 5.

Presenting the Data. After we fully appreciate just what the problem is and the research climate in which it has been investigated, the next consideration is, "What are the facts?" The research document is not a unique production that only you can write. It is, instead, a report that, being given your problem and your data, anyone should be able to produce. As a matter of fact, that is one of the criteria that is frequently cited by which to judge the adequacy of the proposal: the proposal should be so self-contained that should you be unable to complete the research, anyone with the requisite skill and ability could take your proposal and carry the research to its completion.

The second major division of the research report document consists largely of a logical presentation of the data *in terms of the problem* that has been researched. The researcher has gathered a great mass of data. He then codifies, arranges, and separates those data into segments, each of which corresponds to a particular segment of the problem being studied. Presumably, the problem has already been segmented into its component parts, or subproblems, in order to facilitate the management of it. There is then a one-to-one correspondence: certain data which relate to each subproblem. These are then exhibited in logical sequence within the report.

Generally the report is divided into chapters. A logical division is to devote one chapter to a subproblem and its resolution. The subproblem is presented, the data germane to it are presented, and then those data are analyzed and interpreted and the conclusions that those data dictate in terms of the subproblem under investigation are presented. Each chapter normally ends with a summary section in which the findings of that particular chapter are shown in relationship to the problem and the previous subproblem findings.

On the one hand, there is the problem; on the other hand, there are the data. The data should be presented completely. They may, of course, be organized into charts, tables, graphs, statistical summaries, lists of responses to questionnaire inquiries, and so on, but it is imperative that the data be exhibited as evidence for the conclusions that the researcher draws from them. Where the data are extensive and the researcher presents them in summary form in the study, he frequently presents the full array of the data in an appendix to the study. In this way, anyone wishing to take the same data should be able to replicate the results of the research effort, and he should be able to reach substantially the same conclusions reached by the researcher.

Let us not forget that we are testing a hypothesis. Somewhere, therefore, probably in the closing paragraphs of the chapter, some indication should be given as to whether the data do or do not support the hypothesis being tested. The hypothesis should be restated and the researcher's decision should be stated clearly.

Where the data are subjected to statistical analysis, a rationale for employing the particular statistical approach should be presented. It is important to know, for example, not that one employs a particular correlational technique, but why that particular correlational technique was employed. In fact, throughout the research process it is well for you to keep in mind that generally the answer to the question, "What?" is not nearly as important as the answer to the question, "Why?" One of the weakest links in the whole research process is frequently the failure to substantiate *what* one does with the rationale of *why* he does it. We shall have more to say about this in the next section.

The Interpretation of the Data. Too many times researchers feel that having once presented their facts and figures they have done all that needs to be done. This is certainly not the case. To do only that is to have nothing more than a grand compilation. It is not displaying the data which is most important; it is the *interpretation of the data* which is the *sine qua non* of research and the reason for the whole process.

In *Teaching for Thinking*, the following passage epitomizes what we have been saying: "The teacher who asks what the data are (the *who*, *what*, *when*, *where* questions) is concerned with a lower mental process, albeit he elicits the responses with pedagogical flourish. The teacher who gives the student some data and then asks what they mean is concerned with a higher mental process."[1] In fact, without inquiring into the innate meaning of the data, no resolution of the research problem is possible.

Many researchers, however, fail to exploit their data fully. One cannot turn over one's facts too often; look at them from too many angles; chart, graph, and arrange them in too many constellate patterns; inspect them from too many vantage points. Ask simple questions of your facts. "Doodle" with them. This is not to suggest a superficial or trifling approach. It is, however, to indicate that sometimes very simple approaches will afford you startling insights. Have you thought of plotting the data? What has caused the plotted data to "peak?" To reach a plateau? To dip or plummet? Does the behavior of the data have any relationship to events which lie outside the data?

Questions like these may sometimes crack the shell of the data and reveal the meaning within. Every data *gestalt* may not be meaningful. But that is beside the point. What is important is that the researcher leaves no stone unturned, no data configuration unnoticed. As a general rule, data have many more meanings than most researchers discover. This is because having processed the data by one means only they are unaware that other processes applied to the same data may refine many additional meanings from those same facts.

This discussion also suggests another matter. Researchers are sometimes so intent on "proving their point" that their enthusiasm takes control of their better judgment. In the last analysis, the facts speak for themselves; the researcher is only their mouthpiece. He may not like what the facts say. They may not confirm his fondest hopes or preconceived opinions, but the researcher is the servant of the scientific method and that method looks at facts squarely and without subjective prejudice and reports candidly and precisely what the impersonal fact declares.

There is danger here. Every beginning researcher needs to ferret out every generalization, underscore it in red, and then be sure that the facts that are in his tables, graphs, and other exhibits will solidly support his conclusions. It is an academic tradition to defend one's research effort. *Defend* in this sense means "to justify one's conclusions, to support one's statements with the backing of solid fact that has been presented in the document as the result of the research endeavor." Nothing short of this will suffice.

As a final section to the interpretation of the data, the report should close with a chapter entitled "Summary, Conclusions, and the Recommendations." In this chapter all the loose threads should be gathered together. Here is the place for the backward glance, for distilling into a few paragraphs precisely what has been accomplished in each phase of the research activity. One should be able to see the research as through the wrong end of a telescope; clearly, minutely, with all significant aspects brought together in proper proportion. On the basis of this summary, the researcher should state very clearly his findings and the conclusions he has reached with respect to his problem and subproblems under study. These conclusions should be entirely warranted by the facts he has previously presented. Then the researcher is ready for two final steps: (1) to state whether the hypothesis he has posited is supported or not, and (2) to make recommendations for further study, perhaps in those areas which, during his research, he has recognized as worthy of further investigation.

A word should be said about summaries. One of the weakest aspects of all research report writing is the failure of report writers to summarize adequately. They forget human psychology. They overlook the problem of the reader who comes to their report "cold." The whole research project—the problems, the organization of the data, the facts, the figures, the relationships and interrelationships—is so clear in the mind of the writer that he sometimes gives no thought to how these same matters may appear to the reader. The writer

[1] Louis E. Raths, Selma Wasserman, Arthur Jones, and Arnold Rothstein, *Teaching for Thinking* (Columbus, Ohio: Charles E. Merrill Publishing Co., 1967), p. 117.

of the report has spent much time thinking out every detail of his study. In his mind's eye, he knows precisely where each component part of the study belongs and he is entirely cognizant of the master plan. In a very real sense, with respect to the report *he is omniscient.*

But his reader is not in so fortunate a position. As the reader proceeds through the report, he needs to stop occasionally. He needs to look down occasionally to see the terrain he has traversed and to see how his present position is oriented to the goal posts, the triangulation points within the study. Instead of a long, rambling discussion of related literature, the writer may help the reader to keep his bearing by the use of appropriate headings; and at the end of each major section of the discussion, it is proper that he should summarize his facts and tie them in to the larger component of the discussion. At the close of each chapter the writer should pause long enough to summarize for his reader what basically has been happening and what relevance such discussion has to the larger considerations within the report. This is known as keeping one's eye on the goal post in spite of the immediacy of all the action that goes on around one during the frenzy of the game. Pure frenzy can leave us greatly bewildered. Discussions that ramble on and on and on have precisely the same effect.

A Schematic Model of the Research Report

The writer of a research report needs to visualize clearly the total schema of the report. He needs to see what is central and what is peripheral, what is basic and what is ancillary. He should understand the dynamics of the report, and seeing these matters, he should never leave his reader in doubt for a moment as to what is happening during the entire discussion of his report upon his research effort.

At the close of Chapter 1 we presented a diagram showing the cyclical nature of research. At this point in our discussion, we are presenting the same ideas, only in a slightly different way.

Let us conceive of the research problem as metaphorically covering a certain "area" of investigation. The subproblems, then—and we will assume that we have three of them—will each cover one third of the area occupied by the problem. The main dynamics of the research effort will take place in a more or less vertical system of activity which will be localized under the area which indicates the "spread" of the problem under research. Peripheral to the problem will lie those other items whose principal function is to throw light on the problem by explaining the meaning of its terms, delimiting the extent of its boundaries, presenting the assumptions that the researcher will take for granted concerning the problem, delineating the importance and relevance of the study, and outlining the remainder of the report organization. These matters help us to understand the problem, but they are peripheral to it.

In quite the same peripheral relationship is the review of the related literature. This discussion, although helpful in causing us to see the problem under study in relation to other studies, classical and contemporary, merely orients us within the total research environment. It does for us what a map does for a traveler.

The next page shows a schema of a research report. It indicates within the dotted boundary lines what is essential to any research activity. It places outside those boundaries that which is necessary for any research activity but does not constitute the activity itself. At the one extreme is the area of the unsolved research problem; at the other extreme is the realm of the data, where the potential for solving the problem lies. In vertical paths which originate in the problem, but principally in the subproblem areas, is the research activity itself. This activity passes through and is focused in the direction of the facts by the hypothesis. The hypotheses point in the direction of the realm of the data. The activity loop

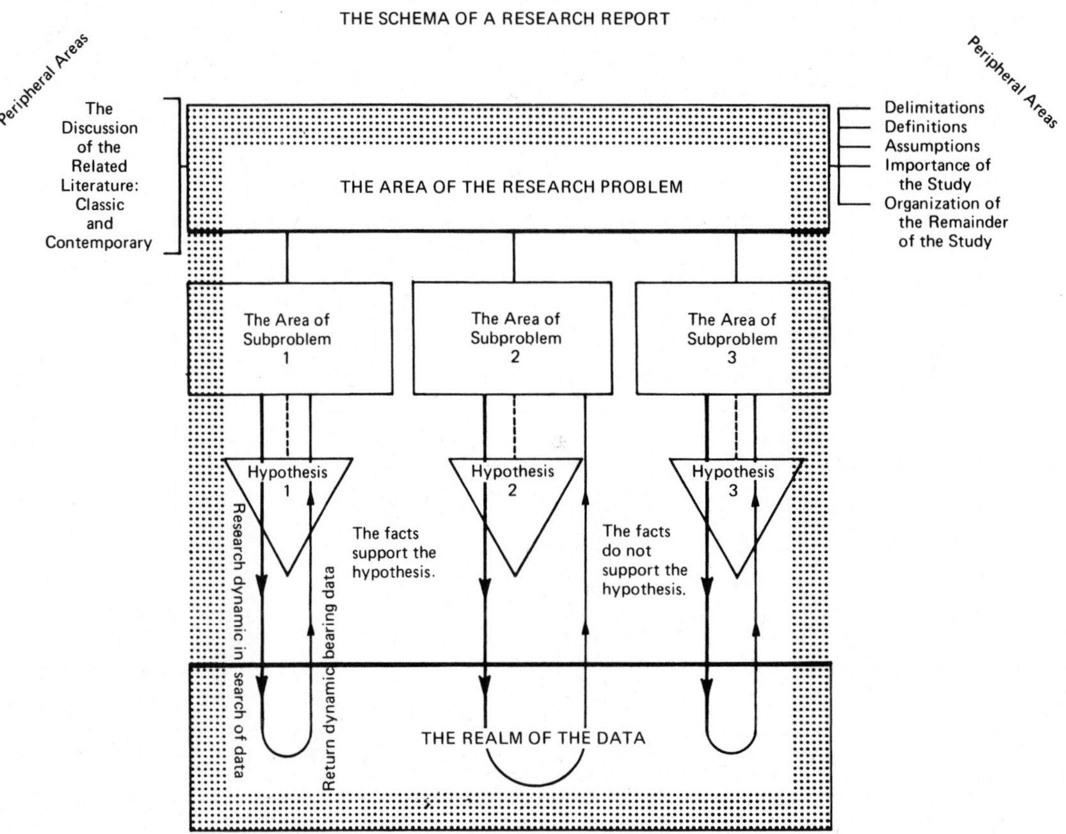

contains two types of energy: *efferent*—the activity that originates in the researcher and in his problem area and goes out into the realm of the data in search of facts—and *afferent*—the return flow on the opposite side of the loop which is the data-bearing dynamic in the system. This returns to the area of the subproblem. If the data support the hypothesis, they pass *through* the hypothesis itself. If they do not support the hypothesis, they miss the hypothesis returning to the subproblem. In the schema, we have indicated that the facts do not support the hypothesis of subproblem 2.

OUTLINE FOR THE RESEARCH REPORT

The following outline is merely suggestive. It is presented in the conventional outline form. It is presumed, however, that when you write your report you will not employ the indented outline form given here but will indicate the organization of your report in the usual professional manner by the use of conventional headings and subheadings as discussed on p. 44 of this book.

The overall consideration in the writing of any report is to present to the reader a document that is both logical in structure and organized in thought. That you will see variant organizational patterns for research documents should not disturb you. One basic criterion should be employed to test every report: Is it at once obvious to the reader what the writer is attempting to do and is the document so organized that the logic of its presentation comes through by a casual inspection of the table of contents or of the text itself? Within the parameters of this criterion, many variant presentations are possible.

We have presented in Appendix A a sample proposal for a research project. Here is the table of contents from the final document which reported on that research.[2]

[2] Arthur Louis Benton, "The Inventoried Interests of Cartographers" (unpublished doctoral dissertation, The American University, Washington, D.C., 1970).

[3] With dissertations and scholarly research especially, copyright is advisable. Application for it is made to the Copyright Office, Library of Congress, Washington, D.C. 20540 on Form A. Notice of copyright is required by law on the page following the title page.

VI. SUMMARY, CONCLUSIONS, AND RECOMMENDATIONS
Summary
Conclusions
Recommendations

BIBLIOGRAPHY

APPENDIXES

Appendix A: Letter of Transmittal

Appendix B: Follow-up Letter

Appendix C: Item Count and Differences in Group Percentages and Scoring Weights Assigned to the *SVIB* Key for Army Cartographers

Appendix D: Standard Score Means and Standard Deviations of the Cartographer Groups on Other Current Scales of the *SVIB*

Appendix E: Significance of the Differences between Cartographer Group Means on Other Current Scales of the *SVIB*

Appendix F: Percentage Overlap of Cartographers on Other Current Scales

Appendix G: Pearson Product Moment Correlations between Scores of the Cartographer Criterion Group on the Cartographer Scale and Other Occupational Scales Incorporated in the 1971 Revision to the *SVIB*

Appendix H: Significance of the Differences between the Mean *SVIB* Scores of Cartographers and Other *SVIB* Occupational Groups

The Preliminary Matter and Appendix Content

The preliminary matter takes in all of that material of an introductory nature which precedes the actual text of the study. This includes the title page and, on the page following, the copyright notice. Copyright is the protection given by the law of the United States (Title 17, U.S. Code) to the authors of literary, dramatic, musical, artistic, and other *intellectual* works. Because of the great expenditure of time, effort, monetary resources and other investment in a scholarly work such as a thesis or dissertation, it would seem only prudent to protect that investment by copyright. The first term of statutory copyright runs for twenty-eight years; a copyright may be renewed for a second term of twenty-eight years. For full information, write to the Copyright Office, Library of Congress, Washington, D.C. 20540.

Some theses and dissertations have later been turned into very remunerative and well-known books. Consider John Livingston Lowes' *The Road to Xanadu.* Sometimes under the pressure of writing a dissertation a student may not realize how important or publishable his efforts may be. For the low cost of protective literary insurance, it may be well, therefore, to have the dissertation or thesis copyrighted, just in case.

The acknowledgments page is usually a gracious inclusion in which the author gives credit to all those who have assisted him in pursuing and completing his research. These may include those who are responsible for providing the researcher with entree to persons and data resources which have aided him in completing his research, those who have guided his efforts and given him counsel—his academic dissertation committee and similar specialists, his faithful typist and proofreader, and his wife and children who (in the case of a dissertation) have endured much so that he might achieve his academic goal. It is gracious, and the guild mark of education, to say thank you to those who have given their time and their assistance. The acknowledgments page is the proper place for such recognition.

The rest of the "front matter" of the document is largely locative. The table of contents is merely a bird's-eye view of what the document contains and its organizational structure. The illustrative material appearing in the manuscript is indicated by two types of lists: a list of tables, a list of figures. A *table* is usually an arrangement of words, numbers, signs, or combinations of them in parallel columns for the purpose of exhibiting certain information in compact and comprehensive form. A *figure*, on the other hand, indicates any kind of graphic illustration other than a table: a chart, graph, photograph, schematic, drawing, sketch, or other illustrative or graphic device to convey an idea by other than verbal means.

The "back matter" usually contains supplementary aids or addenda which may be valuable in understanding the text material more completely but which is not absolutely essential to the comprehension of the body of the report. A rule of thumb is that the material that appears in the appendixes enables one to "go further" with the document, if he so desires. In the dissertation that we cited, the appended data are largely numerical values, scores, statistical computations, mean values, and other similar data, so that if the reader wished to do so, he might "check" the statistics of the researcher to confirm their accuracy. In research reporting nothing is hidden. All the data are laid before the reader. The researcher's integrity is, thus, preserved and his results and conclusions can be readily verified.

The bibliography is in the nature of reference material also. Should one wish to read further in the area of the problem or in corollary areas, the bibliographical items provide that opportunity. The bibliography also speaks pertinently of the researcher's awareness of the literature in the field of his investigation and of his own critical evaluation of his resources. A glance at a bibliography is usually enough to convince us either that the researcher knows the principal scholarly works underlying his area of endeavor or that he does not seem to be aware of them. Bibliographic materials usually may be categorized into two principal classes: the "classic" studies that one might find almost invariably appearing with respect to any particular area and the highly relevant items that are especially appropriate to the problem area under study.

Learn by Looking

Perhaps the best way to appreciate the nature and the various forms of research reports is to inspect them, keeping in mind the points we have emphasized in this chapter. Any university library will have a representative collection of theses and dissertations, and state and federal governmental agencies issue reports of research in many areas.[4] Certain notable reports available are the report of the Surgeon General of the United States on smoking, the numerous reports on research issued by the National Institutes of Health, the American Medical Association, the many learned societies, professional associations, and occupational and trade groups; one needs only to let his imagination roam, to inquire, and to request and soon a research report will be reaching you in the mail. Not all of these will follow the somewhat formal and academic format and style that we have outlined here. All of them should exhibit essentially the basic characteristics of a research report that we outlined in the opening pages of this chapter. Perhaps the best way to become acquainted with what a research report is—and, conversely, to become aware of what a research report is not—is to learn by looking, keeping in mind the guidelines presented in this chapter.

[4]The United States Government Printing Office, Public Documents Department, Washington, D.C. 20402, issues a free periodical listing of published governmental research in a leaflet entitled *Selected U.S. Government Publications.* You should request it from The Superintendent of Documents.

12 Matters of Style, Format, and Readability

TECHNICAL DETAILS AND STYLISTIC MATTERS

We have discussed in the previous chapter and at various other places throughout the book matters of style and format as these have seemed appropriate to the discussion at hand. This chapter will be devoted to methods of presenting the thought upon the page, and some suggestions of practical importance to facilitate the production of the document.

Write on the Right Side of the Paper

Few students know that there is a right and a wrong side of the paper. Every sheet of paper has one side which has a smooth, feltlike appearance. This is called the *felt side.* This is the side on which the typing is done. Typing on the felt side of the paper gives the manuscript a soft, clean appearance, with the letters having a sharp, clear configuration. The reason for this will be seen by taking any sheet of typing paper and looking carefully at one side and then at the other with a high-powered magnifying glass. One side will be, as we have said, soft and felty in appearance. The other side under magnification will look like a window screen. In fact this side is called the *screen side.*

In the paper-making process the pulp and rag issue from the Jordan macerating machine and flow onto the first stage of the paper-making machine as a thin, milklike fluid. This stage is an oscillating trough where the water is drained away, the fibres are oriented, and the soft pulp comes to rest upon a fine screen bed. The impressions made by the webbing of the screening is never entirely eradicated from the surface in the paper-making processes that follow. Because of its pitted texture, the screen side of paper does not register the full force of the typed character as well as the felt side, and although the difference is small, to the observant there *is* a difference. Papers typed on the screen side do not have the snap, the vitality, the finesse of appearance that those written on the felt side do.

With watermarked paper it is a very simple matter to identify the felt side. Hold up the paper to the light, looking at the watermark. When the watermark is oriented in the proper right-side-up reading position, you are facing the felt side of the paper on which you should type. For papers without watermark, the outside wrapper will usually bear the words *felt side* to identify it, but inspection under magnification will always reveal one side as more granular or screenlike than the other. The granular side, the "dead"-looking side is not the typing side.

A further word about paper. In making paper, both wood pulp and rags are used. Wood pulp paper, sometimes merely called pulp paper, is cheaper, less durable, and after a time has a tendency to turn brown and become brittle. Other types of paper are composed of various proportions of rag. Rag content gives paper durability and flexibility that pulp paper lacks. The proportion of rag content in paper is usually indicated as 25, 50, 75, or 100 per cent rag. Many universities specify a particular make and rag content of paper for their dissertations. You should check with your university librarian, registrar's office, or graduate dean's office to ascertain whether, indeed, a special paper requirement is designated for your thesis or dissertation. If it is, it will doubtless be watermarked. Check the orientation of the watermark before you begin typing.

Follow the Accepted Guidelines

If you are writing a thesis or a dissertation, be sure to check with the graduate dean's office to ascertain whether the university has a prescribed set of guidelines for writing theses. Check such matters as paper size, margins, and size and style of type face. (Some universities specify only 12 point Pica; others will accept Pica or Elite face.) Double spacing of manuscript is a universal requirement. Stylistic customs differ. What is permitted in one institution may be entirely unacceptable in another. You should make sure, then, whether your university has a style manual for writing research documents or whether it suggests that you follow a *particular* style manual, and if so, which one. Some of the principal manuals of style are the following:

A Manual of Style. Twelfth revised edition. Chicago: The University of Chicago Press, 1969.

American Mathematical Society, "Manual for Authors of Mathematical Papers." Reprinted from *Bulletin of the American Mathematical Society*, 68 (September, 1962), 5.

Campbell, William G. *Form and Style in Thesis Writing.* Boston: Houghton Mifflin Company, 1970.

Conference of Biological Editors. *Style Manual for Biological Journals.* Second edition. Washington, D.C.: American Institute of Biological Sciences, 1964.

Dissertations in History and English. University of Iowa Studies, No. 183. Iowa City, Iowa: University of Iowa, 1930.

Harvard Law Review Association. *A Uniform System of Citation and Abbreviations.* Tenth edition. Cambridge, Mass.: Harvard Law Review Association, 1958.

Parker, William Riley, compiler. *MLA* (Modern Language Association) *Style Sheet.* Revised edition. New York: Modern Language Association of America, 1951.

Publication Manual of the American Psychological Association. Rev. 1967. Washington, D.C.: The American Psychological Association, 1967.

Trelease, S. F. *The Scientific Paper: How to Prepare It, How to Write It.* Second edition. Baltimore: Williams and Wilkins Company, 1951.

Turabian, Kate W. *A Manual for Writers of Term Papers, Theses, and Dissertations.* Chicago: The University of Chicago Press, Phoenix Books, 1960.

United States Government Printing Office. *Style Manual.* Revised edition. Washington, D.C.: Government Printing Office, 1973.

Footnotes and Documentation

We shall not prescribe any footnote form here. There are too many. Some styles of footnote documentation are preferred for one academic discipline, others are preferred for a different scholarly area. What you need is to get the idea and the purpose of the footnote which lies behind the form of the documentation.

We shall first discuss the idea behind the documentation. The documentary footnote has two principal functions. One of these is to invest the statements within the document with an aura of authority. You buttress your statements with an authoritarian source to establish their validity by citing your authority in a footnote. Another type of footnote acknowledges your indebtedness for quoted material or data. Ethics among writers requires that if material is borrowed from any source, both the author and the source should be acknowledged by footnote citation. Where the quotation is extensive and the writer is contemplating having his document published in any form, or copyrighted, he should secure *in writing* from the publisher or the author of the material—whoever holds the copyright to the material—permission to reprint the material. In addition to the footnote citing the source, the words *Reprinted by permission of the publisher* (or author, whichever may be the case) should be given.

The purpose of the footnote is to convey information. In the documentary footnote, that information may generally be categorized as follows:

1. The authorship data.
2. The source data.
3. The publication data.
4. The chronological data.
5. The locational data.

We shall discuss these items briefly.

The Authorship Data. Generally in footnotes the author's name is listed in the natural order: given name and surname. In bibliographic entries the order is usually reversed. Where multiple authors are involved the names are separated by commas with "and" joining the last name, and the names are usually all presented in given name-surname sequence, with the reverse being followed in bibliographic listings. Academic degrees or titles of respect are always deleted in listing authors' names.

The Source Data. Source data list the source from which the information has come. Generally the entire title is listed as it appears on the title page of the book or on the front cover of a journal. The rule is to put the title in *italics* when the document is a separate publication. (In typing, italics are indicated by underscoring the words with a straight line.) When the reference is a part only of a larger published whole (such as the title of an essay within a book of essays, the title of a poem, or the title of a chapter within a book), then put the title in *quotation marks.* Titles of books and journals are never put in quotation marks. The misuse of the quotation mark is a common fault among writers who do not know how this punctuational device is used. The quotation mark has five specific uses. Quotation marks are not to be scattered willy nilly at the whim of the writer.

The Publication Data. With books the publication data usually consist of the city and state in which the publisher is located and the full name of the publisher. The place of publication is available from the title page of the book or the masthead of the periodical. In the case of books, the title page may carry a list of cities; for example, Van Nostrand Reinhold Company, New York, Cincinnati, Toronto, London, Melbourne. The place of publication is always the *first* city mentioned in such an array—in this case, New York.

The publication information of a periodical is the volume number or the series number. With some periodicals the quarter of publication is also included among the publication information: e.g., winter, spring, summer, fall.

The Chronological Data. With books, chronological information is the year of publication as indicated on the title page or in the copyright notice of the book. The chronological information usually follows immediately the name of the publisher and is separated by a comma. With periodicals the chronological data are usually the year, the month, and in the case of daily or weekly periodicals, the day of the month.

The purpose of all documentation is to permit the reader, if he wishes, to go with the least difficulty to the source cited. To that end, the documentary data should assist the reader. In the case of newspaper citations, the date of issue, section of the newspaper, and column indication are frequently helpful.

The Locational Data. The locational data locate the data by page. Usually this information is the last item cited in the footnote. A widely used convention is to include the abbreviation *p.* or *pp.* for page references with *book* citations and to *omit* the page abbreviations for periodical citations: *Research/Development* 24:33 (1973). In this citation, 24 is the volume and 33 is the page. This journal numbers its pages consecutively throughout the year.

You should think of each *issue* of a periodical as one *section* of a volume. A journal which is issued monthly will have twelve sections which when compiled into a single *volume* will bear the volume number common to those twelve monthly issues.

Bibliographies are usually appended to extended discussions either as a recapitulation of the works cited in the document or as an additional reading list of related literature for the reader who wishes to pursue the subject at greater length.

Two other types of footnotes that we have not mentioned are the *informational footnote*, in which supplementary information (considered by the author as not particularly appropriate for inclusion in the text proper) is placed in footnote position, and the *internal reference footnote*, in which the reader is referred to a page earlier or later in the work in which a particular topic is discussed.

The Prose Style of the Report

The research report is precisely that, *a report.* It is the researcher reporting upon what he has done in the progress of his research effort. As we have said earlier, the researcher is acquainting the reader with the problem, with the data he has brought to bear upon the resolution of that problem, the means he has employed in gathering those data, the processes of analysis to which he has submitted them, the conclusions he has reached. All of this is history.

Because the researcher is reporting upon what has already happened, *the manuscript should be written in the past tense.* The document will also be restricted by another convention of document writing, namely, that—except for the title page or the by-line—the researcher should appear to be nonexistent. The use of the first personal pronoun in any of its forms is particularly taboo. This causes a concomitant problem: it forces the writer to employ the less forceful but the more impersonal *passive voice* style.

In case you are uncertain on matters of grammar, do not confuse past *tense* with passive *voice.* They have nothing in common. Past tense relates events as happening in the past: "The Treaty of Paris *brought* to an end the Revolutionary War." That is a simple statement of an event which happened in the past. The passive voice, on the other hand, is used to indicate that no identifiable subject is performing the act. It is a kind of ghostly form of the verb which causes events to happen without any visible cause being present. We *assume* that someone or something caused the events to transpire; but on the face of the record, no evidence of it appears, unless we specifically identify the perpetrator by a phrase indicating him intentionally. Note the passive voice in this sentence: "A survey *was made* of the owners of Rollaway automobiles." We have no indication of who made the survey. On the other hand we could say, "A survey was made *by the researcher* of the owners of Rollaway automobiles." This is a kind of quasifirst-person intrusion of the researcher and some readers may frown upon it. The passive voice is always identifiable by two features: *it always contains some form of the verb* to be; *it always contains a past participle of a verb.* It need not relate at all to things past: "The test *will have been given*" is a future passive verb form. The underscored words indicate the essential verbal components for the passive construction.

The general rule for the style of the research report is, therefore:

1. *Write it in the past tense as a report of events which have already transpired.*
2. *In the interest of keeping the person of the researcher subdued upon the face of the report, do not hesitate to employ the passive voice in writing the report.*

THE TYPING OF THE REPORT

The report should be a clean, neat, attractive document. City planners are conscious of "open spaces" and include them in their designs. Research report writers should be no less aware of their importance. Between text material and free-standing sideheads ample space should be allowed. Four single spaces between the end of the text material and the sidehead, then three single spaces between the sidehead and the continuing text material give an openness which suggests a definite break in the discussion and a turning to new matter. Two inches at the top, 1 inch at the bottom of the page, 1.75 inches on the left, and 1 inch, minimum, on the right give a page an atmosphere of spaciousness.

Such a page fulfills the specifications laid down by typographers and printers of quality books.

> Enough of the paper is exposed to make its contribution of a surface sympathetic to the type, texture, and pliability pleasant to the touch, and color pleasing to the eye. The classic page relationships are in the neighborhood of 50 percent for type page and paper page respectively. The Gutenberg 42-line Bible has 45 percent for type, 55 percent for paper page area.
>
> The distribution of margins from the esthetic viewpoint is governed by the principles of design relating to spatial areas. This means simply that there should be a pleasing difference between front and back and top and bottom margins.[1]

The proportions of type page suggested above are well proportioned from an esthetic standpoint and the left margin is wide enough to allow room for binding in the case of theses and dissertations. Also a text page area which is 5.75 by 8 inches on an 8.50- by 11-inch sheet of paper covers slightly more than 49 per cent of the total page area.

Chapter headings should be dropped approximately 3.5 inches from the top of the typing page. The first line of text begins six single spaces below the chapter heading. The text extends to within 2 inches of the bottom of the page. The first page of the chapter is drop-folioed; that is, the page number for the first page of each chapter is typed at the bottom of the page, centered, 1 inch from the lower edge of the typing page. All chapter headings are typed in capital letters, centered on the page.

Perhaps one of the most useful devices for typing a manuscript is an easily made typing guide. It measures 2 inches wider than the standard typing paper. On this extra 2-inch extension to the right of the page, the important page features are noted. Also, in diminishing sequence, beginning with maximum number of lines which the page will contain—twenty-five in this instance—and descending in reverse order to 1, each double-spaced line is numbered. The typist knows, therefore, at any given point on the page just how many lines he has left. The page is also divided within the print area into half sections by both

[1] *Typography and Design* (Washington, D.C.: United States Government Printing Office, revised 1963), p. 66.

vertical and horizontal lines. A box is provided for chapter headings and a starting line of the first line of text of a new chapter is indicated. In the upper right-hand corner is the designation for the page number. As we approach the bottom of the page an additional device of ▽ symbols begins to warn us when we have only ten lines until the end of the typing page. We are further alerted by the word *caution* beginning at line 8 and the last five lines are marked by ever-widening rows of inverted-triangle symbols.

A page typed with such a guide will be well proportioned, neat, and attractive.

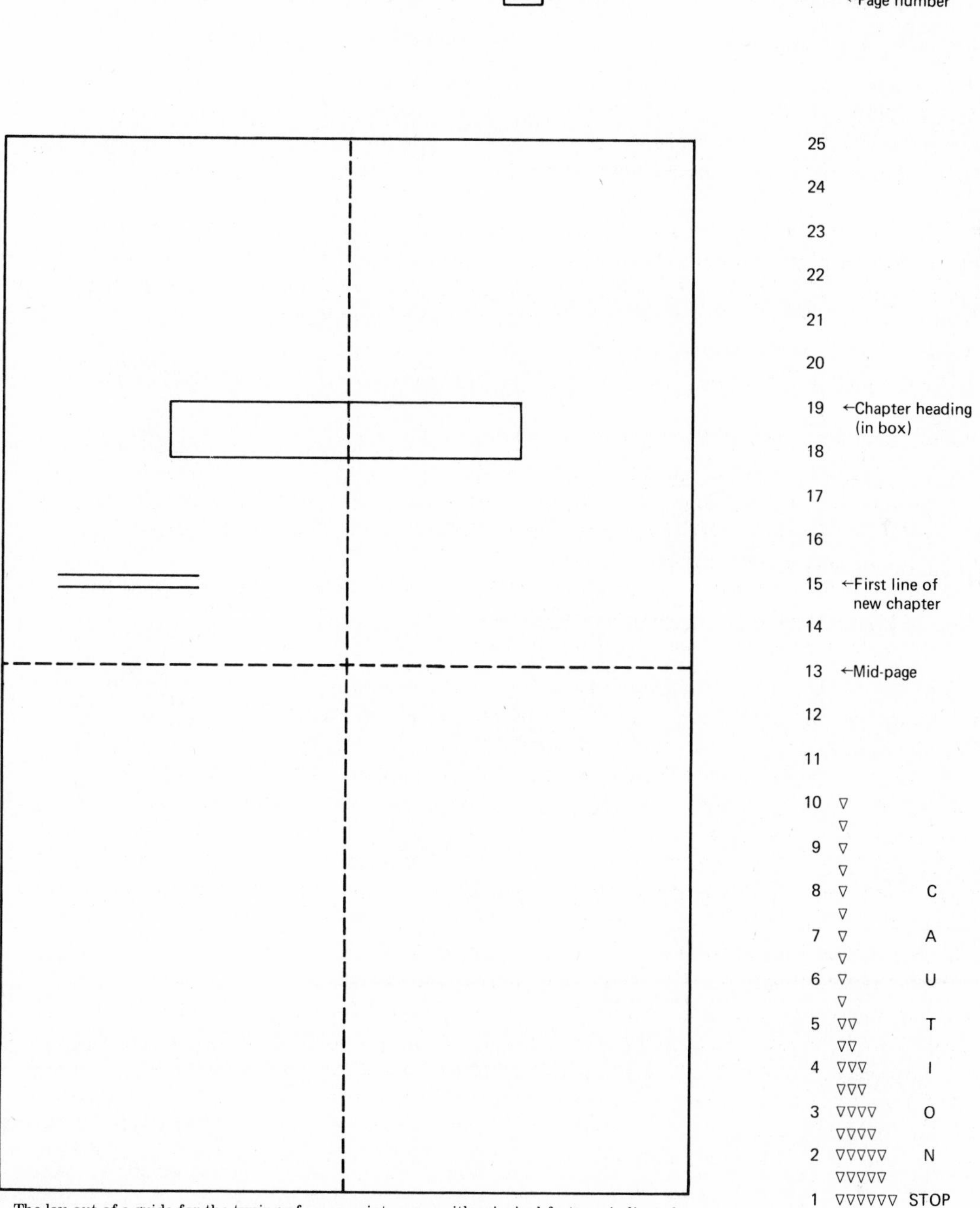

The lay-out of a guide for the typing of manuscript pages, with principal features indicated at the proper locations.

←Page number

The Typing of the Report

The report should be a clean, neat, attractive document. City planners are conscious of "open spaces" and include them in their designs. Research report writers should be no less aware of their importance. A crowded page bespeaks a crowded mind. Between text material and free-standing sideheads ample space should be allowed. Four single spaces between the end of the text material and the sidehead, then three single spaces between the sidehead and the continuing text material gives an openness which suggests a definite break in the discussion and a turning to new matter. Two inches at the top, an inch at the bottom of the page; an inch and three-quarters on the left and a full inch, minimum on the right presents a page whose margins are liberal and which gives an atmosphere of spaciousness.

Such a page fulfills the specifications laid down by typographers and printers of quality books.

> Enough of the paper is exposed to make its contribution of a surface sympathetic to the type, texture, and pliability pleasant to the touch, and color pleasing to the eye. The classic page relationships are in the neighborhood of 50 percent for type page and paper respectively.[1]

[1] Typography and Design. (Washington, D.C.: The United States Government Printing Office, 1963), p. 65.

←Chapter heading (in box)

←First line of new chapter

←Mid-page

▽ ▽ ▽ ▽ ▽ ▽ ▽ ▽ C A U T I O N ▽▽▽▽▽▽ STOP

A manuscript page superimposed on the guide for typing. The type page guide lines and center division broken lines are visible under the manuscript text.

Before you begin typing your final manuscript be sure that you have a well-inked ribbon and that you have thoroughly cleaned your type characters.

Nothing leaves a worse impression than a page typed with ink clogged characters, with lines that come out looking like this specimen.

A soft brush and a can of lighter fluid can correct such a condition.

And, Finally, the Research Report Need Not Be Dull!

There is no reason why the research report should be dull. It is unfortunate that the research report, the academic thesis, the dissertation have been considered an almost certain cure for insomnia. The only reason research reports are dull is because they are the products of dull writers. Phlegmatic attitudes and unimaginative minds will never set ablaze dry, lifeless fact.

Discovery is one of the most exciting of human activities. And research is discovery. It is sailing upon seas where no man has ever been before. It is looking across vast waste lands of mere data and seeing in them features previously unrecognized and characteristics heretofore unnoticed by any human mind. Imagine the attitudes that the men who walked upon the moon must have had. To them it was a thrilling adventure: not because it was the *moon*, primarily, but because in that seemingly dull and lifeless world lurked the facts that might provide an answer to the birth and age of the earth, the origin of the solar system, the birth of the moon. It offered the means of testing our theories. In the gray and lifeless dust, more completely dead than anything that man had ever looked upon in all his long history, lay exciting possibilities of extending human knowledge.

There is no such thing as a dead and lifeless fact. When facts die, something more important than the fact has first succumbed: the imagination, the force of thought within the researcher. When this goes, research dies. The writing of the report then becomes a dull exercise that produces an uninspired account of the researcher's efforts and his factual quarry.

We have come full circle. Now we understand why the selection of a problem which fascinates the researcher is so important. Only by being engrossed with a problem that captivates the researcher will the researcher keep his enthusiasm until the last word of the report is typed. And that enthusiasm is infectious. His words will capture it.

The author many years ago started out to find the origins and to investigate the influences which have been contributory or ancillary to the history and development of reading improvement as an instructional subject at the college level. He expected that his quest would take him back perhaps a quarter of a century and that the causes would have shallow roots. Instead, his study became a quicksand, taking him down, down, down into a historical abyss for which he had not bargained and of whose cavernous reaches he had little dreamed.

Coming back from the historical depths, he brought with him data. Here is what he did with the reporting of pedestrian fact:

> Many reasons contributed to the discouragement of reading in the mid-nineteenth century college. The libraries grew slowly, and even the oldest—and presumably the best—fell far short of what a college library might have been. Harvard and Yale had doubtless the acme of collegiate libraries in America, but even they left much devoutly to be wished by men of vision who saw what books and reading could mean in the educational program of the American college. . . .
>
> While no particular date can dichotomize the moment when the old order ceaseth, giving way to the new, 1876 is an especially noteworthy year. Influences which accumulated strength for years seemed suddenly of a moment to materialize into concrete fact. When this happens, certain historical moments become pivotal. In retrospect, 1876 seemed to be such a moment. . . . In 1876 the American Library Association was formed. Perhaps in the light of this fact Shores says that modern librarianship generally dates from 1876. In this year also R. R. Bowker became the first editor of the newly founded *Library Journal*, a publication that was to voice again and again in its columns the pertinency of reading to higher

education. On the first of January of this year, Daniel C. Gilman, the new president of The Johns Hopkins University, issued his first annual report. In this initial report to the trustees of the new university, President Gilman said,

> The idea is not lost sight of that the power of the university will depend upon the character of its resident staff of prominent professors. It is their researches in the library and the laboratory . . . which will make the University in Baltimore an attraction to the best students and serviceable to the intellectual growth of the land.

And the University in Baltimore did, indeed, have a far-reaching effect upon the "intellectual growth of the land."[2]

The Elements of Style

The elements of style are there; the text has readability. The paragraphs begin with topic sentences. These are elaborated, and the facts are documented. The first three sentences are normal subject-predicate order. The fourth sentence begins with a dependent clause. Then subject-predicate form again. Then a clause beginning, followed by a phrase introduction, followed by an adverb beginning, then a phrase. Variety is the spice of life; it is also the life of a writing style. Short sentences alternate with longer ones. These are all features which make for easy, interesting reading.

You might do well, if you are not sure of what makes readable writing to study two books: *The Elements of Style*[3] and *The Art of Readable Writing.*[4] Eschew the exaggerated expression; look sharply at your ill-advised and thoughtlessly chosen adjectives. Stick to the facts, report them accurately, but in so doing enliven your prose with variety of sentence length and precision of verb and noun.

More do's and don'ts are probably to no avail. Distilled into a brief stanza by an anonymous hand is a broad guideline for all your writing. Follow it.

The written word
Should be clean as bone:
Clear as light,
Firm as stone;
Two words are not
As good as one.

[2]Paul D. Leedy, "A History of the Origin and Development of Instruction in Reading Improvement at the College Level" (unpublished doctoral dissertation, New York University, 1958), pp. 94, 97-98.

[3]K. W. Strunk, Jr., and E. B. White, *The Elements of Style* (New York: Macmillan Publishing Co., Inc., 1959).

[4]Rudolph Flesch, *The Art of Readable Writing* (New York: Harper & Row, 1949).

Bibliography

This bibliography has been selected with the purpose of providing the student with a reading list for further exploration of the areas covered in this text. The second part of the bibliography consists of texts dealing with statistical aspects of research. Each of the works listed will have its own bibliography which will further assist the student.

RESEARCH AND RESEARCH METHODOLOGY

Ackoff, R. L. *The Design of Social Research.* Chicago: University of Chicago Press, 1953.

———. *Scientific Method.* New York: John Wiley & Sons, Inc., 1962.

Adams, J. S. *Interviewing Procedures.* Chapel Hill, N.C.: University of North Carolina Press, 1958.

Ball, John, and Cecil B. Williams. *Report Writing.* New York: The Ronald Press Company, 1955.

Barr, A. S. "Research Methods" in *Encyclopedia of Educational Research,* Chester W. Harris (ed.). New York: Macmillan Publishing Co., Inc., 1960.

Barzun, Jacques, and Henry F. Graff. *The Modern Researcher.* New York: Harcourt Brace Jovanovich, Inc., 1957.

Beveridge, William I. B. *The Art of Scientific Investigation.* New York: W. W. Norton & Company, Inc., 1957.

Blalock, Hubert M., Jr. *Causal Inferences in Nonexperimental Research.* New York: W. W. Norton & Company, Inc., 1972.

Bloch, M. L. B. *Historian's Craft.* New York: Alfred A. Knopf, Inc., 1953.

Boaz, Martha T. (ed.). *Modern Trends in Documentation.* Elmsford, N.Y.: Pergamon Press, Inc., 1959.

Borg, Walter R., and Meredith D. Gall. *Educational Research: An Introduction.* Second edition. New York: David McKay Co., Inc., 1971.

Bowles, Edmund (ed.). *Computers in Humanistic Research: Readings and Perspectives.* Englewood Cliffs, N.J.: Prentice-Hall, Inc., 1967.

Bradley, E. F., and O. T. Denmead. *Collection and Processing of Field Data.* New York: John Wiley & Sons, Inc., 1967.

Brickman, William W. *Guide to Research in Educational History.* New York: New York University Bookstore, 1949.

Bunge, Mario A. *Scientific Research.* New York: Springer Publishing Co., Inc., 1967.

Bush, George P. *Bibliography on Research: Annotated.* Washington, D.C.: University Press of Washington, D.C., 1954.

Chapanes, Alphonse R. E. *Research Techniques in Human Engineering.* Baltimore: The Johns Hopkins Press, 1959.

Chapin, F. S. *Experimental Designs in Sociological Research.* Revised edition. New York: Harper & Row, Publisher's, 1958.

Churchman, Charles W., R. L. Ackoff, and E. Leonard Arnoff. *Introduction to Operations Research.* New York: John Wiley & Sons, Inc., 1957.

Cochran, William G., and Gertrude C. Cox. *Experimental Designs.* Second edition. New York: John Wiley & Sons, Inc., 1957.

Cohen, Dorothy H., and Virginia Stern. *Observing and Recording the Behavior of Young Children.* New York: Bureau of Publications, Teachers College, Columbia University, 1958.

Cohen, Jerome. *The Structure of Forms of Human Inquiry.* Chicago: Adams Press, 1972.

Cohen, Morris R., and Ernest Nagle. *An Introduction to Logic and the Scientific Method.* New York: Harcourt Brace Jovanovich, Inc., 1934.

Collier, R. O., and S. M. Elam (eds.). *Research Design and Analysis: The Second Phi Delta Kappa Symposium on Educational Research.* Bloomington, Ind.: Phi Delta Kappa, 1961.

Cooley, W. W., and P. R. Leonard. *Multivariant Procedures for the Behavioral Sciences.* New York: John Wiley & Sons, Inc., 1962.

Cox, D. R. *Planning of Experiments.* New York: John Wiley & Sons, Inc., 1958.

Coyle, William (ed.). *Research Paper.* Indianapolis, Ind.: The Odyssey Press.

Curti, Merle (ed.). *Theory and Practice in Historical Study.* Social Science Research Council Bulletin, No. 54. New York: The Council, 1946.

Dartmouth College, Amos Tuck School of Business Administration, Committee on Research. *Manual on Research and Reports.* New York: McGraw-Hill Book Company, 1937.

Davies, Owen L. *The Design and Analysis of Industrial Experiments.* New York: Hafner Publishing Co., Inc., 1956.

Dow, E. W. *Principles of a Note System for Historical Studies.* New York: Appleton-Century-Crofts, Inc., 1924.

Edwards, A. L. *Experimental Design in Psychological Research.* Revised edition. New York: Holt, Rinehart & Winston, Inc., 1960.

Edwards, A. L. "Experiments: Their Planning and Execution," in G. Lindzay (ed.), *Handbook of Social Psychology.* Vol. I: *Theory and Method.* Cambridge, Mass.: Addison-Wesley Publishing Co., Inc., 1954.

Englehart, Max D. *Methods of Educational Research.* Chicago: Rand McNally & Co., 1972.

Fenlason, Anne. *Essentials of Interviewing.* New York: Harper & Row, Publishers, 1952.

Festinger, L., and D. Katz. *Research Methods in the Behavioral Sciences.* New York: The Dryden Press, 1953.

Finney, D. J. *An Introduction to the Theory of Experimental Design.* Chicago: University of Chicago Press, 1960.

__________. *Experimental Design and Its Statistical Basis.* Chicago: University of Chicago Press, 1955.

Fisher, R. A. *The Design of Experiments.* Sixth edition. New York: Hafner Publishing Co., Inc., 1951.

Fox, David J. *The Research Process in Education.* New York: Holt, Rinehart & Winston, Inc., 1969.

Freedman, Paul. *The Principles of Scientific Research.* Second edition. New York: Pergamon Press, Inc., 1960.

Gage, N. L. (ed.). *Handbook of Research on Teaching.* Chicago: Rand McNally and Company, 1963.

Galfo, Armand J., and Earl Miller. *Interpreting Educational Research.* Second edition. Dubuque, Iowa: William C. Brown, 1970.

Garraghan, Gilbert J. *A Guide to Historical Method.* New York: The Free Press, 1959.

Gephart, William J., and Robert B. Ingle (eds.). *Educational Research: Selected Readings.* Columbus, Ohio: Charles E. Merrill Publishing Company, 1969.

Good, Carter V. *Essentials of Educational Research: Methodology and Design.* New York: Appleton-Century-Crofts, Inc., 1966.

———. *Introduction to Educational Research.* Second edition. New York: Appleton-Century-Crofts, Inc., 1963.

Good, Carter V., and Douglas E. Scates. *Methods in Research: Educational, Psychological, Sociological.* New York: Appleton-Century-Crofts, Inc., 1954.

Goode, William J., and Paul K. Hatt. *Methods in Social Research.* New York: McGraw-Hill Book Company, 1952.

Gottschalk, Louis R. *Understanding History.* New York: Alfred A. Knopf, Inc., 1950.

Harris, Chester W. (ed.). *Encyclopedia of Educational Research.* New York: Macmillan Publishing Co., Inc., 1960.

Hillway, Tyrus. *Introduction to Research.* Boston: Houghton Mifflin Company, 1956.

Hockett, Homer C. *The Critical Method in Historical Research and Writing.* New York: Macmillan Publishing Co., Inc., 1955.

Hodnett, Edward. *The Art of Problem Solving.* New York: Harper & Row, Publishers, 1955.

Holt, Robert T., and John E. Turner (eds.). *The Methodology of Comparative Political Research.* New York: The Free Press, 1972.

Hook, Lucyle, and Mary V. Gaver. *The Research Paper.* Fourth edition. Englewood Cliffs, N.J.: Prentice-Hall, Inc., 1969.

Howe, George F., et al. *Guide to Historical Literature.* New York: Macmillan Publishing Co., Inc., 1961.

Hubbell, George Shelton. *Writing Term Papers and Reports.* Fourth edition. New York: Barnes and Noble, 1957.

Hyman, Herbert H., et al. *Interviewing in Social Research.* Chicago: University of Chicago Press, 1954.

International Bibliography of Historical Sciences, 1926–. New York: H. W. Wilson Co., 1930–.

Jahoda, Marie, M. Deutsch, and S. W. Cook. *Research Methods in Social Relations.* Two volumes. New York: The Dryden Press, 1951.

Kahn, R. L., and C. F. Cannell. *The Dynamics of Interviewing.* New York: John Wiley & Sons, Inc., 1957.

Kaplan, A. *The Conduct of Inquiry: Methodology for Behavioral Science.* San Francisco: Chandler Publishing Co., 1964.

Katz, Jay. *Experimentation with Human Beings: The Authority of the Investigator, Subject, Professions, and State in the Human Experimentation Process.* New York: Russell Sage Foundation, 1972.

Kempthorne, Oscar. *The Design and Analysis of Experiments.* New York: John Wiley & Sons, Inc., 1952.

Kraus, Michael. *The Writing of American History.* Norman, Oklahoma: The University of Oklahoma Press, 1953.

Lazarsfeld, Paul F., and Morris Rosenberg (eds.). *The Language of Social Research.* New York: The Free Press, 1958.

Madge, John. *The Tools of Social Science.* New York: Longmans, Green & Company, 1953.

Marsh, Marilyn B., and Nadine W. Ricks. *How to Write Your First Research Paper.* Belmont, Calif.: Wadsworth Publishing Co., 1970.

McCormick, Thomas C., and Roy G. Francis. *Methods of Research in the Behavioral Sciences.* New York: Harper & Row, Publishers, 1958.

McGrath, J. H. *Research Methods and Designs for Education.* Scranton, Pa.: International Textbook Company, 1970.

Morse, Philip M., and George M. Kimball. *Methods of Operations Research.* Cambridge, Mass.: Technology Press of the Massachusetts Institute of Technology, 1951.

Mouly, George J. *The Science of Educational Research.* New York: Van Nostrand Reinhold Company, 1970.

Palmer, Arshie M. (ed.). *Research Centers Directory.* Fourth edition. Detroit, Mich.: Gale Research Company, 1972.

Payne, Stanley L. *The Art of Asking Questions.* Princeton, N.J.: Princeton University Press, 1951.

Pugh, Griffith T. *Guide to Research Writing.* Boston: Houghton Mifflin Company, 1955.

Rummell, J. Frances. *An Introduction to Research Procedures.* New York: Harper & Row, Publishers, 1958.

Sanders, Chauncey. *An Introduction to Research in English Literary History.* New York: Macmillan Publishing Co., Inc., 1952.

Sax, Gilbert. *Empirical Foundations of Educational Research.* Englewood Cliffs, N.J.: Prentice-Hall, Inc., 1968.

Scott, M. Gladys. *Research Methods in Health, Physical Education, Recreation.* Second edition. Washington, D.C.: American Association for Health, Physical Education, and Recreation, 1959.

Scott, William A., and Michael Wertheimer. *Introduction to Psychological Research.* New York: John Wiley & Sons, Inc., 1962.

Selltiz, Claire, Marie Jahoda, M. Deutsch, and S. W. Cook. *Research Methods in Social Relations.* Revised edition. New York: Holt, Rinehart & Winston, Inc., 1961.

Sidman, M. *Tactics of Scientific Research.* New York: Basic Books, 1960.

Skager, Rodney W., and Carl Weinberg. *Fundamentals of Educational Research: An Introductory Approach.* Glenview, Ill.: Scott, Foresman and Company, 1971.

Skillin, Marjorie E., Robert M. Gay, et al. *Words into Type.* New York: Appleton-Century-Crofts, Inc., 1948.

Travers, Robert M. W. *An Introduction to Educational Research.* Second edition. New York: Macmillan Publishing Co., Inc., 1964.

Trelease, S. F. *How to Write Scientific and Technical Papers.* Baltimore: Williams and Wilkins, 1958.

Townsend, J. C. *Introduction to the Experimental Method.* New York: McGraw-Hill Book Company, 1953.

Tuckman, Bruce W. *Conducting Educational Research.* New York: Harcourt Brace Jovanovich, Inc., 1972.

Tullock, Gordon. *The Organization of Inquiry.* Durham, N.C.: Duke University Press, 1966.

Van Dalen, Deobold B., and William J. Meyer. *Understanding Educational Research: An Introduction.* New York: McGraw-Hill Book Company, 1962.

Wandelt, Mabel. *Guide for the Beginning Researcher.* New York: Appleton-Century-Crofts, Inc., 1970.

Whitney, Frederick L. *The Elements of Research.* Englewood, N.J.: Prentice-Hall, Inc., 1950.

Williams, Cecil B. *A Research Manual for College Studies and Papers.* Third edition. New York: Harper & Row, Publishers, 1963.

Wilson, E. Bright. *An Introduction to Scientific Research.* New York: McGraw-Hill Book Company, 1952.

Wise, John E., Robert Nordberg, and Donald J. Reitz. *Methods of Research in Education.* Boston: D. C. Heath and Company, 1967.

Young, Pauline V. *Scientific Social Surveys and Research* Third edition. Englewood Cliffs, N.J.: Prentice-Hall, Inc., 1956.

Young, Raymond J. (compiler). *A Directory of Educational Research Agencies.* Second revision. Bloomington, Ind.: Phi Delta Kappa, 1962.

STATISTICS

Anderson, Theodore R., and Morris Zelditch, Jr. *Basic Course in Statistics.* New York: Holt, Rinehart & Winston, Inc., 1968.

Arkin, Herbert, and Raymond H. Colton. *Statistical Methods.* Fifth edition. New York: Barnes and Noble, 1970.

Averill, E. W. *Elements of Statistics.* New York: John Wiley & Sons, Inc., 1972.

Bailey, Daniel E. *Probability and Statistics: Models for Research.* New York: John Wiley & Sons, Inc., 1971.

Blum, Julius R., and Judah I. Rosenblatt. *Probability and Statistics.* Philadelphia: W. B. Saunders Company, 1972.

Burrington, G. A. *How to Find Out about Statistics.* Elmsford, N.Y.: Pergamon Press, Inc., 1973.

Chambers, E. G. *Statistical Calculations for Engineers.* Second edition. New York: Cambridge University Press, 1958.

Cochran, W. G. *Sampling Techniques.* Second edition. New York: John Wiley & Sons, Inc., 1959.

Crow, E. L., F. A. Davis, and N. W. Maxfield. *Statistics Manual.* New York: Dover Publications, Inc., 1960.

Deming, W. E. *Sample Design in Business Research.* New York: John Wiley & Sons, Inc., 1960.

DuBois, P. H. *Multivariate Correlational Analysis.* New York: Harper & Row, Publishers, 1957.

Ehrenfeld, S., and S. B. Littauer. *Introduction to Statistical Method.* New York: McGraw-Hill Book Company, 1964.

Fisher, R. A. *Statistical Methods and Scientific Inference.* Revised edition. New York: Hafner Publishing Co., Inc., 1959.

———. *Statistical Methods for Research Workers.* Tenth edition. Edinburgh: Oliver and Boyd, 1948.

Fisher, R. A., and F. Yates. *Statistical Tables for Biological, Agricultural, and Medical Research.* New York: Hafner Publishing Co., Inc., 1964.

Freund, John E., and F. J. Williams. *Dictionary-Outline of Basic Statistics.* New York: McGraw-Hill Book Company, 1966.

Fruchter, Benjamin. *Introduction to Factor Analysis.* New York: Van Nostrand Reinhold Company, 1959.

[Gosset, W. S.] *"Student's" Collected Papers.* Edited by E. S. Pearson and J. Wishart. Third edition. London: Cambridge University Press, 1958.

Gruenther, W. C. *Analysis of Variance.* Englewood Cliffs, N.J.: Prentice-Hall, Inc., 1964.

Hammond, Kenneth R. *Introduction to the Statistical Method.* Second edition. New York: Alfred A. Knopf, Inc., 1970.

Hicks, C. R. *Fundamental Concepts in the Design of Experiments.* New York: Holt, Rinehart & Winston, Inc., 1964.

Hogben, Lancelot. *Statistical Theory: The Relationship of Probability, Credibility, and Error.* London: Allen and Unwin, 1957.

Huff, Darrell, and Irving Geis. *How to Lie with Statistics.* New York: W. W. Norton & Company, Inc., 1954.

Huntsberger, David V., and Paul E. Leaverton. *Statistical Inference in the Biomedical Sciences.* Boston: Allyn & Bacon, Inc., 1970.

Johnson, N. L., and F. C. Leone. *Statistics and Experimental Design.* Volumes I and II. New York: John Wiley & Sons, Inc., 1964.

Johnson, Palmer O. *Statistical Methods in Research.* Englewood Cliffs, N.J.: Prentice-Hall, Inc., 1949.

Kendall, M. G. *The Advanced Theory of Statistics.* Philadelphia: J. B. Lippincott Company, 1943.

__________. *Rank Correlation Methods.* Second edition. London: Griffin, 1955.

Lacey, Oliver L. *Statistical Methods in Experimentation.* New York: Macmillan Publishing Co., Inc., 1953.

Lerner, Daniel (ed.). *Evidence and Inference.* New York: The Free Press, 1958.

Mood, A. M., and F. A. Graybill. *Introduction to the Theory of Statistics.* Second edition. New York: McGraw-Hill Book Company, 1963.

Natrella, Mary G. *Experimental Statistics.* (National Bureau of Standards Handbook 91.) Washington, D.C.: United States Government Printing Office, 1963.

Peatman, John G. *Introduction to Applied Statistics.* New York: Harper & Row, Publishers, 1963.

Rand Corporation. *A Million Random Digits with 100,000 Normal Deviates.* New York: The Free Press, 1955.

Rickmers, Albert D., and Hollis N. Todd. *Statistics: An Introduction.* New York: McGraw-Hill Book Company, 1967.

Siegel, S. *Nonparametric Statistics for the Behavioral Sciences.* New York: McGraw-Hill Book Company, 1956.

Snedecor, G. W. *Statistical Methods.* Fifth edition. Ames, Iowa: Iowa State College Press, 1956.

"Student," *see* Gosset, W. S.

Ullmann, Neil R. *Statistics: An Applied Approach.* Waltham, Mass.: Xerox College Publishing Co., 1972.

Walker, H. M. *Mathematics Essential for Elementary Statistics.* New York: Holt, Rinehart & Winston, Inc., 1952.

Walker, Helen M., and W. N. Durost. *Statistical Tables: Their Structure and Use.* New York: Teachers College, Columbia University, 1936.

Walsh, J. E. *Handbook of Nonparametric Statistics.* New York: Van Nostrand Reinhold Company, 1962.

Wilcoxon, Frank. *Some Rapid Approximate Statistical Procedures.* New York: American Cyanimid Co., 1949.

Wine, R. L. *Statistics for Scientists and Engineers.* Englewood Cliffs, N.J.: Prentice-Hall, Inc., 1964.

Winer, B. J. *Statistical Principles in Experimental Design.* New York: McGraw-Hill Book Company, 1962.

Wonnacott, Thomas H., and Ronald J. Wonnacott. *Introduction to Statistics for Business and Economics.* New York: John Wiley & Sons, Inc., 1972.

Yule, G. U. *An Introduction to the Theory of Statistics.* Twelfth edition. London: Griffin, 1940.

Zeisel, Hans. *Say It with Figures.* New York: Harper & Row, Publishers, 1957.

Sample Proposal and Practicum in Research

Appendix A

Sample Proposal for a Research Project

On the pages that follow is an exact reprint of the text for a doctoral research project as it was presented to the faculty of the Department of Education of The American University, Washington, D.C.

The proposal is presented here because, by so doing, it may give the student a clearer idea of precisely what a proposal is, the form it should take, and the arrangement of its several parts. Every proposal is essentially the same whether it is for endorsement of a project that a student wishes to pursue or the underwriting of a proposed research endeavor by grant award or for foundation funding. The greater the investment of time, money, and effort demanded by the project, the fuller and more specific will be the proposal requirements. Certainly there are variations to the format here presented. No brief is made for the priority of the format as presented here over any other equally logical presentation. But the essentials of every proposal are those discussed in the text and presented here.

The proposal chosen for presentation was one which dealt with a very practical item of research. Underlying the thinking of the proposal was a substratum of reasoning that ran something like this: People are more likely to succeed if they are doing the things they like to do. If one can find the key to a person's interests, he has, in part at least, the key to probability of that person's success. Interests are identified objectively by measuring feelings of like and dislike toward things and activities. Of the several general interest inventories, the *Strong Vocational Interest Blank* has been the most studied and most frequently used. Interest scales have been developed on the Strong for fifty-four occupational groups. No scale has been developed for cartographers on the Strong or any other interest-measuring instrument.

Cartographers and the nature of their professional activities as map makers is little known to the general public. The annual production of cartographers is only about 1 per cent of the annual requirement. If, therefore, some way can be found to match people who have kindred interests to those of cartographers with occupational opportunities in which there is a wide-open demand, we may have come to grips with a very real problem facing one segment of our national life. It is to a possible solution of this problem that the problem for research and this proposal address themselves.

One further word should be said about the form in which the proposal is presented. As stated, the conventional typescript is an exact reprint of the proposal as presented by the student. Its value to the user of this book will lie (1) in seeing its original form and (2) in seeing how, excellent as it is, even this proposal might have been improved.

Two conventions have, therefore, been employed: the usual proofreading marks to alter the script itself where necessary and a running commentary in the right-hand margin, pointing out both the good qualities of the proposal and the improvements which might be made to make it even more effective.

A STUDY TO IDENTIFY AND EVALUATE THE EXISTING DISCRETE INTERESTS AMONG FEDERALLY EMPLOYED MALE CARTOGRAPHERS AND TO DEVELOP A SCALE FOR THE STRONG VOCATIONAL INTEREST BLANK TO AID THE RECRUITMENT OF CARTOGRAPHERS INTO FEDERAL EMPLOYMENT

This is the title page for the study. Note that what is given here is a title for the study and not the spacing, the balance, the eye-appeal in the format of the page.

A Dissertation Proposal

Presented to

the Faculty of the College of Arts and Sciences

The American University

This section explains what the document is and for whom it is written. The solid line above separates the one type of material from the other.

In Partial Fulfillment

of the Requirements for the Degree of

Doctor of Philosophy

This section explains the rationale for the document and its function.

---

by

Arthur Louis Benton

December 1969

The author's name and the date of the document completes the essential information on the title page.

COMMENTS ON ITEMS WITHIN THE PROPOSAL

THE PROBLEM AND ITS SETTING

Note the use of the headings to indicate the organization and outline of the proposal. Refer to the discussion of this matter in Chapter 3 (p. 44.)

The Statement of the Problem

This research proposes to identify and evaluate the existing discrete interests among Federally employed male cartographers and to develop a scale for the revised *Strong Vocational Interest Blank* to aid recruitment of cartographers into Federal employment.

The phrase existing discrete is useless verbiage. If they are "discrete interests," they do "exist."

Note the underscoring, indicating italics, for published titles.

Note also that only the words are italicized. It is impossible to italicize spaces. Hence, the line is broken and not solid as so often written.

The Subproblems

1. *The first subproblem.* The first subproblem is to determine whether male cartographers employed by the Federal government have a discrete pattern of interests different from those of men in general as measured by the *Strong Vocational Interest Blank.*

The numbering here is superfluous. The ¶ sidehead makes it clearly apparent that this is the first subproblem. No need, therefore, to number it 1.

2. *The second subproblem.* The second subproblem is to construct a scoring key for the Strong Vocational Interest Blank to differentiate ^the interest of^ cartographers from ^those of^ men in general and ^also from the interests of^ other occupational groups.

Here the researcher is not thinking what he is saying. What he says is that he wants to differentiate cartographers. That is not so. He wants to differentiate the interests of cartographers. The edited additions bring the thought into correct perspective.

3. *The third subproblem.* The third subproblem is to analyze and ^to^ interpret the treated data so as to evaluate the discovered interests in terms of their discreteness in recruiting cartographers.

Note the correction in syntax. A correlative connects two like constructions; thus the insertion of the to.

Note that the three subproblems add up to the totality of the problem.

The Hypotheses

Note the spacing between the free-standing sidehead and the first line of text. Such spacing causes the heading to stand out prominently for ease of reading. Crowding is the worst typing fault of most students.

The first hypothesis is that male cartographers employed by the Federal Government have a discrete pattern of interests different from those of men in general.

Note the position of the hypothesis section. It immediately follows the

The second hypothesis is that the Strong Vocational Interest Blank can identify the existing discrete interests of cartographers differentially from those of men in general and those of other occupational groups.

subproblems. It facilitates seeing the one-to-one correspondence between subproblems and hypothesis pertaining to that subproblem.

"Edited-in" words express precisely what the writer of the proposal means.

The third hypothesis is that the development of an interest scale can aid the recruitment of cartographers into Federal employment.

This hypothesis goes beyond the limits of the problem. The researcher does not intend to investigate the actual recruitments of cartogragpers, yet, unless he does he cannot know whether his hypothesis will be supported or not.

The Delimitations

The study will not attempt to predict success of cartographers.

The study will not determine nor evaluate the preparation and training of cartographers.

Delimitations indicate the peripheral areas lying contiguous to the problem which the researcher expressly rules out of the area of his investigation.

The study will be limited to male cartographers who have attained, within the U.S. Civil Service classification system, full performance ratings of GS-09 or higher in Occupation Series 1370.

The study will not evaluate uniformed military personnel.

Again, the researcher is not saying what he means precisely. What he intends to say is: The study will not evaluate any cartographers who may be uniformed military personnel.

The Definitions of Terms

Cartographer.[1] A cartographer is a professional[2] employee who engages[3] in the production of maps, including construction of projections, design, drafting (or scribing), and preparation through the negative stage for the reproduction of maps, charts, and related graphic materials.

Note that the word to be defined is given in the ¶ sidehead. Then follows a complete definition comprising the three parts discussed on p. 55. The small numbers over the first definition indicate: 1 = the term to be defined, 2 = the genera, 3 = the differentia.

Discrete interests. Discrete interests are those empirically derived qualities or traits common to an occupational population that serve to make them distinct from the general population or universe.

Again the definition is formal in that it begins with the term to be defined (discrete interests); it states the genera to which the term belongs (empirically derived qualities or traits); and then the differentia (e.g., common to an occupational population).

Abbreviations

SVIB is the abbreviation used for the Strong Vocational Interest Blank.

This section was not discussed in the text, but it is perfectly appropriate. Whatever makes for ease of reading and aids in giving the problem an appropriate setting is worthy of inclusion in this part of the proposal.

USATOPOCOM is an acronym for the U.S. Army Topographic Command.

CIMR is an abbreviation used for the Center for Interest Measurement Research.

SD is the abbreviation used for standard deviation.

Assumptions

The first assumption. The first assumption is that the need for cartographers in Federal service will continue.

The second assumption. The second assumption is that the revised Strong Vocational Interest Blank will continue in use as a vocational guidance tool.

The third assumption. The third assumption is that the recent revolutionary advances in the cartographic state of the art will not alter the interests of persons in the employment of the Federal Government as cartographers.

The fourth assumption. The fourth assumption is that the criterion group consisting of the population of catographers employed by the USATOPOCOM at Washington, D.C.; Providence, Rhode Island; Louisville, Kentucky; Kansas City, Missouri, and San Antonio, Texas, is representative of the universe of Federally employed cartographers.

Note that the assumptions are set up with appropriate paragraph subheads. Perhaps this is one feature which might have enhanced the presentation of the hypotheses. Had they been set up, as, for example, The first hypothesis, each section would have been parallel in format.

As we said earlier, clarity is most important in the writing and structuring of a proposal. The writer of this proposal has presented his material in a delightfully clear manner.

Note that again and again the writer of this proposal gives evidence of working with care and precision. He does not try to cut corners. Here he spells out fully the name of the state, rather than employ abbreviations.

The Importance of the Study

Cartographers and the nature of their work is little known in American society. The total annual production of graduates, at the bachelor's level, with competence in the broader field of survey engineering within which cartography is subsumed, is currently less than one per cent of the annual requirement. The addition of a cartographer scale to the occupations routinely reported for the Strong Vocational Interest Blank would potentially bring to the attention of everyone involved with the existing vocational guidance system the opportunities within the field of map-making and serve to attract serious and capable students into the appropriate preparatory college programs.

This section gives the reader of the proposal a pratical rationale for undertaking the study. It shows a utilitarian connection between the problem for research and the exigencies of real life.

Here the researcher points out that chance produces less than 1 per cent of graduates required for the demand of the cartographic profession If he can find a way to identify potential candidates for the profession in terms of their discrete interests on the SVIB, it may attract serious and capable students into courses which might prepare and lead them toward cartography as a life's work.

This section makes no attempt to present a complete discussion of the related literature with respect to this problem. It does, however, select a representative sampling of each section from the complete discussion so that the student may see how the discussion of related literature is presented.

THE REVIEW OF THE RELATED LITERATURE

Note the centered heading, all caps. This is the second main division of the proposal, a fact which the position and all-capitalization of the heading indicates. (See p. 44.)

A Historical Overview

The reader is introduced to the problem through the perspective of its historical background. Note that the discussion begins with the earliest reference to interests in the eighteenth century and progresses strictly chronologically from J. J. Rousseau (1712-1778) to Guilford (1965).

The role of interests within the behavioral sciences is not new. Rousseau (1712-1778) in the eighteenth century spoke to the matter of interests:

> . . . Education . . . is a development from within, not an accretion from without; it comes through the workings of natural instincts and interests and not in response to external force; it is an expansion of natural powers, not an acquisition of information; it is life itself, not a preparation for a future state remote in interests and characteristics from the life of childhood.[1]

Extended quotations are single spaced, indented. Ellipsis is indicated by three periods alternating with single space distances (. . .). Ellipsis indicates that words, or perhaps even sentences, have been deleted from the original text. If an entire paragraph is omitted, such omission is marked by an entire line of double-spaced periods:

. . . .

Herbart is discussed as having been interested in the subject of interest.

Herbart (1776-1841) stressed virtue as the ultimate purpose of education but recognized the need for arousal of interest in order to secure the attention and appropriation of new ideas.[2]

---

[1] Paul Monroe (ed.), History of Education (New York: The Macmillan Company, 1909), p. 566.

Here the author should have gone to the original sources,—to the writings of J. J. Rousseau (definitive edition) and cited the location of the quotation from the work in which it appears.

[2] Ibid., p. 752.

Again the reader should be referred to the specific location in Herbart's writings where the idea discussed is found.

Within the same context of educational and psychological thought, James (1842-1910) said:

Note that here the author of the proposal does cite the prime source of the quotation (footnote 3). This is the way the Rousseau and Herbart quotations should have been cited.

Note again that an extended quotation is single spaced, and indented from both margins of the page.

> Millions of items of the outward order are present to my senses which never properly enter into my experience. Why? Because they have no interest for me. My experience is what I agree to attend to. Only those items which I notice shape my mind -- without selective interest, experience is utter chaos. Interest alone gives accent and emphasis, light and shade, background and foreground -- intelligible perspective, in a word.[3]

Psychologists and educators alike have sought to define the desires, interests, and satisfactions that initiate behavior and have applied the term motivation to the concept. Ryan remarked that a postulated "X" which energizes and directs behavior is still the common core across widely different theories of behavior.[4]

Ryan and Guilford are cited and the footnotes refer the reader to the original sources.

Guilford perhaps ~~comes~~ came close to explaining motivation in terms of his informational psychology when he addressed the Nebraska Symposium on Motivation in 1965, saying ". . . there is goal information and this is in the form of the product of anticipation. Human goals are almost entirely developed by experience in the form of anticipated values, and anticipations are implications." [5]

Note the change in tense. Precision of expression is paramount in research writing and reporting. The broad rule for tense usage is generally that since a research report recounts what has been done, the tense employed should generally be the past tense. If present or future tenses are used they should represent facts that will be true at any time the document is read. Here comes is inaccurate. Guilford came close to explaining motivation in 1965 at the Nebraska Symposium. Other changes in tense will be made where necessary.

---

[3] William James, The Principles of Psychology (New York: Henry Holt and Company, 1908), Vol. I, p. 402.

[4] T. A. Ryan, "Drives, Tasks, and the Initiation of Behavior," American Journal of Psychology, LXXI (January, 1958), 74-93.

[5] J. P. Guilford, "Motivation in an Informational Psychology," David Lewine (ed.), Nebraska Symposium on Motivation (Lincoln: University of Nebraska Press, 1965), pp. 313-333.

Since interests involve reactions or inclinations to specific things, then it would appear that they must be learned. Within that field of psychology identified as learning theory, motive ... ed is crucial for Hull,[6] ... ndike,[7] Lewin,[8] and others am ... ed incidenta ... tensive ... ng ... ysis is ... usly app ... geneous scale ... ure research that "after forty years of fact gathering we ... come organizing theory, especially since the computer has made it possible to carry empiricism to ridiculous extremes.

Here the discussion continues for several more pages, dealing with the "Historical Background." We have given enough for you to appreciate how the material is handled. We have, thus, represented a tear in the manuscript and, after the hiatus, we shall take up the next division of the discussion.

This may be a proper place to point out the organization of the discussion of related literature. Note how it proceeds, from the standpoint of the problem, from the broadest consideration — the historical overview — to the specific construction of a scoring key for the SVIB. Here is the organization as represented by the subheadings:

- *The Historical Overview*
  - *Interest Measurement in Counseling and Guidance* [in general]
    - *Measurement of Interests among Cartographers* [in particular]
      - *The Strong Vocational Interest Approach* [Now, a specific way of measuring interests]
        - *The Validity and Reliability of the Strong Approach* [A discussion of a particular phase of the Strong approach]
          - *The Construction of a Scoring Key* [And so, the discussion of related literature has come full circuit. Refer to the problem and you will see that this is the object of the research: "to develop a scale" for the SVIB].

Note how each section becomes of narrower and narrower scope.

(See pp. 61-62.)

<u>Interest Measurement in Counseling and Guidance</u>

There appears to be universal agreement in the relevance of interest measurement as a guidance technique. In the words of Cronbach:

> . . .Historically, interest tests have always been a method for helping the individual attain satisfaction for himself rather than a method for satisfying institutions. . . . The aim in counseling should be to give the student a more sophisticated view of the world of work, of the choices open to him, and of his own range of potentials for achievement and satisfaction.[12]

Although there is agreement on the use of interest inventories, preferences vary when it comes to the selection of a specific instrument. Perhaps even more important, however, is how the results obtained through the instrument are used in counseling situations. Again quoting from Cronbach:

> . . . It is most unwise to concentrate the interview upon an analysis of scores for specific occupations . . . It is absolutely essential that the student go beneath occupational labels and stereotypes, that he should understand the variety of roles different members of the same occupation play, that he should understand the differences between the demands of the occupations, and that he should recognize the shifting nature of occupations.[13]

Here is a second extended quotation from Cronbach. The source is the same, except for the page location, as the previous quotation; hence, the footnote reference Ibid. [<L. <u>ibidem</u> = the same].

Routine interest testing, as a part of college entrance programs is a relatively recent development. The University of Minnesota was among the early institutions to add interest testing; first appearing in the 1940's so as to provide students with the opportunity to consider

---

[12]Cronbach, <u>op. cit.</u>, pp. 431-432.

[13]<u>Ibid.</u>, p. 433.

Op. cit. [<L. opere citato = the work cited] is an abbreviation meaning "in the work already cited by the author whose last name is given."

vocational alternatives.[14] The function of guidance at the college level, according to Humphreys and Traxler, should be to assist the student to (1) recognize the need for fundamental skill improvement, (2) choose an appropriate curriculum of studies, (3) select a vocation wisely and with insight, (4) make better social and personal adjustment.[15]

Mild dissent ~~comes~~ came from Ginzberg, who ~~feels~~ felt that difficulty is encountered in the translation of interests into realistic choices compatible with goals and values, ~~contending~~ having contended that the individual is not necessarily unaware of his interests. He ~~does~~ did agr... hat

the indivi... osess such as ... of

... r vocati

... ests ~~are~~ were so ... ed in counseling ...

... rea of guidance and vocational guidance which has been extensi...

has devoted an entire volume to the Counseling Use of the Strong Vocational Interest Blank.[19]

Again, to be absolutely accurate in expressing the thought, the verb must be in the past tense because it was actually in 1951 that Eli Ginsberg voiced his "mild dissent" in a book entitled Occupational Choice, published by the Columbia University Press.

Again, a hiatus in the manuscript.

In the previous section, we were discussing "Interest Measurement in Counseling and Guidance" generally. Now the subject narrows to the measurement of interests among a specific occupational group, viz., cartographers.

Measurement of Interests Among Cartographers

The literature ~~contains~~ contained no references directly to the measurement of interest among cartographers nor to the skills subsumed therein, i.e. photogrammetrist, map-analyst, geographer, surveyor, geodesist, or compiler.

Note tense change. When the researcher searched the literature (in the past) the literature "contained."

Research done with the SVIB has resulted in some fragmenting of the broader vocational fields. The physician scale, for example, ~~is~~ was based upon a composite made up of nine specialties plus interns.[20] Similarly, the engineer criterion group ~~includes~~ included mining, mechanical, civil, and electrical engineering.[21] In the latter case, Dunnettee has

Note the footnote form here for citations with reference to journals. Here for the volume the writer uses Roman numerals, the date in parentheses, and merely the numbers—without pp.—for the pages. There are several forms for footnote citation which we shall discuss later in the text.

---

[14] Ralph F. Berdie, "Guidance Between School and College," College Admissions, III (1956), 99-100.

[15] J. Anthony Humphreys and Arthur E. Traxler, Guidance Services (Chicago, Illinois: Science Research Associates, 1954), p. 14.

[19] W. L. Layton, Counseling Use of the Strong Vocational Interest Blank (Minneapolis, Minnesota: University of Minnesota Press, 1958).

[20] Campbell (1968), op. cit., p. 26.

[21] Campbell (1966), op. cit., p. 59.

Note that the author cannot use ibid. here. He is referring to two different works by Campbell: one published in 1968, the other in 1966.

compared the responses of several types of engineers to the SVIB and concluded that the SVIB potentially ~~can~~ could discriminate between the fields within the engineering disciplines.[22]

Note that the tense has again been changed to the past: could is the past tense of can. Also, would, should, and might for will, shall, and may.

In present practice, Campbell ~~reports~~ reported that counselors usually extrapolate from the available SVIB scales to occupations not listed on the profile.[23] This technique, although weak, might be appropriate to parcel out the geologist from potentially relevant engineer and chemist scales. However, to apply the technique when a larger number of existing scales appear applicable to the occupation would considerably weaken any resulting interpretation. The presently available scales ~~do~~ did not identify a single occupation even remotely related to cartography.

The Kuder Preferential Record, the Minnesota Vocational Interest Inventory, the Guilford-Sheidman-Zimmerman Interest Survey, the Occupational Interest Inventory, and the Vocational Interest Analysis ~~are~~ were not scored for cartography nor for any related occupation.

Again, the discussion narrows from the broad discussion of "measurement of interests among cartographers" to a particular method or means of measuring interests among cartographers; namely, the Strong Vocational Interest approach."

The Strong Vocational Interest Approach

The research generated by the SVIB ~~is~~ was probably exceeded only by that of the Rorschach.[24] The SVIB is so well known as to need no description in detail. To repeat here all the information available on the construction of scoring keys for particular occupations does not seem at all pertinent. But the necessary information which is relevant to the

When the research "generated by the SVIB" was exceeded by the Rorschach was in 1969, when Benton wrote his proposal.

Also note the insertion of "that of" expresses precisely the thought the author wished to express.

[22] M. D. Dunnette, "Vocational Interest Differences among Engineers Employed in Different Functions," Journal of Applied Psychology, XLI (October, 1957), ... -273; see also M.

Another hiatus in the manuscript.

procedures to be used in this research were also used by Roys to construct a scoring key to identify potential male administrators in community recreation.[31]

The Validity and Reliability of the Strong Approach

Now the author discusses the matter of validity and reliability of the Strong approach to assessing interests.

The criteria for judging the value of a test have long constituted a controversial issue and are beyond the scope of this review. The American Psychological Association, attempting to aid both the test-maker and the test-user, has published a helpful document, "Technical Recommendations for Psychological Tests and Diagnostic Techniques."[32] Cronbach also ~~includes~~ included an excellent coverage of the subject of test evaluation in his work on psychological testing which has been mentioned earlier in this review.[33]

Note the way in which the author has delimited the discussion by openly stating whatever he feels is beyond the province of his discussion.

Note the general discussion of test validity here.

There are three validities of concern to the test user: content, concurrent, and predictive validities. The validity of the SVIB in each of these traditional areas ~~is~~ was discussed in detail by Strong,[34] by Campbell,[35] and by others.[36] Campbell, in his recent report of factor analysis study found occupational choice determinative.

Now the topic narrows to three validities.

Then we come to Strong and the discussion of these validities as they apply to the Strong approach.

---

[31] K. B. Roys, *op. cit.*

[32] American Psychological Association, "Technical Recommendations for Psychological Tests and Diagnostic Techniques," *Psychological Bulletin Supplement*, LI (March, 1954), 1-34.

[33] Cronbach, *op. cit.*

[34] E. K. Strong, Jr., *Vocational Interests Eighteen Years after College* (Minneapolis, Minnesota: University of Minnesota Press, 1955).

[35] Campbell (1966), *op. cit.*

[36] Buros, *op. cit.*

The degree of separation between scales of the SVIB is generally indicated by a determination of the per ce[illegible]f overl[illegible]ping occasioned

If we go back to reread the problem for this research effort we will see how the author has kept his goal constantly in mind while planning his discussion of related literature. In the statement of the problem the author specifically announces as one of this research objectives is to "develop a scale for the revised Strong Vocational Interest Blank to aid recruitment of cartographers."

The Construction of a Scoring Key

Although Strong has published his procedures for the construction of keys for the SVIB, the literature indicated that refinements in techniques have subsequently occurred. The blanks in scoring and in the weighting system; the format and the items were relatively unchanged.[44] Originally weights of 30 were used. Subsequently, they were reduced to 15; then to 4, and with the current edition, to 1.

That is precisely what he is discussing here, "the construction of a scoring key—the developing of a scale—to aid in isolating the interests of cartographers from men in general.

Here is a discussion of the evolution of the "revised" SVIB key.

The rationale for adoption of unit weights and reduction in the number of items scored from 400 to 298 ~~is~~ was fully discussed in Strong's last contribution to the literature, published posthumously.[45]

The current procedures, and those to be used in this study, for constructing a scoring key are: first, the SVIB is administered to a criterion group of people in a specified occupation. Length of time employed and the individual's liking of the work are specific requirements for the criteria. Second, the percentage responses for the group

The author finally comes to the announcement of the procedures, following those of Strong, that he proposes to use in his study.

[44] E. K. Strong, Jr., et al., "Proposed Scoring Changes for the Strong Vocational Interest Blank," Journal of Applied Psychology, XLVIII (April, 1964), 75-80.

[45] Ibid.

are determined for each response and contrasted to men in general. Item choices different for the criterion group and also for the men-in-general group are separated out for use in the scale. Third, all members of the criterion group and the men-in-general group are scored on the new scale. Fourth, the norms and standard scores are established if the scale has adequately separated the two groups.

In the original document, the discussion of the construction of a scoring key runs on for several pages.

Until the current revision, the weighting system in use em-

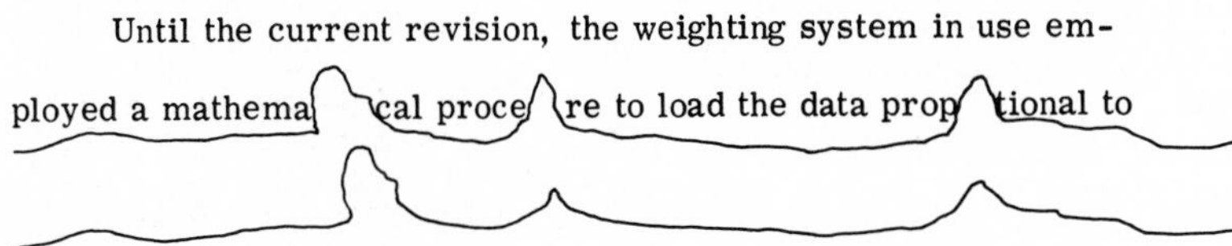

Summary

The extent of research done with the SVIB and its value and reliability as a counseling aid ~~is~~ was well stated by Cronbach in his summary of the application of interest inventories:

The heading of this section is somewhat of a misnomer. Actually this is not so much a summary of the discussion of the related literature as it is a justification, by citing an authoritative opinion, for the choice of using the Strong approach over and against any other approach which might have been selected.

> The Strong blank is undoubtedly the most highly developed and best understood of the inventories; indeed it ranks near the top among psychological tests of all types . . . The great number of keys make interpretation both rich and complex . . . But its length and complexity, together with its research foundation, make the Strong the preferred instrument of most highly trained counselors and psychologists.[56]

[56] Cronbach, op. cit., p. 434.

THE DATA
AND THE TREATMENT OF THE DATA

The Data

The data of this research are of two kinds: primary data and secondary data. The nature of each of these two types of data will be given briefly below.

The primary data. The responses to the SVIB by cartographers are one type of primary data. The demographic responses to the questionnaire appended to the SVIB comprise another type of primary data.

The secondary data. The normative data and current occupational scales for the SVIB constitute one type of secondary data. The published studies and texts and the unpublished dissertations and theses dealing with interest measurement are another type of secondary data.

COMMENTS ON THE TEXT OF THE PROPOSAL

We have now come to the section of the proposal which is its very heart. This section should, indeed, be the strongest of all the sections of the research proposal in setting forth precisely what it is that the researcher intends to do and precisely how he intends to do it.

The format suggested in this section, if followed scrupulously, will prevent the researcher from becoming nebulous and inexact when he is faced with difficult problems to solve.

The researcher should begin by describing broadly the types of data he plans to use in the study. The statements are direct and informative: "The data of this research are of two kinds...." Each type of data is then clearly described.

The study will utilize two categories of primary data.

The secondary data are described. More detail with respect to both of these types of data will be given later under the heading in each subproblem entitled "The Data Needed."

This is the first page of a new section of the proposal. Note the format, and the very effective way in which "open space" has been used.

First pages of chapters and new sections place the folio (page number) at the bottom, centered.

The Criteria for the Admissibility of the Data

Only the revised SVIB for men, completed in accordance with the test publisher's instructions, will be used in the study.

Only responses from criterion group cartographers with three or more years of cartographic experience and who indicate on the SVIB that they like their work will be used in this study.

For the researcher merely to amass data is not sufficient. Data in its raw form is frequently defective or contaminated. The researcher should, therefore, state unequivocally what standards his data must meet or under what conditions he will accept the data that comes to his attention. Here the researcher has provided a screening process through which the data must pass in order to be acceptable for use in the study.

Immediately after stating what the data are, we state the standards which they must meet to be acceptable.

The Research Methodology

Although Hillway pointed out that vague description of the approach to research is indicative of poor understanding of what is to be done and such research potentially will be ineffectual, the classification of educational research method is essentially an arbitrary process.[1] Identification of the method or techniques must also include a description of the schema if ambiguity is to be avoided. The classification system suggested by Barr[2] includes the grouping of data-gathering techniques and data-processing methods among others. Within that framework, this research uses the survey method for data gathering and actuarial prediction for data-processing.

Having presented the types of data and their refining criteria, the next item to be settled is the methodology which will be chosen for handling or processing those data. That is the purpose of this section on the "The Research Methodology."

Here is the statement of methodology: the survey method will be used. Now we know the methodological framework within which we are operating.

Further description of the data-gathering procedures is suggested by Mouly.[3] His system would classify the data-gathering method proposed for this research as a self-report descriptive survey and the data-processing methods as statistical empiricism.

Now the author goes one step further and suggests that the method will be more closely pinpointed as a descriptive survey—using Mouly's definition—and that the data processing methodology will be "statistical empiricism."

---

[1] Tyrus Hillway, Introduction to Research (Boston: Houghton Mifflin, 1956), p. 126.

[2] Arvil S. Barr, "Research Methods," Chester W. Harris, (ed.) Encyclopedia of Educational Research (New York: The Macmillan Company, 1960), pp. 1160-1166.

[3] George J. Mouly, The Science of Educational Research (New York: American Book Company, 1963), pp. 300, 301.

The author has buttressed his comment on method by citing from a standard text on research methods.

A second citation justifies his own choice of method.

The methods and procedures used in this study are those developed by E. K. Strong, Jr. over a period of forty years and continued by David P. Campbell, Director of the CIMR. Interest measurement research continues to evolve, however; and in spite of the prolific literature centered on the SVIB, the current procedures for scale development are not in print.

Here is an interesting comment. The author indicates that the methods and procedures used in this study are those that the developers of the instrument that he is using have developed "over a period of forty years." He also lets the door open for new developments.

Now we come to the heart of the proposal: the specific treatment of the data for each subproblem. Until now we have been dealing in generalities. No more! Now we cannot be too specific.

Specific Treatment of the Data for Each Subproblem

Subproblem one. The first subproblem is to determine whether male cartographers employed by the Federal Government have a discrete pattern of interests different from men in general as measured by the SVIB.

The author begins by restating the subproblem. Let's get it before our eyes and know precisely what it is we are attempting to resolve.

Each subproblem will be considered under four headings:
The Data Needed
Where the Data Are Located
How the Data Will Be Secured
How the Data Will Be Treated.

The Data Needed

The data needed for the solving of subproblem one are (a) the names of the cartographers within the employ of USATOPOCOM who meet the criteria established earlier in this proposal, (b) the responses of the criterion group to the SVIB, and (c) the responses of the normative men-in-general group to the SVIB.

Here the author states what data he needs to solve the subproblem. Note how specific he is in specifying the data needed.

He is in the same position as a builder who must specify exactly what materials he needs to construct the part of the building he is erecting.

While some researchers may feel that the format that we have suggested here is somewhat pedantic, it may be well for you to force yourself to articulate precisely where the data are located which you will need. The author of this book has seen entirely too many students who know what data they need but when asked where the data are located, they bewilderingly begin: "Well, I guess it is in... " Let's not guess. There is no guessing in this proposal. We should know with such precision where the data are located that we could send another to get the data for us with specific instructions as to where to get it.

Here we could go to the personnel files of USATOPOCOM (if we had proper credentials) and to the office of CIMR at the University of Minnesota. We know where the data are.

The Location of the Data

The identification data are located in the personnel files of the USATOPOCOM, Washington, D. C.

The responses of the criterion group are located within that population.

The responses of the normative men-in-general group are located at the CIMR, University of Minnesota.

The Means of Obtaining the Data

The identification data will be requested of the Personnel Officer, USATOPOCOM. Prior verbal permission for release of the data has been obtained. Appendix A exhibits the letter requesting these data.

All right; you know what data you need and where they are located. The next question is: How will you secure them?

The responses of the criterion group will be obtained by written request from the Commanding General, USATOPOCOM, accompanying the mailed SVIB to the individual members of the criterion group. Appendix B contains a copy of the cover letter. In order to preclude possible compromise and to avoid infringement of copyright, a copy of the SVIB is not included in the appendices to this proposal.

This section spells out the answer to that question without any ambiguity.

Note that for even the criterion group provision is made for obtaining the data. No loose ends remain!

If you are tempted to pass any of these sections off with a generalized comment such as, "The data will be obtained from the sources where they are located," be suspect of such an answer. It usually indicates either that you don't know how you will get them, or that you are too careless to bother to spell it out. Either situation will defeat you finally.

The responses of the normative men-in-general group will be obtained from Dr. David P. Campbell, Director, CIMR, University of Minnesota, 101 Eddy Hall, Minneapolis, Minnesota 55455. Appendix C contains the prior letter offering assistance, and Appendix D displays the letter requesting the data.

The Treatment of the Data

The student should study the format of the headings in this section of the proposal. Note that the centered heading, unitalicized, follows the paragraph sidehead, and that the next paragraph sidehead has its principal words capitalized to distinguish it from the first paragraph sidehead format. Read the headings consecutively under "The Treatment of the Data" and you will see how logically the author of this proposal proceeds.

How the Data Will Be Screened. The completed blanks returned by the criterion group will be screened to eliminate those where the respondent fails to meet the criteria for experience and job satisfaction and those forms improperly filled out.

The subsection on "The Treatment of the Data" is the vital center of the proposal. Unless this section spells out without any equivocation or ambiguity precisely what the author of the proposal intends to do, the proposal is a failure.

How the Item Analysis Will Be Made. The criterion group response data will be treated by performing an item analysis to determine which of the three responses, *i.e.*, "Like," "Indifferent," or "Dislike," have been made to each of the 298 items on the blanks that are currently used in scoring. The number of persons among the total group selecting each response to each item will be converted to a per cent value, and this value will be numerically compared with the responses of men-in-general.

The criterion for this section should be that it ought to explain accurately precisely what is to be done to the data that, were you inaccessible, anyone competent to do the research could carry out your research project without your assistance.

Scoring weights will be assigned for each item where the difference in response between cartographers and men in general is 20 per cent or greater. The items will be assigned positive values whenever the difference is in the direction of the cartographers and minus values when the reverse is true.

What is the rationale for 20 per cent? The researcher should tell us. Why not 10, 15, 25, 30 per cent instead of 20?

Table I is hypothetical so far as the data it exhibits, but it is illustrative of the way the data will be treated.

Note the inclusion of Table I. Many students will say: "A table will be presented," and nothing more. It is not enough to know that a table will be presented but precisely, what the table will indicate, and what will be its data components. To show this treatment of the data, the skeletonized "hypothetical" table is presented on the next page.

TABLE I

DETERMINATION OF WEIGHTS FOR CARTOGRAPHER SCORING KEY FOR THE SVIB

(Hypothetical Data)

Items on SVIB	Percentage of Men in General Tested			Percentage of Cartographers Tested			Difference in Percentages Between Groups			Scoring Weights for Cartographers		
	L	I	D	L	I	D	L	I	D	L	I	D
Architect	37	41	22	63	31	7	25	-10	-15	1	0	0
. . .												
Zoologist	27	41	32	87	11	1	60	-30	-31	1	-1	-1

Note the format of the table. It is entitled TABLE I (all capital letters). Roman numerals are used to number tables. Double lines indicate the boundary top and bottom of the table with the column headings separated from the data arranged under them by a single line.

Perhaps an asterisk after the first "L I D" would explain these cryptic letters for those who do not know the SVIB. These letters are three choices which the respondent has to the item: L = "Like," I = "Indifferent," D = "Dislike."

How the Data Will Be Interpreted. The data will be interpreted by counting the number of weighted items and comparing the resulting total to Strong's criterion.[4] That is, weighted response variance on the last forty items will be construed to mean that cartographers possess a discrete pattern of interests as measured by the SVIB.

Note that we have come full circle. The subproblem sought to determine whether cartographers possessed discrete interest patterns as compared to men in general.

After you have finished with the "Treatment of the Data" section it is always well to go back to read your subproblem again to see if what you have done does indeed provide an answer to the subproblem.

Subproblem two. The second subproblem is to construct a scoring key for the SVIB to differentiate cartographers from men in general and also from other occupational groups.

Now under the "Treatment of the Data," we come to the second subproblem. As before, it is stated (repeated) here so that the reader does not lose sight of what it is we are structuring a solution for.

The Data Needed

The data needed are the scoring weights for the 298 items of the cartographer-criterion group, their original responses to the SVIB, as well as responses from a separate group of male cartographers in the Federal employ, the scoring keys for all other available occupational groups, and their normative data.

Again we go through the same ritual as with subproblem one. The careless researcher will not have the patience and precision to work out each subproblem with meticulous detail. If not, it is an unhappy augury for the remainder of his research effort. All that he does will probably be careless and imprecise. A proposal carefully and meticulously worked out is 50 per cent of the research effort completed

[4] E. K. Strong, Jr., et al., "Proposed Scoring Changes for the Strong Vocational Interest Blank," Journal of Applied Psychology, XLVIII (April, 1964), 75-80.

The Location of the Data

Data collection and treatment to be conducted as part of subproblem one will obtain the responses of the cartographer-criterion group and produce, in Table I, the scoring weights. The response data from a separate group of cartographers are located among the male cartographers employed by the U.S. Navy Oceanographic Office, Washington, D.C., and the U.S. Air Force Aeronautical Chart and Information Center, St. Louis, Missouri. The other available occupational scales and their normative data are located at the Center for Interest Measurement Research, the University of Minnesota, Minneapolis, Minnesota.

So accurate are these locations that, again, we could send another with proper credentials to get the material for us.

The Means of Obtaining the Data

The responses of the cartographer-criterion group and the scoring weights will be available at the conclusion of the prior subproblem. The respective commanders of the U. S. Navy Oceanographic Office and the U. S. Air Force Aeronautical Chart and Information Center will each be requested by letter to furnish Strong Vocational Interest Blank responses from a selected sample of sixty cartographers meeting the established experience criterion. A visit will be made to each of these installations to select randomly from the personnel files every fourth name and to facilitate the distribution and return of the blanks. Appendix E contains the letter requesting the data.

Note the way in which the researcher has provided for randomization of his sample: every fourth name in a file.

Letters are important. Note that the researcher exhibits the letter in Appendix E which he will use requesting the data. This gives us an opportunity to see the whole process of selection of the data.

The other available occupational scales and their normative data will be requested from David P. Campbell, Director, Center for Interest Measurement Research, University of Minnesota, 101 Eddy Hall, Minneapolis, Minnesota, 55455. Appendix C contains the letter requesting this data.

Another letter is spread upon the record.

The Treatment of the Data

Scale Construction. The new cartographer scale will be construed by selecting those *Strong Vocational Interest Blank* response items from Table I that discriminate with a 20 per cent or greater variance. The scoring key will be comprised of all items having weights of +1 or -1.

The researcher might have strengthened his proposal at this point by giving us the rationale for setting 20 per cent as an arbitrary—or seemingly arbitrary—figure.

Normalizing. Norms for the cartographer scale will be established by:

(1) scoring the criterion group of answer sheets on the new scale,

(2) computing standard scores for the results,

(3) assigning letter ratings to appropriate ranges of standard scores for the criterion group.[5]

Note how clearly the author of this proposal outlines his next three steps. We shall now note each of these steps with specific emphasis.

The criterion-group answer sheets will be scored to obtain the algebraic sum of the previously selected items. Their range and arithmetic mean score will be determined. The standard deviations will be computed by the formula:[6]

←STEP 1

Where statistics are involved it is well to give the formulas that will be used, together with the meaning of each symbol employed in the formula. This was not done here. The authority or origin for the formula should also be given (here Downie and Heath; see footnote).

A slight weakness is discernible at this point in the proposal. The researcher should have told us not only what he was doing statistically, but why he needed to do it. Why does he need the standard deviation?

$$s = \sqrt{\frac{x^2}{N-1}}$$

The raw scores will be converted to standard scores by the formula:[7]

←STEP 2

Of course, we see why he needed the "s" in the next formula: to derive the standard score.

$$\text{Standard score} = \frac{(x-\bar{X})}{s}(10) + 50$$

Where

x = an individual raw score

$\bar{X}$ = criterion group raw-score mean

s = criterion group raw-score standard deviation

Here the researcher does give us the symbols and their meaning. This is always a desirable practice.

Letter ratings will be assigned to the distribution of standard scores expressed as percentages in the manner developed by Strong.[8,9] The data will appear in Table II and Table III.

←STEP 3

---

[5]Campbell (1966), *op. cit.*, p. 9.

[6]N. M. Downie and R. W. Heath, *Basic Statistical Methods* (New York: Harper and Row, 1959), p. 45.

[7]*Ibid.*, p. 61.

[8]Strong (1943), *op. cit.*, p. 64.

[9]Campbell (1966), *op. cit.*, p. 9.

TABLE II

CARTOGRAPHER-CRITERION-GROUP-LETTER-GRADE DISTRIBUTION

Rating	Standard Score	Per Cent of Normal Distribution	Value in S.D.	Per Cent of Cartographers
A	45 & above	69.2	-0.5 and above	- - -
B+	40-44	15.0	-0.5 to -1.0	- - -
B	35-39	9.2	-1.0 to -1.5	- - -
B-	30-34	4.4	-1.5 to -2.0	- - -
C+	25-29	1.6	-2.0 and below	- - -

Again, a skeleton table shows exactly how the data which have been assembled from "raw" sources will be displayed.

No researcher should ever be content merely to say: "A table will be presented . . . " Always that table should be shown in sufficient fullness for the reader to appreciate precisely what the table will show and, thus, be in a position to judge whether, with such data, the subproblem can be solved or the research goal achieved.

The criterion group answer sheets will be scored for each available occupational scale, converted to standard scores and percentages as was previously done for the cartographer scale. The results will appear in Table III.

To avoid unnecessary repetition, the researcher may refer back to the description of a data treatment which was delineated in an earlier subproblem.

The object of a proposal is not to make it repetitious, but clear.

Cross Validation. The responses of the cross-validation group will be screened to eliminate those blanks where: (1) the respondent failed to meet the previously established criteria for experience and job satisfaction; and (2) the respondent filled out the forms improperly.

The responses will then be scored with the newly developed (Table I) cartographer scale and all other available occupational scales. The results will be converted to standard scores and percentages. The data will appear in Table III.

Note the progress through this section of the Treatment of the Data for the second subproblem: The research task as enunciated by the subproblem is to construct a scoring key. The author, therefore, constructs the new cartographer scale, establishes norms for it (presenting the statistics for so doing) and now cross-validates the scale, and —as we shall see next—establishes the validity and, finally, the reliability for the newly developed scale. Read the subheads. That is the complete story. No researcher could do more than that.

The statistical nature of the data will be determined by comparing the difference between the means by using the $\tilde{z}$ test:[10]

Note how carefully the author of the proposal spells out precisely how the statistical matters will be handled.

He also footnotes the authority for each statistical operation. There is, therefore, no question about the appropriateness of the statistic for the research task in which he is applying it.

Scale Group	Cross-validation Group
$\bar{X}_1$ = __________	$\bar{X}_2$ = __________
S_1 = __________	S_2 = __________
N_1 = __________	N_2 = __________

All of the values which will be later employed in the formulas are presented here for each group.

Standard error for $\bar{X}_1$ Standard error for $\bar{X}_2$

$$S_{\bar{X}_1} = \frac{S_1}{\sqrt{N_1}} \qquad S_{\bar{X}_2} = \frac{S_2}{\sqrt{N_2}}$$

Now the computation of the standard error of the mean for each group takes place.

Standard error of the difference between the means:

$$S_{D_{\bar{X}}} = \sqrt{S_{\bar{X}_1}^{\,2} + S_{\bar{X}_2}^{\,2}}$$

Then the computation of the standard error of the difference between the means.

$$\tilde{z} = \frac{\bar{X}_1 - \bar{X}_2}{S_{D_{\bar{X}}}}$$

And now, the computation of the $\tilde{z}$ test.

[10]Downie, op. cit., pp. 124-125.

The resulting data will appear in the $\tilde{z}$ column of Table III.

And, finally, an indication of the disposition of the data in Table III.

Validity. The similarities between cartographers and other occupational groups will be determined by the degree and direction of of correlation between the standard scores of the criterion group on their own scale and their scores on other scales. The responses, after scoring, will be converted to standard scores by the use of the previously stated formula. The standard scores will then be used to compute the Pearson's product-moment by the formula:[11]

Now, the validity of the new scale will be determined by comparing by means of the Pearson product moment correlation technique the similarities between cartographers and other occupational groups.

Note that the author of this proposal is careful to footnote his source of even so common a technique as the Pearsonian r formula. No opportunity is given for the reader of the proposal to question the integrity of the research approach.

$$\underline{r} = \frac{\Sigma xy}{\sqrt{(\Sigma x^2)\ (\Sigma y^2)}}$$

The data will be included in Table III.

The amount of overlap between the criterion group and other occupational groups will be determined using the method devised by Tilton:[12]

Here, then, is the statistical procedure to determine the amount of "overlap" between the two groups—again, firmly documented to establish the validity of the statistical tool.

$$Q = \frac{M_1 - M_2}{\frac{SD_1 - SD_2}{2}}$$

Where

M_1 is the mean of group one,

M_2 is the mean of group two.

SD_1 is the standard deviation of group one.

SD_2 is the standard deviation of group two.

The resulting data will appear in Table IV.

Again, the writer indicates the disposition of the statistical data by showing in skeletonized form how he will present them in the research report.

---

[11]Downie, op. cit., p. 127.

[12]Tilton, op. cit.

TABLE III

SIGNIFICANCE OF THE DIFFERENCE BETWEEN
THE SVIB MEAN STANDARD SCORE
FOR CARTOGRAPHERS AND MEN-IN-GENERAL
SCORED WITH THE CARTOGRAPHER SCALE

Group 1 (Criterion)	Group 2 (Cross Validation)	$X_1 - X_2$	$\tilde{z}$	Significance	Pearsonian Correlation Coefficient
Criterion	Men-in-General				
Criterion	Navy Cartographers				
Criterion	Air Force Cartographers				

A $\tilde{z}$ value of 1.96 is significant at the .05 level.

In this table all of the data are gathered together which have been derived during the treatment of the data for subproblem two.

With a design such as this, all the researcher needs to do now is to gather the data, process it statistically as he has indicated earlier, and fill in the table at the appropriate places with the appropriate data.

With a carefully thought-out proposal design the research is as good as completed!

Recall what we said earlier: A proposal is like the plans for a house. If the plans are carefully worked out, the contractor has no trouble in constructing the building. The simile is equally appropriate for the research effort.

TABLE IV

MEANS AND STANDARD DEVIATIONS OF RAW SCORES OF
THE CARTOGRAPHER GROUP ON OTHER
CURRENT OCCUPATIONAL SCALES
AND THE PERCENTAGE OF OVERLAP

Scale	Mean	Standard Deviation	Percentage Overlap
Actor	- -	- -	- -
Architect	- -	- -	- -
Artist	- -	- -	- -
- -			
- -			
- -			
- -			
- -			
- -			
Zoologist			

The table will present data comparing the cartographer group on other current occupational scales and the percentage of overlap.

Obviously the occupations are to be arranged alphabetically in this table and the respective values for each column will be entered, from Actor to Zoologist.

Reliability. The reliability or internal consistency of the newly developed cartographer scale will be determined by computing a Pearson product-moment correlation between odd-even split halves and correcting the correlation by applying the Spearman-Brown formula:[13]

Where many a less experienced researcher would have stopped, the writer of this proposal carries his data one step further: he establishes by statistical means the reliability or internal consistency of his newly developed cartographer scale.

$$r_{tt} = \frac{2r_{oe}}{1 + r_{oe}}$$

Where

r_{tt} = the reliability of the original test

r_{oe} = the reliability coefficient obtained by correlating the odd items with the even items

Meaning of symbols is again given.

Interpretation of the data. The discreteness of cartographer's interests derived from responses to the SVIB will be interpreted in statistical terms by comparing the resulting numerical values of validity and reliability with standards established through precedence in similar research.

Finally, subproblem two is wrapped up in the final step which describes the manner in which the statistical data will be interpreted. This is the capstone for all that has gone before. Here we see an indication for the use of the "other" data, which the researcher indicated he needed back on p. 207. "The other available scales and their normative data . . . ."

Note also that the researcher has used the data in this subproblem in the order in which he listed having need for it. (See p. 207.)

Subproblem three. The third subproblem is to analyze and to interpret the treated data so as to evaluate the discovered interests in terms of their discreteness in recruiting cartographers.

We come now to the third and last subproblem.

As with the other two, it is stated at the beginning of the section on the treatment which the researcher will give to the data pertaining to it.

The Data Needed

The data needed are: (1) all treated data developed in previous subproblems, (2) pertinent and selected secondary data gleaned from the literature, and (3) the normative data for the SVIB.

Again he states clearly the data he needs to solve this subproblem.

The Location of the Data

The data will be contained in Tables I, II, III, and IV of the study.

He indicates where the data are found.

[13]Downie, op. cit., p. 192.

The secondary sources -- textbooks and journals containing reports and research conducted with the SVIB -- are located at the Library of Congress, the Battelle-Tompkins Library on the campus of The American University, and in the microfile publications of University Microfilms, Inc., Ann Arbor, Michigan (which may be secured at the Library of Congress or at the Battelle-Tompkins Library, The American University).

On page ***203****, we indicated the need for secondary data. The reader may have thought that the researcher had forgotten about those data. Not so! Here is the subproblem in which those data will be appropriate. Now we see the comprehensiveness with which he planned. This is the way proposals should be.*

The Means of Obtaining the Data

To many readers this section may seem superfluous. Not to this researcher. He is entirely too careful for that. The section takes only a few sentences and he deems these well worth while in order to present the information completely.

No problems exist with obtaining the primary data for this subproblem. All of the data are those which have previously been secured, and reside in treated form within Tables I, II, III, and IV.

The secondary data will be secured at the Library of Congress and from the stacks of the Battelle-Tomkins Library, The American University. The material will be reviewed in place and xerox copies of whatever materials requiring further study will be secured.

A complete statement of how the data will be secured.

Pertinent unpublished dissertations and theses have been obtained through interlibrary loan or purchased from University Microfilms, Inc., Ann Arbor, Michigan.

The section in the Selected Bibliography will indicate the meaning of pertinent. Here those dissertations are fully listed.

The normative data for the SVIB will have been obtained from the CIMR.

The Treatment of the Data

The most as well as the least descriptive discrete interest characteristics of cartographers will be selected from the scoring weight data contained in Table I. Similar and dissimilar occupations will be identified from the data appearing in Tables III and IV. Descriptions of allied and alien occupations will be extracted from the literature.

The researcher will now deal with extremes in terms of cartographer interests.

He will also analyze the data in Tables II and III for similar and dissimilar occupation interest patterns.

The data will be interpreted by consolidating the discrete characteristics into a composite and elucidative description of cartographer interests as compared to and contrasted with other occupations.

Now comes a synthesizing of all of the data into "a composite and elucidative description of cartographer interests."

Turn at this point to p. 192. Read again what the purpose of the research was as stated in the problem. We have indeed come full circle!

THE OUTLINE OF THE PROPOSED STUDY

PRELIMINARIES

- The Preface and the Acknowledgments
- The Table of Contents
- The List of Tables
- The List of Figures

I. THE PROBLEM AND ITS SETTING

- The Statement of the Problem
- The Statement of the Subproblems
- The Hypotheses
- The Delimitations
- The Definitions of Terms
- Abbreviations Used in This Study
- The Importance of the Study

II. THE REVIEW OF THE RELATED LITERATURE

- Interests as Theoretical Concepts
- Interests in Counseling and Vocational Choice
- The Measurement of Interests
- The Strong Approach
- The Measurement of Interests among Cartographers

III. THE POPULATION OF CARTOGRAPHERS

- The Population of Cartographers: Distribution and Genesis
- The Criterion Group
- The Cross-Validation Groups

IV. GENERAL PROCEDURE

- Response Data
- Collection Procedures
- Treating the Data

Many beginning researchers seem to feel that the outline of the proposed study is nothing more than the outline of the proposal. Nothing could be further from the truth.

You do in this section what the architect does when he draws an elevation of the various exposures of the building before a shovel of dirt has been lifted from the site for the foundation.

You envision what the completed study will be. What will you have in Chapter I, Chapter II, Chapter III, etc?

Note how the outline of the study departs from the outline of the proposal.

The first chapter is fairly consistent with the proposal, merely because we need the same information to orient us to the problem and to give us its setting.

The review of the related literature section is also almost comparable to what we have done in the proposal with the exception of its updating with recent studies.

Now organizationally we depart from the proposal. Chapter III of the proposed study will describe the population of the study and the various subgroups within the population.

Chapter IV will outline the general procedures by which the data will be handled. If the data were to be computerized, here would be a full discussion of the computerization process and the programming of the data.

V. THE RESULTS

The Criterion Group Returns

The Cross-Validation Group Returns

The Cartographer Scale

Other SVIB Scores of Cartographers

The Hypotheses

Hypothesis 1

Hypothesis 2

Hypothesis 3

Other Findings

Summary of Results

In this chapter the results of processing the data are set forth. It will doubtless consist of many tables of summarized data.

Now we come to seeing whether the data have supported the hypotheses.

There are always miscellaneous findings. These are presented.

Finally, the summary.

VI. SUMMARY, CONCLUSIONS, AND RECOMMENDATIONS

Summary

Conclusions

Recommendations

This chapter brings the research to a resolution point. Here we have summarized for us the findings, the conclusions reached, and the suggestions for further research in the area.

BIBLIOGRAPHY

The bibliography is always an indispensable part of any study. It lists all of the literature referred to in the study.

APPENDIXES

A. Letter of Transmittal

B. Follow-up Letter

C. Item Count and Differences in Group Percentages and Scoring Weights Assigned to the SVIB Key for Army Cartographers

D. Standard Score Means and Standard Deviations of the Cartographer Groups on Other Current Scales of the SVIB

E. Significance of the Differences between Cartographer Group Means on Other Scales of the SVIB

F. Percentage Overlap of Cartographers on Other Current Scales

G. Pearson Product Moment Correlations between Scores of the Cartographer Criterion Group on the Cartographer Scale and Other Occupational Scales Incorporated in the 1971 Revision to the SVIB

H. Significance of the Differences between the Mean SVIB Scores of Cartographers and other SVIB Occupational Groups

The appendixes contain the very important matter which has facilitated the research.

The appendixes also contain a set of displays of the "raw" data and the statistical computations that are so necessary if anyone would wish to check your results, redo the study, or compare point for point the results of a later study to your data.

This material, too bulky for inclusion in the main study, is extremely valuable for anyone who might wish to check your statistics or do other computational study on the basis of your data.

SELECTED BIBLIOGRAPHY

Books

Blum, Milton L., and B. Balinski. Counseling and Psychology. New York: Prentice-Hall, Incorporated, 1951.

Buros, Oscar K. (ed.). The Sixth Mental Measurement Yearbook. Highland Park, New Jersey: The Gryphon Press, 1965.

Campbell, D. P. (revised from E. K. Strong, Jr.). Manual for the Strong Vocational Interest Blank for Men and Women. Stanford, California: Stanford University Press, 1966.

Clark, K. E. Vocational Interests of Non-professional Men. Minneapolis, Minnesota: University of Minnesota Press, 1961.

Clark, K. E., and D. P. Campbell. Minnesota Vocational Inventory. New York: Psychological Corporation, 1965.

M. N. Appley. Motivation, ry and Research. New York: ley & Sons, 1964.

This is but a partial page of the Selected Bibliography section. This section is indicated as dealing with books. Other sections of the bibliography deal with periodical and journal materials; publications of government, learned societies, and other organizations; and unpublished materials (dissertations, theses, etc.).

Note: For personal reasons, the section preceding the Selected Bibliography entitled "The Qualifications of the Researcher" has been omitted. It forms, however, an essential part of every research proposal. Information concerning the competence of the researcher to engage in the research (and in professional research vitas of the participants) is always an expected component of every proposal. This material usually precedes the bibliographical material.

Appendix B

Practicum in Research

This manual aims to give you an opportunity to develop those skills which are the mark of a qualified researcher. To be able to recognize genuine basic research from pseudo-research is one of the first abilities a researcher should possess. To develop this skill, you should read critically and evaluate already existing research studies.

PROJECT 1: PART 1

Evaluative Survey of Recent Research

Your first project in research is to make a survey of various types of existing studies and to evaluate them against a checklist of criteria that has been discussed in Chapter 1.

Select at least fifteen or twenty recent studies which purport to be research—dissertations, theses, articles which appear in recent professional research journals.[1] By using the following checklist, which contains those features which should generally appear somewhere in the study, evaluate each of the studies you inspect.

If you wish, you may use regular 8.5- by 11-inch sheets of manifold (onion skin) paper. Each piece will then be approximately the size of a page in this book. By placing it over the printed evaluation form, the items on the form and the check columns may easily be seen.

Always keep the paper aligned. Place the manifold paper on the page and mark the points + and —. When checking each item, be sure that the two marks are directly over the marks in the book. If you want to refer to the checklist after you have removed it from the

[1] A partial list of journals for this assignment will be found in Chapter 2.

book, all you have to do is to position the marks over those in the book and you will have the check sheet in its proper position.

Locational [+] Mark

Locational [-] Mark

CHECKLIST FOR EVALUATION OF RESEARCH

Author ____
Last Name First Name Initial

" ____ "
Title of research report/thesis/dissertation

appearing in ______________________________, (_____, ____), _____.
Journal (title) Volume Month Year Pages

Directions: Place a check mark in the appropriate column after carefully inspecting the research report to see if it contains the item designated.

Factor	*Yes*	*No*	*Comment*
1. Is the central problem for research clearly stated?			
2. Are the subproblems clearly stated?			
3. Does the research evidence plan and organization?			
4. Has the researcher stated his hypotheses?			
5. Are the hypotheses related to the principal problem or the subproblems of the research?			
6. Is the research methodology which has been employed clearly stated?			
7. Did the researcher interpret the data, i.e., tell what the facts mean?			
8. Are the conclusions which the researcher presents justified by the facts presented?			
9. Is there any indication whether the hypotheses are supported or rejected?			
10. Is there any reference to or discussion of related literature or studies by other researchers?			
Number of tally marks in each column (Enter these here) →			
Multiply the total of each column as follows	x 10	x 0	
Total Score (Column 1 only)		0	

PROJECT 1: PART 2

Conclusions with Reference to the Above Survey

You have made a brief sampling of some research studies. At this point, look over your findings. What conclusions can you reach in terms of what you have discovered?

1. How much of the research that you reviewed seemed to have the qualities of genuine basic research? (Average the scores of all your samples.)

☐ 100% ☐ 80%-90% ☐ 50%-70% ☐ 30%-50%

☐ 10%-30% ☐ None of it.

2. What were the areas of greatest weakness in the studies which you reviewed?

☐ Failure to state the problem clearly.

☐ No subproblems stated.

☐ Research poorly planned and organized.

☐ Hypotheses were not stated.

☐ No seeming connection between problem being researched and hypotheses stated.

☐ No research methodology is indicated.

☐ Data are poorly presented.

☐ Data are merely presented; no interpretation of what data mean.

☐ Conclusions do not seem to be justified by facts presented.

☐ No indication of support or rejection of hypotheses.

☐ Related literature is not discussed.

3. Which factors seem to be most generally present in these studies?

☐ Problem statement

☐ Subproblems stated

☐ Good organization

☐ Hypotheses present

☐ Problem-hypothesis closely related

☐ Methodology stated

☐ Data clearly presented

☐ Data clearly interpreted

☐ Conclusions logical outcome of facts

☐ Hypotheses supported or rejected

☐ Relevant literature discussed

4. From your review of the studies as a whole, what conclusions can you formulate about the studies in general? ____________________

____

____

5. Additional comments (list in space below):

PROJECT 2

Assignment in Discovering the Resources of the Library

Researchers often need varied items of information which, if one is skillful in using the library, may be secured directly and without the need for the librarian to look it up for the researcher. Effective library skills save time and effort and make you self-sufficient to secure the information you need by knowing just where to go to get it.

The procedure for the following searches will be very simple:

1. Consult one of the eight Master Keys to locate bibliographical references to the works where the information is likely to be found.
2. Go to the card catalog in your own library to see if these reference works are owned by your library.
3. If the library owns the reference work, copy down its author, title, edition, and call number.
4. Go to the reference stacks, secure the work, and, using the table of contents and/or the index, look for the information you seek.

With any reference work it is always very important to study the individual volume to see how the author or the compiler has arranged the information within it. Brigham's *History and Bibliography of American Newspapers, 1690-1820* is arranged geographically, by state. An overview of the particular work with an eye to seeing its plan of arrangement frequently will facilitate your search. Read again pp. 17–20, 21 in the text. Then proceed to follow a similar procedure in finding the answers to the following questions for library data search:

1. What Wilmington [Delaware] newspapers probably carried the story of the inauguration of Thomas Jefferson when he took office for the first term? Where may I find a copy of these papers in order to read the account firsthand?
2. What was the original meaning of *pedagogue* in Greek? What was its earliest meaning in English? What year did it first come into the English language? Who first used it? In what work? Is that work now in print and, if so, who publishes it?
3. In writing a paper for a course in education, I wish to find an article entitled "Education as an Adjustment," written by J. M. Long, which appeared in an American periodical during the last half of the nineteenth century. Find the title of the periodical in which the article occurred, the year of publication. I live in Lincoln, Nebraska. What is the nearest library which has a copy of the periodical containing the article?
4. In 1916, John Dewey published *Essays in Experimental Logic.* The London *Times Literary Supplement* reviewed the book. How may I find, in part at least, what the review said?
5. In the District of Columbia, the *Washington Chronicle* was published from 1861 to 1911. I am a history professor at the University of Chicago, and I wish to find an account of the battles of Gettysburg and of Vicksburg which took place simultaneously during the early days of July, 1863; I also want to see what was said of these battles in the *Washington Chronicle.* What is the nearest library where I may find the copies of this paper for July 1, 2, 3, 1863?

The following information search routing form may assist you in facilitating your search for the preceding facts.

ROUTING SHEET FOR LOCATING INFORMATION

To Find:	Look in Master Key Under Heading of:	Referred to Reference Work Listed Below:	Call Number	Pages Consulted

PROJECT 3

Indication of Thought Organization and Structure

We have been discussing in Chapter 3 the organization of the thought in a research proposal and the indication of its subordination by means of headings and subheadings. A report, a chapter in a textbook, a pamphlet—any written item, for that matter—if well written and organized should evidence that organization by the use of appropriate headings.

Collect a group of such items and *by means of the headings alone* reduce each item to an outline merely by inspecting the headings and subheadings.

If you are in school or college, make a survey of the students (or the professors in charge of various courses) to see how many of them:

1. Require (in the case of the professors) their students to organize their papers and express that organization by appropriate headings.
2. Are aware (in the case of students) of the use of headings to show organization of thought.
3. Use (in the case of professors) such heading organization indications in the professional papers or reports that they write.
4. Expressly use (in the case of students) appropriate headings to show the organization of their thought.

PROJECT 4, PART 1

Basic Preliminaries to Selecting a Problem for Research

The purpose of this project is to help you to select an *area of interest* and, ultimately, a problem for research. We shall proceed deductively from the general considerations to the specific problem. Every problem for research is a very small point of investigation in the much broader territory of one segment of human knowledge. We will, therefore, proceed "funnel" fashion.

Enter in the following spaces (1) the broad area of knowledge in which your primary interest lies; (2) the specific subarea (or subdivision) of that larger area in which you have unanswered questions or basic curiosities.

1. The broad area of knowledge in which you are interested: ____________________

____

2. The specific subarea in which you have particular interest: ____________________

____

3. Now list on the following blanks the various unanswered questions you have with respect to the subarea. State your questions in *complete sentences.* Mark the one or two which intrigue you most with an asterisk (*):

a. ____

b. ____

c. ____

d. ____

e. ____

PROJECT 4, PART 2

In Part 1 of this project you narrowed your research interests down to certain questions to which you would like to give your prime attention. Now you are ready to zero in on one of those questions, stating it fully and, thus, articulating a problem for research.

This you may do in one of two ways: either as a question or as a statement of purpose. In any event, remember what we have just been saying in the text about the importance of writing a *complete* statement. Note in the examples given in the text (see p. 49) that statements 1 and 3 were stated in the form of a question: statements 2 and 4, as statements of purpose.

In the following space write your problem. After you have completed it, check it against the criteria that follows.

CHECKLIST FOR EVALUATING THE PROBLEM

The following checklist will assist you in evaluating your problem. It may indicate to you those aspects of your problem that need further refinement. In using the following checklist, *be realistic.* Read the problem as you have it written; read the checklist statement; then, to the best of your ability, try to decide whether the checklist item is applicable. There is no value at this point in wishful thinking. Either the item is applicable or it is not. Check the appropriate column.

Faults Resulting from Lack of Understanding of the Nature of Research	Yes	No
1. Problem seems to be merely an exercise in gathering data on a particular subject. ("I don't know anything about the subject; I'd like to learn more by 'researching' it.")	___	___
2. Problem seems to be little more than a simple comparison.	___	___
3. Problem can be resolved finally with a yes or no answer.	___	___
4. Problem seems to indicate that all you will have ultimately is a list of items.	___	___
5. Problem seems to indicate that your study will be little more than an exercise in finding a correlation coefficient—the discovery that there is a relationship between various data.	___	___
6. Problem has no identifiable word within it which indicates the need for interpretation of the data.	___	___

Diagnosis of your difficulty: If you have checked any items in the yes column, you need to go back to the text and study pp. 3–8 and pp. 46–49. After you have read these pages and restudied your problem again in terms of the items 1-6, check this box. ☐

Faults Relating to Pseudoproblems

	Yes	No
7. You do not have a problem per se but rather an expression of an opinion which you would like to defend or "prove."	___	___
8. Your problem does not focus on *one* research aim or goal but rather diffuses into several problems.	___	___
9. The problem is too broad; it attempts to research too much: too large a geographical area, too great a population.	___	___
10. The problem seems to suggest that you wish to learn more about the particular area you propose to "research" and that you are using the research project as a means of gathering such information.	___	___
11. The problem seems to be more in the area of *applied* research than in that of *basic* research: you wish to research the problem merely because it has a practical application—"it needs to be done"—rather than because it seeks to discover the basic truth underlying the practical application.	___	___

Diagnosis of your difficulty: If you have checked any items in the yes column in the preceding section, you need to go back to text and study pp. 1-5, 47-48. After you have read these pages and restudied your problem again in terms of items 7-11, check this box. ☐

Faults Relating to the Language and Manner in Which You State the Problem

	Yes	No
12. Problem statement is a meaningless fragment: you have no sentence.	___	___
13. Read your problem *literally, phrase by phrase.* Are there any areas in the wording where the words do not say precisely what you *mean?* Is there any "fogginess" in the statement?	___	___
14. Problem is stated in cliches or in other inexact or involved language which does not communicate clearly.	___	___
15. You use reference words which have nothing to which they refer: pronouns without antecedents.	___	___
16. You have additional discussion: a preamble, apology, statement why you have an interest in the problem area, or other discussion. You have written more than simply the statement of the problem.	___	___

Diagnosis of your difficulty: If you have checked any items in the yes column in the preceding section, you have trouble in an area which is corollary to the domain of this book: you need to learn some matters pertaining to written English. Many people have difficulty in putting their thoughts in written form. Read again pp. 49-50 in the text and follow the suggestions given there.

After you have read the preceding pages (and whatever other sources were necessary) and have edited your work and are satisfied with it—and do not be too easily satisfied with your own efforts—check this box. ☐

Now rewrite the statement of your problem on the next page precisely as you wish it to stand after checking it out and editing it according to the preceding sixteen criteria.

PROJECT 4, PART 3

Stating the Subproblems

On a separate sheet of paper, copy the problem for research that you have written on the previous page. Allow considerable space between the lines. Now do the following, after inspecting the problem carefully:

1. Box off within the problem those areas that must receive in-depth treatment if the problem is to be fully explored. Number each of the boxed-in areas consecutively.
2. Enclose within dotted lines those specified words within your statement of the problem which indicate your intention to interpret the data.
3. Below the problem, which has been thus treated, write in complete sentences the several subproblems for your study.

The Other Items to Complete the Section Entitled "The Problem and Its Setting."

Now having stated the problem and the subproblems, you are ready to finish the entire first section of your proposal. Turn to the sample proposal and study it carefully. Note especially the running comments in the right-hand column. These comments will guide you with respect to important points to be observed. Note carefully the use of the headings in presenting the material in a clear, logical format.

Now do the following:

☐ *Write the hypotheses.* Read again what has been said about hypotheses in the body of the text (pp. 6-7, 56, 192). Study the way in which the author of the sample proposal posited his hypotheses. They are precisely parallel with his subproblems.

Write the delimitations. Review again what was said on pp. 55, 193. Study the way in which the author has ruled out in the sample proposal those areas which, although contiguous to his research effort, his study will not consider.

☐ *Write the definitions of terms.* Before writing your definitions read again pp. 55, 193. It may help to number 1, 2, 3 the parts of the definition as we did in the text or to "box in" the several parts of your definition, labeling each as "term," "genera," or "differentia." Study the handling of the definitions section in the sample proposal. (Take out the numerals in the final draft of the proposal.)

Write the assumptions. Read again pp. 55-56, 193-194 and study the section of the sample proposal dealing with assumptions.

☐ *Write the section dealing with the importance of the study.* In a short, succinct statement point out to the reader the importance of your study. Generally, you will not need more than two or three well-written paragraphs. Edit out all but essentials. Study the section which establishes the importance of the study of the sample proposal.

As you complete each item, check the box preceding the directive.

Using now the sample proposal as a format, type up *your* proposal, observing the amenities of style and format as suggested by the sample proposal.

You now have the first section of your research proposal completed. After you have your proposal typed and positioned on the page, compare the appearance of your page with that of the sample proposal. Do they resemble each other? They should.

PROJECT 5

Defining the Scope and Indicating the Sources of the Related Literature

The purpose of this project is to help you plan in a systematic and organized manner the search of the related literature with respect to the problem that you delineated in Project 4.

The literature that you will review is related only to your problem and to nothing else. In order to keep that fact foremost in your mind, write your problem in the following space:

Step 1

Step 2. Now read the problem analytically and insert ①, ②, ③, ④, and so on, before each separate subarea of your problem, thus isolating the several subareas of your problem into topics under which you might look in indexes, abstracts, bibliographies, and similar reference works in order to find specific items related to your problem. List the key words or phrases which will guide you in your search in the following spaces:

______________	______________	______________	______________
______________	______________	______________	______________
______________	______________	______________	______________
______________	______________	______________	______________

Step 3. Begin your search of the related literature by consulting the following eight keys to reference materials (see pp. 17–18, 21), noting in each instance the library where the

book was consulted, the edition, the pages on which relevant material was found, and any comments that you may wish to make.

MASTER KEYS TO REFERENCE MATERIALS

Title	Library	Edition	Pages	Comments
Alexander & Burke, *How to Locate Educational Information and Data*				
Burke & Burke, *Documentation in Education*				
Chandler, *How to Find Out: A Guide . . .*				
Gates, *Guide to the Use of Books . . .*				
Hoffman, *The Reader's Adviser*				
Murphey, *How and Where . . .*				
Shores, *Basic Reference Sources*				
Winchell, *Guide to Reference Books*				

Step 4. On the basis of the references suggested to you in the several master reference works, represented in the preceding chart, make up a bibliographic reference card similar to the following and duplicate it in sufficient quantities for your use. This is the first step in locating specific items: to go to the indexes, abstracts, bibliographies, and similar works to find the particular bibliographic item in the literature. A suggested 3- by 5-inch bibliographic reference card might contain the following information:

BIBLIOGRAPHIC REFERENCE CARD
For Abstracts, Bibliographies, Indexes, etc.

Type of Reference

Title ______________________ Abstract (Check) [ ]

Volume ________ Date ______________ Bibliography [ ]

Categories consulted: Index [ ]

Library ______________ Book call number ______________

See other side for additional notes

Step 5. Finally, using the suggested bibliography card given on p. 60, copy down the specific references in the literature as given in the abstract, bibliography, or index. Use one card for each item. Fill in the author's name, the title of the article, the title of the journal in which the article is to be found, together with the volume of the journal, the pages, and the month and year of publication, and finally the source of your information (the bibliographic reference that you are using). You are now ready to go to the library to begin reading.

A reduced copy of the bibliography card follows. It may be well for you to read the section in the text entitled "How to Begin a Search for Related Literature," pp. 59-61, before you actually begin collecting the data for the related literature discussion.

Serial No. ________

Author(s) ____

(Last names first, first name, initial)

Title of article ____________________________________

Journal title ______________________________________

Volume ________ Pages ________ Month ________ Year ________

Place of Publication, Publisher, date (books only) ________________

________________________________ Edition ________

Source of bibliographic information ________________________

Library where information is located ________________________

Call number of book ____________

How item relates to problem: ____________________________

____

Use reverse side for additional comment. (If used, check here ☐.)

PROJECT 6, PART 1

Understanding the Nature of the Data

We have been discussing the care with which a researcher regards data. A study of the diagram of the research process, p. 66, suggests many alternatives to a unilateral interpretation of any quantum of data.

Let us take a specific instance:

A woman screams.

Now with the philosophical structural diagram of the research process, let us fit the happening (the data) into the research structure:

Absolute Truth of the Situation	*The Impenetrable Barrier*	Data Reaching the Observer	*First Barrier: Single Sensory Channel (Hearing)*	Channel of Perception	*Second Barrier: Limitations of Human Ear*	Limits (Barrier) of the Channel	*Third Barrier: Data Beyond Reach of the Observer*	Meta-* perceptual Data (Confirmatory)	*Fourth Barrier: Human Reason and Deductions from Data*	Probable Meaning of the Perceived Data
?		Scream		Human ear (hearing).		Frequency limits of hearing. Human hearing can perceive only within certain limits.		Blood pressure rise. Muscular tension. Adrenalin content.		Fear motivated the scream.

*Meta is a combining form from the Greek which means "beyond." Metaperceptual data, therefore, are those available data which are beyond the receptive and sensory channels available to the observer.

Perhaps it should be pointed out that the last column contains only *one* deduction which the observer has made. It could be that this deduction is entirely wrong. The woman may have screamed in surprise; she may have screamed in delight, or in laughter. We cannot be sure, merely by *hearing* a woman scream—without other confirmatory data—that she indeed has screamed in fright.

The following is a list of data-bearing situations. Using the skeleton table which follows, try to consider each of these situations in terms of its possible interpretation.

Data Reaching the Observer	Observer's Channel of Perception	Limits of the Channel	Metaperceptual Data*	Probable Meaning of the Situation	Other Conceivable Meanings

*Metaperceptual data are those data beyond the sensory mode through which the data reach the observer. They are confirmatory data which may assist in substantiating the probable meaning that he deduces from the available data that he has.

Here is a list of situations. Fit each into the preceding table format:

A low moan.
A fireball in the night sky.
The smell of acrid smoke.
A man collapsed on the sidewalk.
The wailing of a siren.
A slight tremor of the house.
A distinctly bright spot on the equator of a newly discovered planet.
All of the lights in a room go out.
A sudden flash in a dark area.
An automobile which suddenly swerves off the road into a ditch.

PROJECT 7

Practicum in Historical Research Writing

Historical research evidences broad variations, depending upon the historian and his style of writing. We made the point in Chapter 12 (pp. 177–178) that research writing need not be dull. This statement is certainly obvious when reading some historians. Their pages are as varied and as interesting as life itself.

To appreciate how various historical scholars have handled the same subject matter, take *one* significant event in history—the Peloponnesian War, the Sacking of Rome by Alaric in 410 A.D., the Battle of Tours, the march of Hannibal across the Alps—and compare the treatment of the event by various historical writers. In view of the matters discussed in Chapter 7, compare the various historical accounts on the basis of the following criteria.

Criterion or Evaluative Standard	Yes	No	Your Comment Based on Your Observations
Are the accounts essentially the same? If not, what is the difference between them?	___	___	
The accounts reveal some attempt at textual criticism of sources.	___	___	
The accounts show an awareness of "historical time."	___	___	
The accounts show some awareness of "historical space."	___	___	
The account is a prose form of chronology.	___	___	
The account is interspersed with interpretations of the historical data presented.	___	___	

General critical reactions:

Author: ______________________	Author: ______________________
Title: ______________________	Title: ______________________
Source 1	Source 2

Perhaps for the preceding project it may be well to look up some event in the *Cambridge Ancient (or Medieval, or Modern) History* and to choose the identical event in, for example, Will Durant, *The Story of Civilization.* The purpose of this project is to give you an opportunity to develop a critical evaluation of historiography and historical research: to react to standard historical works in review of the topics discussed in Chapter 7.

PROJECT 8, PART 1

The Descriptive Survey: Questionnaire Construction

If your research methodology falls within the area of the descriptive survey and you intend to gather some or all of your data by means of a questionnaire, you should duplicate as many of the forms for the construction of a questionnaire as you will need to accommodate all your questions. Beginning in the left-hand column with the statement of the question which you should write out clearly and completely, you should then proceed to analyze that question in terms of the following channels, moving toward the right. With an analysis of each question in this manner, there will be much less chance that you will produce a questionnaire that may be grossly faulty or that may have in it major defects that might impair your study and cast a shadow of credibility upon you as a researcher. The following form is merely to help you to put into practice some of the principles discussed in Chapter 8.

GUIDE FOR THE CONSTRUCTION OF A QUESTIONNAIRE

Write the question clearly and completely in the space below	What is the basic assumption underlying the reason for this question? How does the question relate to the research problem?	Type of question				How do you expect to relate this question to the research effort?
		Multiple Choice	Yes/No Answer	Comple-tion	Counter-check*	

*A "countercheck" question is one included to countercheck the reply given on another question in the questionnaire.

PROJECT 8, PART 2

The Descriptive Survey: Population Analysis

Take any population and make an analysis of its structure and characteristics. First, identify the population on the following line:

____

Now ask the following questions with respect to the *structure of the population:*

	Yes	No
1. Is the population a conglomerate mixture of homogeneous units?	___	___
2. Considered graphically, could the population be considered as consisting generally of equal "layers" each of which is fairly homogeneous in structure?	___	___
3. Considered graphically, could the population be considered as being composed of separate homogeneous layers but differing in size and number of units comprising them?	___	___
4. Could the population be envisioned as isolated islands or clusters of individual units, with each cluster apparently the same or similar to every other cluster, but upon close inspection being composed of distinctly heterogeneous units?	___	___

What is the *randomization process,* i.e., the means of extracting the sample from the total population? (Describe on the following lines:)

____

____

____

By referring to the table on p. 101, is the technique of randomization appropriate to the characteristics of the population? ☐ Yes ☐ No

Has the maximum of fortuitousness and at the same time the equality of representativeness of the various components of the population been guaranteed? ☐ Yes ☐ No

If the preceding answer is yes, indicate *how* this has been done. Explain simply on the following lines:

____

____

____

Indicate what means will be employed to extract the "hard facts" from the sample:

____

____

____

What are the weaknesses inherent in this method of securing the data?

____

____

____

What safeguards have you established to counteract the weaknesses of the data extraction approach? Be specific.

____

____

____

PROJECT 9

Guide to the Management of Data for the Analytical Survey

If your research methodology falls within the area of procedure normally considered to belong to the analytical survey methodology, the following guide to the consideration and management of the data will help you with the necessary groundwork for such a study.

The Characteristics of the Data

1. Are the data ☐ discrete or ☐ continuous?
2. What are the characteristics of the data? Are they
   - ☐ nominal
   - ☐ ordinal
   - ☐ interval
   - ☐ ratio
3. What do you want to do with the data?
   - ☐ Find a measure of central tendency? If so, which?__________
   - ☐ Find a measure of dispersion? If so, which?__________
   - ☐ Find a coefficient of correlation? If so, which?__________
   - ☐ Estimate parameters? If so, which?__________
   - ☐ Test the null hypothesis? If so, at what confidence level?__________
   - ☐ Test of significance? If so, which?__________
   - ☐ Other (specify)__________
4. With respect to correlational techniques, what are the characteristics of the variables?
   Independent variable: (identify)__________
   Nature of the data?__________
   Dependent variable: (identify)__________
   Nature of the data?__________
   Correlational technique for dealing with these types of data:__________
5. State clearly your rationale for planning to process the data as you have indicated you intend to do in sections 3 and 4:

The Interpretation of the Data

6. After you have treated the data statistically to analyze its characteristics, what will you then have? (Explain clearly and succinctly.)

7. Of what will your interpretation of the data from a research standpoint consist? What has the statistical analysis done in terms of solving any part of your research problem? (Explain precisely.)

8. What yet remains to be done before your problem (or any one of its subproblems) can be resolved? In other words, what further needs to be done so that the data will result in a resolution of the problem or any of its integral parts?

9. What is your plan of procedure for further carrying out this interpretation of the data? (Explain clearly.)

PROJECT 10

Practicum with Respect to the Experimental Method

1. You have a pretest-posttest control group design. When you have the statistical data collected, what statistical treatment of the data would be the recommended procedure to use?

2. Researchers talk so much about the importance of the "pretest" in the pretest-posttest design experiment. Name ten instances where life phenomena do not lend themselves to pretesting techniques.

3. In such instances as those cited above, indicate how you would employ the experimental method of research to resolve problems associated with them.

4. We have cited the instance of Fleming and experimentation with penicillin as an example of the

$$O_1 \rightarrow O_2 \rightarrow O_3 \rightarrow O_4 \rightarrow X \rightarrow O_5 \rightarrow O_6 \rightarrow O_7 \rightarrow O_8$$

design. Name some other experimental situations that would be appropriate for testing by the same design structure.

5. You have two types of material (conventional textbook and programmed textbook). You wish to test experimentally the effectiveness of the use of the one type of material as against that of the other type. Indicate what experimental research design you would employ and give the procedure in paradigm form.

Index